BIG NOISE FROM NOTRE DAME

FOR MIKE,
MY BEST CRITIC!
YOUR PAL,
JOE

BIG NOISE FROM

A History of the

NOTRE DAME

Collegiate Jazz Festival

Joseph Kuhn Carey

University of Notre Dame Press
Notre Dame, Indiana

Library of Congress Cataloging in Publication Data

Carey, Joseph Kuhn.
  Big noise from Notre Dame.

  "Collegiate Jazz discography": p.
  Bibliography: p.
  1. Collegiate Jazz Festival. I. Title.
ML38.N69C6443 1986   785.42′07′977289   85-41009
ISBN 0-268-00677-6 (pbk.)

Manufactured in the United States of America

For my grandfather,
JOSEPH KUHN,
whose world of silence
these past fifty years
has cried out for a book of sound

If there is any future for jazz, it will be guided by the hands, horns and minds of college musicians. — Leonard Feather, 1963

CONTENTS

AUTHOR'S NOTE

In an ephemeral artform such as jazz, for a celebration to exist for several years, let alone for nearly three decades — as the University of Notre Dame Collegiate Jazz Festival has done — is extraordinary. It is for this reason (and many others) that the book before you has been written.

The purpose of this work has been to allow the festival to come to life, to try and capture the year-by-year excitement, essence, and spontaneity that the event has created on the Notre Dame campus for each of the past twenty-eight springs. The book has also attempted to explore a festival's development and growth as it helped to educate others, particularly the yearly listening audiences and youths gifted enough to be able to express themselves through their instruments and the raw power of their music.

In addition, the book has tried to bring to light the unsung role of the festival's student organizers. For, though it is most definitely a festival for musicians, the Collegiate Jazz Festival is also created by those who often must remain on the sidelines once the onstage activity begins, people who craft the yearly toe-tapping trappings out of sheer love for the music itself. To give some insight into inner festival workings, an expanded, first-person, behind-the-scenes look at the event is offered for 1979 — my own year as chairman of the Collegiate Jazz Festival.

In a larger sense, then, this book is for those involved with the CJF and other such festivals around the world, who rarely receive credit for the often arduous, but ultimately rewarding tasks they undertake. For them, as well as the student musicians, the professional musician/critic/educator judges, and, most importantly, the festival audiences past and present, this work, like the event itself, is a gift, dedicated to the mysterious joys, jumps, and journeys of jazz.

ACKNOWLEDGMENTS

Although *Big Noise From Notre Dame: A History of The Collegiate Jazz Festival* is the result of five years of intensive research in Illinois, Indiana, Iowa, New Hampshire, Florida, Massachusetts, and New York, the book itself could never truly have taken final shape without the contributions, recollections, support, and counsel of numerous concerned, patient, and enthusiastic individuals, each of whom evidenced a warm affinity for the author's efforts and, most of all, for the colorful event around which the project revolved.

Among this select group of festival "friends," I would especially like to extend thanks to Dan Morgenstern for reading a final draft of this work. I remain indebted to readers of portions of earlier drafts over the years, including Jerrold Hickey, Michael O'Donnell, Robert Share, Charles Suber, and Bernie Zahren.

Thanks are also offered to a long list of past festival chairpersons, judges, student musicians, committee members, critics, fans, and Notre Dame jazz band and combo alumni, who kindly consented to interviews and provided historically pertinent programs, tapes, correspondence, and other festival-related paraphernalia during the course of research for the book, including: Nat Adderley, Mike Ahern, Warren Albright, Willard Alexander, Gene Bertoncini, Bob Brown, Jethro Burns, Tom Cahill, Jack Carr, John Cerabino, William R. Coulson, Charlie Davis, Robert "Gus" Duffy, Allan B. Dreyer, Larry Dwyer, Jim Long of Electro-Voice, Inc., Clark Galehouse of Crest/Golden Crest Records Inc., Bill Graham, Chet Grant, Charlie Haden, Jim Hayes, Dick Klarich, Bill LaFortune, Dr. Paul Leavis, Nathaniel Madison, Carl Magel, Roger Mills, George Milton, Greg Mullen, Jim Naughton, John Noel, Con J. Nolan, Bill O'Connell, Bob O'Donnell, Larry Powell, Steve Rodby, Tim Ryan, Duncan P. Schiedt, Paul Schlaver, Robert Share, Neil Stalter, Charles Suber, Tom Tafelski, Paul Willihnganz, John S. Wilson, Jim Wysocki, and Bernie Zahren.

Kudos must also go out to the ever-helpful music library staffs of the Berklee College of Music, Boston University, Northwestern University, and the University of Iowa, as well as to the staff of the South Bend Public Library. Special thanks are also offered to Jim Hobbs and the Listening Center of Northwestern University's music library for mastering and transferring fragile reel-to-reel tapes of 1959-61 award winning groups to cassettes to insure listening access. (Located by Dave Sommer in his Minneapolis basement in 1983 after persistent prodding by the author, the tapes served to firmly dispel any remaining doubts about the prowess and inventiveness of collegiate jazz talent in early festival days.)

For the photos included in this book—the majority of which were taken by Notre Dame students—I am deeply indebted to: Ed Brower, *The Commercial Appeal, down beat* magazine (particularly editor Art Lange, former managing editor Charles Doherty, and Maher Publications president Jack Maher, for allowing me to scour *down beat* photo files), Sid Davis (of the *Musical Merchandise Review*), Leo Hansen, Bruce Harlan, Karen Klocke, Dave Larsen, Tom Paulius, Kevin Pritchett, Dave Sommer, *South Bend Tribune* photo editor Roger Baele (for the opportunity to sift through twenty-five years of festival negatives in the newspaper's photo morgue) and staff photographer Joe Raymond, United Press International and the Bettmann Archive, Bill Wheeler, and Paul Willihnganz.

Finally, I would like to thank Janet Burroway, typist Donna Carswell, Rich Cromonic of Boston's *Sweet Potato* magazine (for the chance to write about jazz), the countless collegiate jazz program directors across the United States and Canada who responded—sometimes at surprising length—to questionnaires on several occasions, Byron Faust of Direct Mail Letter Service Inc. (who kindly allowed me to spend a day climbing up and down the walls of his South Bend printing shop, joyfully kicking up large quantities of dust and retrieving mint-edition copies of many past festival programs and posters), Janice J. Feldstein (for knowledgeable, sympathetic editing), Steve Katz, Doug and Marjorie Kinsey (for unbeatable hospitality and a snug place to stay during several South Bend research trips), the National Association of Jazz Educators, Ken and Beryl Nordine (for being there), the University of Notre Dame Office of Public Relations and Information Services, Jim Langford and the University of Notre Dame Press (for believing in the book's possibilities), the University of Notre Dame Archives (particularly Charles Lamb and former staff members Richard Cochran, Carolyn Mankell, Michele Pacifico, and Mo Uliciny), and Mrs. Everett Warren.

Lastly—and most importantly—I thank my parents and family for their advice, humor, love, and unfailing support, but for which no ink would have ever reached the page.

Chapter 1

BEGINNINGS

An Idea Emerges

South Bend winters set in hard and fast. They grip the campus of the University of Notre Dame in ice, thrash it with over-the-Indiana-plains winds that whip the snow in lazy, taunting curls around the center-piece Golden Dome. Students hidden behind scarves and parkas scurry in and out of collegiate ivy-covered buildings, cursing the classes so far away or the miserable backbone chill inseparable from daily treks to South Dining Hall meals. Thoughts of football, coach Terry Brennan's blue-and-gold-clad 1958 minions' frequent fall punts, kicks, and passes, the traditional postgame Saturday-night dances, or just an easy stroll along the tree-lined walk of nearby St. Mary's College with a girl underarm fade into the all-encompassing glum of cold. It stings. It's South Bend. It's a student body under ice.

Over hot cups of coffee and routine inspection of infamous "Huddle" hamburgers in the renovated LaFortune Student Center, the unrest in young, clean-shaven, crew-cut-topped faces begins to show. Nothing. Nothing to do, nothing to see, nothing new anywhere to crack the igloo mood, nothing exciting to spark the slow, snow pace of life. "Nothing." The oldest Notre Dame complaint, handed down from class to class, year to year, alumnus father to freshman son. And never once a lasting move by those in appropriate positions of power to do anything about it.

One day late in 1958, something small and seemingly insignificant happened to change all that. An idea, a simple concept, perhaps the most unlikely solution of all to thaw a conservative Catholic bastion's deep-set case of winter blues: jazz.

1

1958–59: The Midwest Collegiate Jazz Festival

Making his usual rounds of the University of Notre Dame's LaFortune Student Center, a small, eccentrically designed building that had once housed the glider experiments of American aeronautics pioneer Albert Zahm, and now included a rathskeller, ballroom, student-government office, and popular "Huddle" restaurant (all the result of a sizable early-fifties donation by Tulsa oilman/1916 alumnus Joe LaFortune), senior telecommunications major Tom Cahill was definitely exhibiting his finest late-fall 1958 semester puzzled look. As "Affairs Commissioner," it was his responsibility to tap the student pulse and determine what the Notre Dame "natives" needed in the way of diversion. Occasionally running dry of ideas, he would wander throughout the Student Center to pick up various bits of trend, conversation, anger, or activity and, so far as he could tell, this "tour" was as uneventful as the rest. That was, except for the tightening mood around him, the usual approaching winter noose he, in fact, felt himself and about which something had to be done.

Speakers, he knew, came and went. An occasional top-notch author or poet might shuffle out to a Washington Hall stage podium and find a decent audience, but, those infrequent exceptions aside, literary drawing power was limited, not nearly enough. On a larger scale, the annual "Mardi Gras" extravaganza came complete with gambling booths, old athletic Fieldhouse or Navy Drill Hall atmosphere, and music as well.

Football, of course, was the perennial fall frenzy, but even Terry Brennan, the former Notre Dame star running back, whose legions had shattered Bud Wilkinson's Oklahoma Sooner winning streak of forty-seven games the year before, couldn't stave off two consecutive "down" seasons (by Notre Dame standards) of 7–3 and 6–4. Something else was needed, something that could grab the students and make them shout as they had in Frank Leahy days. Something big, but at the same time, down-to-earth and entertaining, something even, perhaps, put on by people their own age. Something collegiate for collegians. Music, music, Cahill began to realize, might just be the key.

Continuing his walk through the LaFortune corridors, Cahill mulled these thoughts over, pausing briefly from time to time to listen to lively bits of student discussion or to chat with an acquaintance who happened to brush by. Relaxing for a moment near the end of his 'stroll,' he let himself ease back into the fresh, crisp, catchy strains of music often encountered in the Center. There was always a musician or two practicing away in some room, unwinding notes from an out-of-tune piano or somewhat hesitant horn. Always some sort of music there to catch the ear. Always something like jazz, which intrigued and added a sort of excitement, a mystery to the often uneventful walk. Music, music, Cahill began to realize, might just be the key.

Leaning lightly against a nearby wall, he recalled the fall football dances, held, regardless of game results, each Saturday night in the Navy Drill Hall, a huge barrackslike structure with a hard-on-the-dancer's-feet cement floor located on the easternmost side of campus, directly behind the Old Fieldhouse and the LaFortune Student Center. Flanked by fenced-in Cartier Field, the football and baseball practice ground, to the south and the married-student housing area known since the end of World War II as Vetville, to the north, the Drill Hall's dirigiblelike maze of metal innards would rapidly fill with couples on those nights, all maneuvering the latest dance steps to the not unswinging sounds of the official Notre Dame dance band, the Lettermen.[1]

A jazz buff himself, Cahill had often noted the eager student looks and vocal responses at these affairs as dashing architecture student/guitarist/band leader Gene Bertoncini put his band through the Basie-ish swing paces of numbers like "Just Us," written and arranged by lead trombonist Charlie Armstrong. In fact, the upbeat Armstrong original had become so popular that the post-Army-game dance crowd had requested—and received—Lettermen versions of the song three times.[2] Even on the slower tunes, Cahill had noticed, the students seemed to relate to the sounds and the group that was made up, for the most part, of other Notre Dame students their own age.

A few members of the Lettermen, such as Bertoncini and Armstrong, were, of course, musically trained and even had professional experience. The rest, though, like pianist Wally Jones or drummer Paul Willihnganz, were English or mechanical-engineering majors and played in the group primarily for fun. They got a kick out of performing for their friends and the student body at large, and the crowds more often than not responded with an instant excitement and rapport unlike anything Cahill had experienced before. Even when things didn't go right on a given night, the 'good time' earnestness of the young musicians was still infectious (pianist Jones had even made something of a minor legend for himself during a Freshman Mixer engagement that fall, when he gave a "yogi-istic" performance at a legless, floor-mounted Student Center grand piano).[3]

Jazz . . . Cahill pondered it for awhile, now fully removed from the bobbing tide of sound around him. Jazz. It wasn't quite established in the colleges yet, was taught only at a few ground-breaking institutions like North Texas State, Boston's Berklee School of Music, or the

Westlake College of Modern Music out in Hollywood, but the lure was there. There were some terrific musicians in the college ranks, musicians who just weren't being heard or given a decent chance to listen to other jazz aspirants their own age.

Jazz . . . so much of it to choose from, so many ways to make the wrong—or right—pick. Perhaps some sort of mix of it all, some sort of festival . . . but with college groups, not professionals. College groups . . . raw and exciting . . . untested . . . meeting and competing together in an old "battle of the bands" format. Jazz . . . collegiate jazz. The Lettermen and a smaller Bertoncini-led group had been slipping it into the Notre Dame/South Bend community now for years, and Cahill believed it might just work. Jazz would be just the thing to pull the students together and break the inevitable icebound campus blues. Head full of possibilities, a no-longer puzzled Affairs Commissioner ended his LaFortune walk and returned to his office to map the idea out.

A few days later, an obviously enthusiastic Tom Cahill got in touch with his good friend Bill Graham and outlined his still sketchy plan. Graham, who also happened to be student-body vice president, was immediately taken by the concept.[4] The idea of a festival devoted solely to college jazz was unique. There was no real precedent for it, outside of a few scattered, thoroughly stuffy such events in the country. And the Midwest definitely needed jazz. Outside of Chicago, unless you turned to the colleges, there simply wasn't any of it to be found.

As for the Notre Dame student body, Graham was confident they would go for it; after all, what student didn't like jazz? It was unadulterated Americana and exuded a power and attraction other sounds just didn't. More importantly, it was (at least in some eyes) an established art form, unlike the recent burst of "rock and roll" that had swept the nation (a brand of "crowd-exciting" music the quiet Fathers of Notre Dame might not be particularly keen on allowing on campus in festival form). Placed alongside the "outrageous" swivel-hipped sexuality of Elvis Presley, jazz, though long a "four-letter" word, looked comparatively "clean," a festival of collegiate jazz even "cleaner," and just the thing to let the world in on where music education in the schools (particularly in regard to jazz) was at. But how, came Graham's considered reply, could they corral a number of collegiate bands, acquire a proper space to play in, and, above all, procure the services of knowledgeable judges to sort out the chaos such a "festival" might well create?

When no easy answers were forthcoming, Cahill and Graham immediately sensed their idea was already getting out of hand. Even if they could pull the festival off, it couldn't possibly take place in a week or two. The process of putting it all together would take months, until February, March, even April at the earliest. Worse still was the fact that though the event could obviously be modeled on the professionally run jazz festival held each summer in Newport, Rhode Island, there was simply too much in the planning and execution that neither of them had any idea about. It was just too big to handle alone. On an impulse, they decided to turn to *down beat* magazine, one of the foremost sources of knowledge about jazz in America since its inception in mid-1934.

Loaded with high hopes and unbridled enthusiasm, the two Notre Dame students set about arranging a trip to *down beat*'s Chicago home office. A call was placed to publisher Charles Suber, to inquire if he might spare some time and hear out an embryonic jazz idea. To Cahill and Graham's surprise, Suber took the call and, fulfilling their wildest expectations, told them to come in and present the concept in person.

Wrapped in thick coats and hats, armed with festival "plans" mapped out on various pieces of paper and a gnawing desire to find out where it would all lead, Cahill and Graham stepped on the rattling, unpredictably heated orange cars of the notorious South Shore train line that covered the unendingly dull ninety-mile distance between South Bend and Chicago in a little under two and a half hours. All the way, past La Porte, past Michigan City, past the stifling steel fumes of Gary and assorted Indiana stops in between, they hashed out the concept, nixing certain ideas, expounding others, wondering above all how to present the whole thing to the jazz brass at *down beat*.

Arriving at Chicago's Randolph Street Station by early afternoon, the two bundled figures disembarked and moved purposefully out into the cold Windy City streets to find the magazine's 2001 Calumet Avenue office. Inside the building, recovering from a blast of frigid Lake Michigan air, they shrugged off their coats, located *down beat*'s door, gulped, and walked in.

After a few minutes, a short, vigorous, dark-haired man of thirty-five emerged from his small, book-and-paper-jammed office, introduced himself as Charles Suber, and motioned for them to come in. Moving back to his chair behind a large, document-strewn desk, he sat back, smoothly lighted an unpretentious "magazine-publisher's" black pipe, and prepared to listen. Puffing disinterestedly for awhile as Tom Cahill and Bill Graham began to talk, Suber slowly leaned forward to put his arms on top of the desk and listened some more, his eyes suddenly lighting up with excitement at the prospect being laid before him. A collegiate jazz festival, featuring just collegiate talent. An unheard-of showcase for young musicians from across the Midwest. It was a very good idea.[5]

Involved in the push for music (particularly jazz) education in schools for years, Suber's keen jazz sense quickly spotted something in the project that could be truly dynamic and worthwhile, not to mention a fantastic spur to the growth of the already strong "Stage Band" (dance-jazz band) movement in high schools and colleges that he and others were helping to bring about.[6] For years the movement had been searching for a way to show the dramatic progress that had been made, and to have such a knockout solution dropped in his *down beat* lap by two kids in crew cuts and all-American smiles was little short of a godsend. Without hesitation, then, Charles Suber, publisher of *down beat*, man of innumerable contacts and jazz-festival connections, threw his total support behind the idea, promising to help line up capable judges, organize some of the more difficult festival aspects, and publicize the event in his widely-read magazine.[7] Best of all, Suber selflessly handed over the name of another lead for festival support, that of Frank Holzfiend, owner of the legendary Blue Note Jazz Room in Chicago.

Stunned by the success of their talk with Suber, Cahill and Graham stumbled out once more into the Chicago chill and, not a little like lightheaded gamblers hoping to keep a lucky roll alive, headed for 3 North Clark Street and the Blue Note. A Chicago jazz staple since 1947 at various locales, but now firmly entrenched at the "barnlike" upstairs Clark Street address, the club gave equal time onstage to both big-name musicians and complete unknowns. Though struggling a bit to keep its head above the financial waters (as were most jazz clubs of any consequence in the late fifties), the 1958 Blue Note was still the premier downtown Chicago jazz spot. Cahill and Graham knew well that, despite Suber's enthusiasm, it was a definite long shot that a busy man such as Holzfiend would turn an ear to the problem at hand.

Climbing up the long flight of stairs that stretched from street-level to the club doors, the two young jazz entrepreneurs soon found themselves displaying their clean-cut smiles, crew cuts, and dream of collegiate jazz once more. Story ended, they sat back slowly inside the cavernous club and awaited the white-haired, former bowling-alley proprietor's response. Amazingly, Frank Holzfiend fell right in step with Charles Suber, offering wholehearted backing and the all-too-generous donation of a Blue Note engagement for the eventual festival winner.[8]

Delighted, delirious, more than a little tired, but definitely on their way, Tom Cahill and Bill Graham wrapped themselves back up in coats and hats, shook the last Chicago hand of the day, and sprinted off to catch the South Shore train back to South Bend. Few, if any, words

were exchanged during the return trip, as the two could only sit looking at each other in glass-eyed glee, unable to believe what had just
been wrought. It had been an extraordinary day with extraordinary
men. There was electricity in the air, and a collegiate jazz festival was
on its wobbling way.

Returning to Chicago and the *down beat* offices a few weeks later
to finalize plans and smooth out the event's multitudinous rough edges
(Cahill and Graham, idealists, were also Cahill and Graham, businessmen enough to demand everything—Frank Holzfiend's booking commitment included—in writing),[9] the now-familiar Notre Dame duo had
a number of things to report. Already, a festival committee had been
organized and a small budget procured. In addition, the date of Saturday, April 11 (one of the few remaining open slots on the student-
government spring calendar) had been selected for the event. Despite
these achievements, however, there remained the nagging lack of a
festival locale.

During this second *down beat* trip, Graham ventured a call from
Charles Suber's office to St. Mary's College (the all-girls school run
by the Sisters of the Holy Cross just across the Dixie Highway from
Notre Dame) to determine whether the festival could be put on in
the auditorium there. The ensuing conversation had some surprising
results.

"Hello, Sister," intoned Graham on making contact with the proper
department, "This is the vice president of the Student Council at Notre
Dame calling. I . . . I was wondering if you would perhaps give permission to hold our jazz festival at St. Mary's and . . . Pardon me?
Oh . . . Oh I see, Sister. Yes, yes, I understand." Conversation ended,
Graham slowly put the phone back down and looked over at his wide-
eyed, saddened partners. "Doesn't the Sister like jazz?" asked a puzzled
and hurt Tom Cahill, to which the somewhat stunned Graham could
only shake his head. "Oh no," he responded. "It's not that. She just
doesn't want any conflict with the George Shearing date she has
booked."[10]

Undaunted, Cahill and Graham returned to South Bend and examined other possibilities, including aged Washington Hall, and finally settled on the Old Fieldhouse, the only building on the Notre
Dame campus both available and large enough to house such an event.
It was the most logical, if not the most atmospheric choice.

As yet not quite undone by age, but definitely headed down that
route (as the word "old" already seemed to hint), the Fieldhouse was
the repository of countless memories of Notre Dame sports events and
performances. Originally constructed out of Georgia pine in 1899 and

rebuilt after a devastating fire in November 1900, the "new" Fieldhouse (rededicated on March 10, 1901) quickly became the center of Notre Dame athletics for the next half-century. Sporting an indoor track, a boxing room, handball, wrestling, and baseball facilities and, after a 1925 enlargement, a fencing room and movable hardwood basketball court, the Fieldhouse's unusual size also made it a natural haven for other large campus events and activities: concerts, commencement exercises, the famous yearly student boxing "Bengal Bouts" (held under the watchful eye of fireplug-shaped-trainer Dominick J. Napolitano), and, of course, the legendary Friday-night, pre-football-game pep rallies, a Notre Dame tradition for years.[11]

Huge, rectangular, topped by a long, arched roof supported by ten semicircular iron trusses resting in turn on the fireproof brick walls, the Fieldhouse, though often guilty of swallowing musical performances whole, was indeed ideal for a jazz festival. It could house several thousand listeners without difficulty. It was comfortable and, above all, familiar to students and the surrounding community, who knew of the famous play of 1930s All-American basketball star (and later athletic director) Edward "Moose" Krause, as well as the down-court feints and swishes of current high-scoring standout Tom Hawkins. And, though it would obviously take some doing to turn the basketball court at the east end of the place into something resembling a stage, the area was at least there for the sculpting.

By now, in addition to the committee (consisting of seven students) and the Fieldhouse locale, the "idea" also had a name: the Midwest Collegiate Jazz Festival. Its scope, as determined by Cahill, Graham, and the others with Charles Suber's essential over-the-shoulder aid, would be regional and would therefore include college bands from all over the central United States: Illinois, Ohio, Indiana, Iowa, Michigan, Minnesota, Wisconsin, and more. Designed to allow groups in these areas, many of them quite good, a chance to appear publicly and perhaps go on to the ranks of professional jazz, the festival's purpose would also be to provide "good, solid entertainment" for the student body and the South Bend community at large.[12]

To that end, Cahill, Graham, and company set out on a high-speed publicity campaign, forwarding pertinent information to schools throughout the Midwest with the hope that someone, somewhere, might indeed reply.[13] Open to any college jazz group able to muster up a modest registration fee, the festival soon found itself awash with over thirty-five applications (some even accompanied by audition tapes), from which sixteen groups, ranging from trios to big bands, were selected.[14] Set up as a one-day affair, the event was now slated to feature two distinct music sessions: a preliminary round stretching from 1 P.M. to 6 P.M. and an 8 P.M. to 10 P.M. head-to-head finalists' bout.

With the unequalled assistance of *down beat*'s Charles Suber, the festival committee rapidly assembled a panel of diverse, well-known judges that included Suber himself, Blue Note club owner Frank Holzfiend, Chicago radio/television station WGN music director Robert Trendler, and popular jazz accordionist Art Van Damme, winner of *down beat*'s "Reader's Poll" for the last seven years (as of late March, the Reverend Norman O'Connnor, one of the creators of the Newport Jazz Festival, was also tentatively scheduled to attend).[15] Not only did these talented men lend instant prestige and structure to the event, but they insured the festival's commitment to jazz education as well.

In such capable judging hands, festival winners would be carefully sorted out, the final decision in each case depending fully on deep-rooted jazz experience and knowledge and not merely an audience reaction (which had, in truth, been the only "judge" in the old Savoy Ballroom band battles in Harlem during the thirties and forties between groups led by Chick Webb, Count Basie, Jimmie Lunceford, and Fletcher Henderson). Even more importantly, for the first time on the collegiate level, the panel would make use of a judging sheet adapted by Suber and *down beat* from the Music Educators National Conference, thereby establishing judging criteria such as tone, blend, intonation, dynamics, balance, and more.[16] Thus, each participating group in the festival would be assured of an individual, written critique from four (and, with luck, five) different, dedicated jazz sources after the event had ended.

Working with a limited budget and staff the festival crew constructed a wooden platform stage (backed by a heavy blue velvet curtain that served to block out much of the unappealing wall, basketball scoreboard, and wooden exit doors) at the southeast end of the Fieldhouse basketball floor as the actual festival date drew near. Lighting, admittedly primitive, was acquired from the Washington Hall Theater Department, and committee fears of acoustical nightmares were quietly quelled by an adequate miking and amplification system put together from various local sources, most notably the student-run radio station on campus, WSND, which, oddly enough, had less than a decade ago located its broadcasting facilities in the Fieldhouse boxing room.[17]

Although pieces seemed to be falling into place, there was no easing of tensions for those in charge as the festival day approached. This, of course, was mainly due to the fact that no one on the committee itself could accurately predict which of the bands contacted would actually show up at all. Even worse, neither Cahill, Graham, nor anyone else had the slightest idea what to do in that event, or in case any of a hundred other things went wrong. Millions of unanswerable questions filtered down through the minds of the young, ceaselessly active Notre Dame jazz cohorts, but, fortunately, several hard facts existed to bolster their occasionally flagging musical spirits.

First of all, there were festival sponsors: *down beat*, the Blue Note, the Notre Dame Student Government, and, most recently, the Elkhart, Indiana-based music companies of C. G. Conn Ltd. and H & A Selmer, Inc., which volunteered to take care of all the prizes for individual soloists at the festival. Second, the committee had cash awards and engraved plaques to offer the festival winners; third, they had acquired an atmospheric locale and, lastly, they had arranged a tantalizing smorgasbord of top-notch collegiate jazz. Still, there was no festival yet, and though it all seemed set, the appointed date was taking forever to roll around. Finally, the day arrived.

The judges pulled in first: Blue Note owner Frank Holzfiend and Charles Suber maneuvering the distance from Chicago with another noteworthy passenger in tow, the Reverend George Wiskirchen, C.S.C., a 1951 graduate of the University of Notre Dame and overworked resident music instructor at Notre Dame High School for Boys (unaffiliated with the university in South Bend) in Niles, Illinois, since 1956. A renowned pioneer of the "Stage Band" movement, jazz educator, and author in his own right, Father Wiskirchen's high-school jazz band, "The Melodons," had been etching a name for itself in the national music consciousness by playing consistently amazing, sophisticated jazz at festivals, events, and on radio. Interested in any development that might foster jazz-education in the schools, and a friend of Charles Suber's, Father Wiskirchen gladly accepted the ride to see what might be happening down at his South Bend alma mater this day.

With the arrival of Art Van Damme and Robert Trendler by late morning, the panel of judges was present and accounted for (the Reverend Norman O'Connor, unfortunately, could not attend). For Cahill and Graham, that was critical step number one. But what about the bands? Slowly, surely, they began to trickle in. Just after noon, festival committee members nervously fingering fresh copies of the tiny, four-page blue paper program suddenly looked up to find that, incredibly, each and every one of the groups scheduled to attend had found a way there.

The judges, already on familiar terms, made small talk with one another, not a little intrigued by the dirt floor and white-painted, brick-wall surroundings as endless gaggles of crew-cut, coat-and-tied musicians began to fill Fieldhouse niches with warm-up chatter and nervous instrument sound. Art Van Damme consented to sign a few autographs; Holzfiend, Trendler, and Suber strolled around the stage, sizing up the decorations and massive Fieldhouse look before moving to the long, wooden judges' table, set up near the northwest corner of the basketball court for premier viewing and listening.

Amid the chaotic scramble, the table full of nicely sharpened pencils, neatly stacked judging sheets and programs, silver water pitchers, and sparkling, face-down glasses seemed a welcome refuge of order. Noting that the time was rapidly approaching the hour of 1:00, the trio sat down in the comfortably padded chairs, waved over Art Van Damme, and waited for the event to begin.

The first band took the stage and arranged its equipment as a crisp, ineluctable jazz tension hung like a hundred high-wire balancing acts in the air. Microphones in place, lighting in order, bits of daylight streaking through the partially paint-blackened, rafter-high east windows to illuminate eerily the American flag that dangled far above the stage from loose ceiling ropes, the festival, much to the committee's relief, was with one drumbeat and fingersnap just what it had been intended to be: an idea of jazz. It was swinging. It was exciting. It was April 11, 1959, 1:03 P.M. on the campus of the University of Notre Dame, and the Midwest Collegiate Jazz Festival couldn't be stopped.

Still, the fans, outside of a scattering of the curious, just weren't there. To the musicians in attendance, however, the ones already comparing styles and techniques and warming up elbow to elbow in the assorted cubbyholes of the Fieldhouse and nearby LaFortune Student Center, this initial lack of audience couldn't have mattered less. They had come to play and to listen, to "compete" healthily with one another in a new jazz environment as they kicked up the aged Fieldhouse dust with jazz in all its multifaceted glory. It was their arena, their place to learn and give their own learning back. For once, regardless of those many or few who came to listen, they could breathe deeply in an unconfined jazz air.

To the festival committee, of course, the lack of spectators meant something entirely different. Fortunately for all concerned, Tom Cahill had arranged for the student radio station WSND to broadcast early portions of the festival, along with interviews and other related publicity blurbs. As a result, a gradually wakening-to-collegiate-jazz campus was suddenly up and hustling toward the Fieldhouse to join the swelling, cheering crowd.

By the midpoint in the five-and-one-half-hour preliminaries (from which the six evening finalists would be chosen), nearly 1,200 people were packed in for the fifteen- to twenty-minute collegiate jazz sets.

With additional radio publicity continuing throughout the day, the crowd and the number of calls about the festival coming in to an already overwhelmed university switchboard could do little else but expand. By the time the evening session unfurled, close to 2,000 fans were roaring along with the music onstage.[18] Jammed to east-end capacity, the Fieldhouse appeared about to burst with some gigantic musical pep-rally that didn't know how to stop.

Back against one of the Fieldhouse walls, Cahill, Graham, and the other committee members whistled together in quiet awe of the crowds, the music, and the proceedings that were going so magnificently well. They talked over the day, the judges, and, most of all, the memorable performances caught in snatches in the midst of running around: 233-pound Lois Nemser of the University of Cincinnati churning through slow, soulful ballads like "Blue Moon" with a guitar and bass trio; tenor saxophonist Sonny McBroom throwing out thick solo after solo over a hard-pushing Ohio State University brass section that didn't seem as if it could ever quit;[19] Purdue University's dazzling jazz accordionist Bob Sardo swinging through a rousing eight-minute original called "Some Blues";[20] the hard-driving sounds of the University of Detroit's Bob Pierson Quartet with talented drummer Ben Appling in tow;[21] the infectious improvisations produced by University of Illinois sextet alto-saxophonist Dave Hutson and flautist/tenor-saxophonist Joe Firrantello (who would soon change his last name to Farrell); and, finally, the Southern Illinois All-Stars Band, which included a young baritone saxophonist by the name of Hamiet Bluiett in its swinging jazz midst. Those and all the other individuals and groups from DePaul University, Marquette, Oberlin College, Indiana University, Michigan State, St. John's (of Minnesota), and Notre Dame brought the collegiate jazz sound and the Old Fieldhouse to life as never before.

From the six finalist bands (the Yeomen of Oberlin College, the Chuck Lewis Sextet of Michigan State, Dave's Band of Indiana University, the UJW Quartet of the University of Minnesota, The Bob Pierson Quartet of the University of Detroit, the Ohio State Jazz Forum Band, and a vocal group, The Ivy's of Western Michigan), the judges, after retiring to confer in the cramped student-manager's office, selected the festival winners. First place as best overall group went to the UJW (University Jazz Workshop) Quartet, led by "Zoot Sims-like" tenor saxophonist/classics scholar Gary Berg.[22] A collegiate hodgepodge of talent possible only at an event such as the one just spinning down, the group also featured chemistry major/part-time beer salesman Herb Pilhofer on piano, a psychologist, Tim D'Andrea, on drums, and, as might have been expected, a music major, Tim Hughart, on bass.[23] Rehearsing for but a few weeks previous to the festival, the quartet garnered a three-week Blue Note engagement and a student-government sponsored $200 cash award.

Second place and $100 went to the crowd favorite, Dave's Band of Indiana University, led by trombonist Dave Baker. Featuring no less than six trumpets and five trombones (as well as comely vocalist Arlene Martel), the group was also named Best Band (one notch below the top UJW Quartet slot). Third and $75 belonged to the seventeen-piece Ohio State aggregate led by Lowell Latto, and, finally, fourth place and a cash award of $50 went to the Bob Pierson Quartet of the University of Detroit, a group also selected as Best Combo in the "quintet or smaller" category.

Another finalist, the Ivy's, an admittedly difficult-to-"pigeonhole" Four Freshmen-esque group that accompanied itself on bass, snare drum, and electric piano, received a special merit award, along with unexpected WGN radio and television bookings at the behest of judge Robert Trendler. Vocalist Lois Nemser, tenor man Sonny McBroom, alto-saxophonist Dave Hutson, and accordionist Bob Sardo snared individual awards, while the latter also managed to take in the festival's Outstanding Instrumentalist category as well.[24] Asked to comment on the young Sardo's jazz prowess, Art Van Damme wryly remarked, "I'd like to step on his fingers."[25] Pausing a moment to take in festival memories as musicians and fans milled about the judges' table, a more serious Van Damme added, "It's the finest affair I've ever been to; it just knocked me out."[26]

"I've renewed my faith in jazz,"[27] chimed in Frank Holzfiend (who was presently set to engage two other festival groups besides the UJW Quartet for his club) as he stood near a beaming Charles Suber, the two men joking lightly about booking agents like Freddie Williamson of Associated Booking Corporation cornering some of the young jazz talent during the festival to "talk shop."[28] Beneath the humor, though, Holzfiend and Suber realized the importance of the event as a potential spawning ground for as yet unheralded jazz voices and softly predicted to one another that there would be a day when hordes of recordmen, festival promoters, and bookers would descend upon South Bend to ply their trade. That was, of course, if there was to be another festival. With the size of the evening's crowd still fresh in mind, Charles Suber, for one, had a hunch he might well be back in the Fieldhouse next spring. "Five years from now I'm going to be very glad to say I was here at the first one," he remarked before moving off quickly to congratulate a tired-looking group of young festival committee men in crew cuts.[29]

The first Midwest Collegiate Jazz Festival was now in the delicate process of winding down. Judges and fans who had come to see and hear collegiate jazz were now happily headed home on a stratospheric "jazz-high," most of them unaware that it had taken until spring to crack a student body's stubborn case of winter blues. And all because two students, Tom Cahill and Bill Graham, had put a thought and hope in motion, a thought and hope about jazz. "From an embryonic idea has grown what may well become, within the span of a few short years, the ultimate in collegiate jazz competition," read the enthusiastic, though perhaps näively conceived opening lines of the small festival program now tattered, rolled, and worn inside a couple of weary student-government hands. Little did the writers know how true those very words would ring, through twenty-seven festival springs to come.

Dashing architecture student/guitarist Gene Bertoncini leads the popular dance band Lettermen through their swinging 1958 paces at the Navy Drill Hall. (Photo courtesy Paul Willihnganz)

Led by Gene Bertoncini (center), a smaller University of Notre Dame jazz combo made up of drummer Paul Willihnganz (left), pianist Wally Jones (second from right), and vocalist Vince Mauro (right), played both in the South Bend area and on campus during 1958-59. (Photo courtesy Paul Willihnganz)

University of Cincinnati singer Lois Nemser belts out another slow, soulful ballad like "Blue Moon" en route to a '59 Best Vocalist award. Accompanist Don Miller didn't fare too badly either, taking the top prize on guitar.
(Photo courtesy David B. Sommer)

Tirelessly throwing out solo after solo over a hard-driving Ohio State Jazz Forum band, hornman Sonny McBroom led his group into the '59 finals and snared a Best Tenor-Saxophone award.
(Photo courtesy David B. Sommer)

The UJW Quartet from the University of Minnesota, led by tenor-saxophonist/ classics scholar Gary Berg (front left), took first place as Best Overall Group at the 1959 Midwest Collegiate Jazz Festival. With that honor went $200 in cash and a three-week engagement at Frank Holzfiend's Blue Note in Chicago.
(Photo courtesy David B. Sommer)

Led by trombonist Dave Baker (left), Dave's Band of Indiana University quickly won over the 1959 festival crowd and was named Best Band.
(Photo courtesty David B. Sommer)

The University of Detroit's Bob Pierson Quartet, led by flautist/saxophonist Bob Pierson, snared 1959's Best Combo award, as well as Best Bass (William Wood, center), and Best Drums (Ben Appling). Also pictured (right) is pianist John Griffith.
(Photo courtesy David B. Sommer)

Chapter 2

THE SIXTIES

I got to meet a lot of musicians and got to hear what they had to say. I wanted to hear what the *world* was saying. —Trumpeter Carmell Jones, speaking of the 1960 Collegiate Jazz Festival

The Hippest College Bash of Them All

1960 One month after the Midwest Collegiate Jazz Festival sounded its last strain, Charles Suber made good on the final clause of his *down beat* pact. Stressing the refreshing absence of "goatees and jive talk," Suber's glowing "First Chorus" review offered high praise for the caliber of musicianship at the festival, crowd behavior, overall concept, and, most of all, the "bang-up job" done by organizers Bill Graham, Tom Cahill, and the rest of the Notre Dame crew. "Many a commercial promoter could take lessons from the students in charge of arrangements," wrote the *down beat* publisher and festival "father figure," who went on to declare, "They even had the piano retuned after the afternoon session!"[1]

Closer to the University of Notre Dame campus, the *Scholastic's* opening commentary the week following the festival offered additional kudos to Tom Cahill's Student Affairs Commission for putting on "probably the most important student function of the year." Noting that the event had courageously overcome such "paramount obstacles" as "initial student apathy" and "poor acoustics" (a topic diplomatically sidestepped by Charles Suber, who diverted *down beat* reader attention to the "well-draped" Fieldhouse instead), the *Scholastic* went on to congratulate Bill Graham and the festival committee and dub the festival an "all too short" and "near professional show."

15

"The almost unlimited potential for student satisfaction which last week's performance revealed," the publication continued, made plain the need to retain the festival and expand the following year into a "two-day affair."[2] By May 1959, it became excitingly clear that a new festival committee and a now "financially convinced" sponsoring student government would heed the journalistic advice and do just that.

Unfortunately, this second festival would not be able to make use of the fast-accumulated jazz expertise of Tom Cahill and Bill Graham. Scheduled to graduate in May and go their separate ways in the world outside Notre Dame, the two entrepreneur/friends could only (with understandable reluctance) turn the festival reins over to someone else. A successor had to be found. Eventually, one was—'59 jazz festival committee member Jim Naughton.

A twenty-one-year-old senior from Painesville, Ohio, majoring in communication arts, Naughton combined an unbridled, though occasionally thoughtful and scholarly enthusiasm for jazz (prior to the 1959 festival, he had penned a *Scholastic* article containing jazz-literature references dating back as far as 1917) with a firsthand working knowledge of festival operations and complexities. Still, despite these obvious qualifications, there was little to be gleaned about running a two-day jazz event from the departing festival heads; they had had only one day to deal with, and (as he well knew) it had been difficult enough at that. The arrangements, the number of attending bands, and the crowd size would all have to increase dramatically, as would the already too apparent risks.

On a more positive note, Naughton was assured of continued help and support from *down beat*, Selmer, and a much more cooperative student government, and, at the very least, that was a firm festival foundation upon which to build. With these things in mind and the 1960 festival committee loosely organized, Jim Naughton dug in and began to work. To his surprise, he began to find help in practically every musical corner in which he chose to look.

In part due to the critical success of the first National Stage Band Camp organized in 1959 by South Bend, Indiana, businessman Ken Morris, Dr. Eugene Hall of the University of Michigan Music Department and popular band leader/jazz idol Stan Kenton[3] (as well as the growing Stage Band movement in the high schools and the sudden rise of college jazz), the musical world was more than ready to deal with this persuasive young man from Notre Dame and get in on a good thing. To Jim Naughton's unknowing good fortune, 1960 just happened to be the year in which everything began to click.

Professional band leaders and promoters like George Wein, Woody

Herman, and Stan Kenton were suddenly on the prowl for fresh, young, exciting talent no longer available on the evaporating jazz-club scene; a collegiate jazz festival offered them a potent new showcase from which to pick and choose. Musical-instrument companies noting the rapid growth of student-musician ranks and highly evident hints of an approaching boom in instrument/sheet-music sales looked upon the Notre Dame spring rite with a fondly misted corporate eye. Jazz-club owners and record executives immediately sensed in the event a source of inexpensive, enthusiastic music to help heal recession wounds. Music educators viewed it as a year-long goal, a gauge of the progress made in jazz education in a number of universities, as well as a method of measuring teaching ideas and techniques against those of professional peers. In short, the festival by 1960 was many things to many people, and that, in itself, suited Jim Naughton just fine.

Working an average of forty hours a week throughout the summer and fall of 1959, Naughton (who, like predecessor Bill Graham, was both jazz-festival chairman and student-body vice-president) made the necessary headway. By November, he had not only lined up prize bookings at the Blue Note in Chicago, *down beat* scholarships, and mammoth traveling trophies, but had arranged an astounding festival advisory board (with Charles Suber's help) as well.

Included in this wide-ranging list of names assembled from the world of entertainment and music were Fred C. Williamson (vice-president of Joe Glaser's Associated Booking Corporation), Louis Lorillard (president of the Newport Jazz Festival), Dr. Eugene Hall, Larry Berk (director of the Berklee School of Music), Ken Morris (director of the National Stage Band Camp), Dave Garroway, Steve Allen, Frank Holzfiend, the Reverend Norman O'Connor, Marian McPartland, Benny Goodman, Duke Ellington, and John J. Maher (chairman of the board of Maher Publications, publishers of *down beat*, and other publications).[4] In addition, Naughton had organized and expanded the previous year's college mailing lists and released informational letters delineating eligibility requirements, application procedures, and festival rules.

Most importantly, the name of the event had been altered. Instead of using the self-limiting appellation "Midwest," Naughton and crew substituted the open-ended Collegiate Jazz Festival, or CJF, as it would soon become colloquially known. A two-day March gathering of collegiate jazz clans, the event would, according to a small *down beat* blurb in late 1959, "accommodate forty bands"[5] (this number as immediately suspect as the grossly inflated figure of "eighty bands" predicted by *down beat* — working no doubt with information acquired from overenthusiastic Notre Dame committee members — for the inaugural jazz fest).[6]

With the change in festival size and name also came a change in scope. Taking advantage of what was felt to be a "grass roots" jazz-education mandate in colleges and universities, the 1960 Collegiate Jazz Festival (under Naughton and Suber's guiding hands) would look not only in the Midwest for talent, but across the entire United States as well. In that way, it was rationalized, a more accurate cross section of musical ability (not to mention a tremendously diverse, exciting format) could be achieved.

That being the direction, as the early months of 1960 rumbled around (Notre Dame's winter blues as deep-set as ever after yet another lackluster 5–5 football season under new coach Joe Kuharich) and the piles of more than fifty reel-to-reel audition tapes now required of all applicants, along with a standard $15 fee, began to be whittled down to an acceptable twenty-six, it became apparent that, indeed, the festival's character would be entirely different. School combos and big bands selected to attend in 1960 would not only represent familiar Midwest states such as Indiana, Ohio, Michigan, Iowa, Illinois, and Minnesota but previously untapped places such as Texas, Vermont, Tennessee, New Hampshire, Washington, D.C., West Virginia, Nebraska, Colorado, and Kansas. This was a major step toward establishing an event of national scope, the next step necessary if the Collegiate Jazz Festival was to tap the pulse of U.S. collegiate jazz.

In addition to these developments, the judging panel was to be expanded by one. Seeking to adhere to the critic/educator/club owner/jazz-musician balance established the previous year by Suber, Cahill, and Graham, Jim Naughton looked hard to acquire big-time names on each count. Phone calls were placed day and night, week after week, month upon month, tracking down jazz notables through secretaries, associates, musicians, girlfriends, and wives until Naughton and his committee members were well on their way to racking up the highest phone bill in student-government history.[7] By February of the new year, however, the work and cost had more than paid off.

The new "national" look of the second festival would include in its judging panel not only regulars Charles Suber of *down beat* and Blue Note-owner Frank Holzfiend, but renowned Washington, D.C. "Voice of America" jazz programmer/broadcaster and perennial Newport Jazz Festival master of ceremonies Willis Conover. Not satisfied with this prestige-adding minor coup, Naughton soon snared Robert Share, administrator of Boston's Berklee School of Music, one of the top jazz-education institutions in the United States. Finally, for the last judging spot, Naughton and Suber obtained the services of the musician who was considered by many the biggest professional jazz name in 1960: Stan Kenton.

At the end of the Fifties, Stan Kenton was perhaps the most influential musician in big-band jazz and, therefore, so were his arrangements or "charts" in high-school and college Stage Band repertoires. Utilizing explosive talent over the years such as drummer Shelly Manne, trumpeter Maynard Ferguson, alto-saxophonists Art Pepper and Lee Konitz, tenor-wizard Stan Getz, composer/arrangers Pete Rugolo, Johnny Richards, Shorty Rogers, and more, Kenton's varying groups had moved into the jazz-world spotlight during the last decade with a new "progressive" sound.

Though the critics were often intimidated by Kenton's music and his attempts to extend jazz's "legitimacy" by integrating classically orchestrated sounds into his works (hence the "progressive" label), the dapper, articulate band leader had become a frequent visitor to plush concert halls and college campuses. By the late fifties, then, Kenton, in the public eye, was the "man" and his group was the "sound." Most of all, though, he was an exemplary teacher who (no doubt recalling his own difficult early days trying to pry hints and praise from jazzmen in California clubs) went out of his way to work with aspiring, young musicians, eventually going so far as to donate his valuable presence and time to the National Stage Band Camp free of charge.

That such a national figure would agree to come to a fledgling festival located in South Bend, Indiana (the most unlikely mecca for collegiate or professional jazz) was extraordinary. And, if such a national figure were actually to attend and enjoy the jazz proceedings, there was no telling what might come the festival's way. That, too, suited Jim Naughton just fine.

Naughton also liked the way the prize list was shaping up. As of March, roughly $5,000 worth of instruments and trophies awaited the festival winners.[8] Individual soloists selected as the "festival best" on their respective instruments would, instead of plaques and pats on the back, receive new instruments, courtesy of music manufacturers such as Selmer, Conn, Rogers, Gibson, Kay, Wurlitzer, and the Voice of Music Corporation. Incredibly, these acts of industry "goodwill" meant that winning young trumpeters would acquire new trumpets, piano players brand-new electric keyboards, bass players string basses, and drummers full sets of drums! There had never been anything like it for American collegians, and Jim Naughton knew this was the best way to display the festival's aim of providing the best possible environment for collegiate jazz.

Along with the attractive lure of professional engagements at Chicago's Blue Note and the upcoming summer Detroit Jazz Festival, "prize" goods of this nature did much to insure the attendance of bands from far-off locales. After all, what sane, struggling collegiate jazz band or leader would pass up the chance to play before Stan Kenton, Willis Conover, the publisher of *down beat*, club owners, and booking agents and possibly miss garnering a bit of this festival prize luster and loot? More than that, awards brought credit to individuals and groups and gave tangible proof of a collegiately "approved" music, as well as the united effort of musical interests in backing this necessary educational tool. As of 1960, awards were the stuff that stood for legitimacy and progress and a jazz-education movement that could no longer be summarily ignored or pushed aside.

Somewhere in the midst of all this progress though, Naughton and his hardworking committee of twelve sensed trouble. Too much commercialism, glitter, festival hoopla, and prize "gold" for the attending musicians could (if handled the wrong way) turn the well-intended event into a cutthroat competition of the worst kind. And yet, suddenly to turn away the outpouring of instruments and newfound media attention would also seriously damage hopes for future growth. Fortunately, there was another way. So long as the jazz trappings couldn't be rearranged on short notice, Naughton and crew decided that the basic festival philosophy could. Though still based on a "battle of the bands" format, this second festival would have to begin the move away from out-and-out competition to the true meaning of the name "festival." To those close to jazz and CJF orchestrations, such as WSND disc jockey/jazz critic Pete Herbert, this shift or, rather, "reemphasis" of original festival ideals was welcome indeed.

"Since its conception not much more than a year ago," wrote Herbert in a thoughtful *Scholastic* piece the week before the 1960 Fieldhouse affair, "the Collegiate Jazz Festival at Notre Dame has helped to close the gap between talent and recognition; a gap that has forced many a young musician into early retirement." "But," he continued, "stress should be placed on the fact that this is not essentially a contest but rather a festival: if you've got something to say, come here and be heard: this is the lure of the CJF."[9]

Without such reexamination of festival values, it would indeed have been easy for Jim Naughton to step into a lighthearted ego-waltz, for on the first day of the event, Friday, March 18, reporters from *Time* magazine, the *Saturday Evening Post*, *down beat*, the *Jazz Review*, the *Chicago Sun Times*, the *South Bend Tribune*, and numerous other local papers were on hand to explore and record this curious collegiate sight.

Following the guidelines set down in 1959, the first "preliminary" music session was scheduled to begin at 1:00 P.M., with each participating group allowed twenty minutes to display its jazz wares before the panel of distinguished judges and a no-less-distinguished but much more highly charged and vocal crowd.

The atmospheric Fieldhouse, once again "well draped" but exhibiting a much improved lighting and sound system, was the logical site. By the designated opening afternoon starting time, the Ralph Mutchler-directed Jazz Workshop Band from Northwestern University had taken the stage, the judges were comfortably in place, and the usual crowd of stragglers was beginning to swell. Suddenly, as if induced by a mystic cannon shot, the Fieldhouse was crackling again with collegiate jazz in a way it hadn't since April 11 of the previous year.

Before the session ended four toe-tapping hours later at 5 P.M., ten riveting bands and combos had appeared, including the Stan Cowell Trio of Oberlin College, the Behm-Martin Sextet of the University of Iowa, the University of Nebraska Varsity Five, the Allan Beutler Quartet of Michigan State, a smartly uniformed USAFA Jazz Trio from the Air Force Academy in Colorado, solo pianist Ran Blake of New York's Bard College, and Notre Dame's own Lettermen, minus Gene Bertoncini and consisting of Wally Jones (piano), Jack Carr (drums), Len LaRose (bass), Charlie Armstrong (trombone), and saxophonist Bob Brown. Set for the 7–11 P.M. preliminary competition were familiar faces such as the UJW Quartette from the University of Minnesota, mysterious unknowns from Washington, D.C.'s Catholic University of America, Wayne State, the University of Kansas, and Randolph-Macon College of Virginia, and two particularly intriguing aggregates, the North Texas State College Lab Band and Rev. George Wiskirchen's Niles, Illinois-based Notre Dame High School band, the Melodons.

The appearance of North Texas State's premier Lab Band (the term "lab" originating at North Texas in 1946 as the shortened heading for "dance-band laboratory" classes designed to "experiment" with new musical ideas) at the Collegiate Jazz Festival in 1960 had from the start seemed to Jim Naughton and those in charge little short of a jazz-education match made in heaven. Establishing the standard for jazz studies within a respected university years before, in 1946, North Texas had begun to offer a jazz-specialized Bachelor of Music degree in 1955. In addition, an extensive library of band arrangements had evolved for student study and use, thereby keeping pace with the Lab Band, which was ever expanding in diversity and size.

Entered in a nationwide College Dance Band contest in 1952 by Lab Band director/program conceiver Eugene Hall, only to place fifth, the North Texas group had finally catapulted to major U.S. recognition in 1959 by reaching the finals of a national Best New Band Competition sponsored by the American Federation of Music. Stunning a field of 187 groups, the North Texas State Lab Band was selected along with three other bands (all professional) to play in the finals held at the Roseland Ballroom in New York City. To everyone's surprise but their own, they finished third.[10] Music educators and jazz personnel nationwide took note: something was happening down amid the sand dunes in Texas.

Though presently directed by Leon Breeden (who assumed band and program directorship after Dr. Eugene Hall departed to start a new system of jazz studies at Michigan State), the band was still poised to make new, exciting contributions to the energetic world of collegiate jazz. And, in the spring of 1960, there was no better way to do that than by performing at a festival like the one at Notre Dame. To be sure, there had been other festivals (at which North Texas State usually swept all the awards), but nothing quite like this, with national coverage and top-notch personalities on hand. It was a show that couldn't be passed up, and Breeden's Lab Band (after sending in its application fee and audition tape and receiving a prompt affirmative reply) bided its time in Denton, Texas, raising funds for the long, hard cross-country bus ride to South Bend.

In addition to this stellar college group, Naughton had invited Father Wiskirchen and his precocious Notre Dame High School Melodons (recent winners of the Chicago Area High School Stage Band Competition), to attend the 1960 Collegiate Jazz Festival as a guest band in the Friday-evening preliminaries. Already intrigued by the music he had witnessed and absorbed the previous year, Wiskirchen readily agreed to come. Known to many as a driving force behind the move toward high-school jazz education in the mid-to-late fifties, Father Wiskirchen had singlehandedly transformed the music department of the newborn Notre Dame boys high school of Niles, Illinois, into a wide-ranging contemporary and classical-music workshop for young musicians.

Ordained into the priesthood in 1955 upon completing studies in Washington D.C. and Portland, Oregon (barely four years after his graduation from the University of Notre Dame), Father Wiskirchen had come to Notre Dame High School that same year and quickly made efficient use of the modern music facilities available to him to teach the school's first freshman class. A proficient cornetist and former University of Notre Dame concert-band member long interested in all types of music—classical as well as jazz—Wiskirchen soon had students thriving in both realms under his tireless tutelage in everything from varsity and cadet bands to marching ensembles, not to mention orchestras, choral groups, and swing bands. His pride and joy, though, were the "jazz lab" Melodons, who for the past few years had been knocking out audiences with their collegiate-level jazz prowess and exciting, fresh sound.[11]

If North Texas State in 1960 stood for what was possibly the pinnacle of collegiate jazz, the Melodons and Father Wiskirchen represented the finest in high-school Stage Bands. Best of all, both were coming to South Bend to flex their ensemble muscle and to show the jazz world what they could do. Even more importantly, band directors Leon Breeden and Father Wiskirchen were two more top-level emissaries of jazz education in the schools to add to already flush festival VIP lists. Jazz, so it seemed, was indeed at long last going to college.

Along the "academia versus jazz" lines, a strange and humorous meeting took place during opening festival hours in the lobby of the Morris Inn, the university-run hotel located at the end of the tree-lined southern approach to the Notre Dame campus. As chance would have it, at the same time the Collegiate Jazz Festival was blasting out at the Fieldhouse, a quiet academic conference was in session at the Inn less than a half-mile away. Consisting of one hundred scholars assembled in South Bend for the eleventh annual meeting of the Metaphysical Society of America in order to discuss the nature of Being and Reality, the gathering was a natural target for queries on the nature of jazz. Fortunately, one *South Bend Tribune* reporter, Walter Collins, couldn't resist.

Cornering Yale professor of philosophy/Metaphysical Society founder Paul Weiss on his way to a lecture on "Experience" and presenting him with a tall, green 1960 Collegiate Jazz Festival program for quick perusal, Collins engaged the metaphysician in some truly surprising academic talk, which, of course, Collins kindly transcribed in print the next day for the hip, CJF/*South Bend Tribune*-reading crowd. The result went something like this.

"Metaphysics and jazz are both somewhat offbeat," began Weiss (whom, Collins noted, the "foot-stomping" audience at the festival might have "dug"). "Jazz is impossible without some awareness of classic beats. . . ." the professor continued, "and metaphysics is impossible without a classic background." (Translation/Collins: "You gotta feel it Dad, but you gotta know why.") "Both metaphysics and jazz are concerned with breaking new ground." (Translation/Collins: "It's Kenton or Brubeck.") "And both are seeking the truth in their own peculiar ways." (Translation/Collins: "Someone's on the line and I'm readin' him clear.") Shaking a few hands, Weiss then revealed to the reporter that he was writing two books on philosophy of art (Translation/Collins: "That music, that jazz, like it's art, too, like painting and stuff") and then concluded hastily, "Our way doesn't make much noise, but we hope it produces some light." (Translation/Collins: "Crazy, I'm blinded.")

Hustling off to his appointed meeting (a metaphysical tune-up for a later session on the "Categories of Being"), the professor expressed interest in the nearby jazz festival on campus, but politely declined an invitation, citing a lack of available time. "It was a shame they couldn't have gotten together," noted the wry reporter in his journalistic wrap-up, "If nothing else, the jazz fans and the philosopher could have compared beards." Unfortunately, related a bemused but cryptic Collins, "Paul Weiss doesn't wear a beard."[12]

A chance meeting of these two extremes—collegiate jazz and higher academia—had ended, and each had, unfortunately, once more, gone its separate way. Obviously, Jim Naughton and his cohorts were doing their best back in the Fieldhouse to avoid a similar schism, and, to their surprise, were finding themselves in the midst of a musical success.

Though the talent in the 1960 Collegiate Jazz Festival was perhaps not as outstanding as it had been in 1959, there could be no faulting the smooth production and professional manner with which the festival was being brought off. Bands and equipment moved on and off stage like clockwork, aided by additional Notre Dame student muscle recruited at the last minute. Announcements between performances were informative, and, fortunately, short-winded. The needs of both musicians and judges were attended to with thoughtfulness and speed. In fact, whatever formula Jim Naughton had hit upon to expedite a two-day jazz festival was surpassing even the highest expectations. And then, too, there was the crowd.

Numbering between 2,000 and 3,000 for the Friday-night preliminary session and 3,000 for the finals on Saturday evening, the audience was stunningly well-mannered, enthusiastic, and unstinting in whistled or applauded praise that did so much to urge the college musicians on.[13] "Clean-cut" in the best sense of the word, the people (some collegiate-jazz-festival "veterans" from the 1959 fest, others novices experiencing it all for the first time) were there for the sheer exhilaration of the event. Regardless of the gaps in musical knowledge, though, there was one thing everyone in attendance agreed upon by the second festival day: they couldn't get enough of the collegiate big bands, particularly those from North Texas State, Ohio State, and Northwestern University.

One reason for this was the imbalance between bands (four) and combos (twenty-two) at the festival, which made the comparatively rare appearance and sound of a large group a refreshing change from smaller combo work. In addition, the larger instrumental section of a big band enabled young musicians to cloak lapses in musical ideas, directions, and techniques more successfully, whereas such flaws stood out boldly in a smaller-group format, often deflating otherwise exciting, well-intended jazz performances.

Noting this festival trend, judge Willis Conover wisely remarked, "It's tough for a youngster to play jazz in a small group."[14] Fortunately for all concerned, however, there were several outstanding individual and collective performances that impressed judges, audiences, and critics alike.

Vocalist Lois Nemser was back again (with the Four Axemen of the University of Cincinnati) to wow judges with professional versions of "Gone With the Wind," "My Funny Valentine," and "Guess Who I Saw Today?"[15] Bob Sardo, last year's Outstanding Instrumentalist, returned with a well-rehearsed quartet (including the searing trumpet of Gary Barone) that took on difficult tempos, exhibited fine swing and played numbers like "Summertime" with a rare "togetherness."[16]

Trombonist Dave Baker's outstanding quintet from Indiana University (made up of Dave Young on tenor saxophone, Austin Crow on piano, Larry Ridley on bass, and Paul Parker on drums) left both crowd and assorted student musicians agog with their mature, original jazz sense and their approach to demanding material such as Ornette Coleman's "The Sphinx" and Baker's own "Kentucky Oysters."[17] (Unfortunately, Baker's group, clearly on its way to a second consecutive festival band award, would be excluded from judging consideration because it could not attend the final Saturday-evening session.) Meanwhile, trumpeter Carmell Jones sparked the University of Kansas Jays with his highly individual "Clifford Brown" sound and dexterity both during the festival on Ornette Coleman's "Dig" and "When Will the Blues Leave?" and at early-morning, downtown-bar jam sessions that left other musicians "shaking their heads."[18]

The UJW Quartette of Minnesota and the Bob Pierson Quartet of the University of Detroit ripped enthusiastically through challenging material with unusual collegiate confidence and rapport, while Ohio State big-band hornman Sonny McBroom returned to vie for yet another tenor-saxophone award. Finally, two new big-band soloists emerged: trombonist Loren Binford of Northwestern's Jazz Workshop Band and a trumpeter by the name of Marvin Stamm from North Texas State.

Not everyone, of course, could win an award or become one of the "chosen" Saturday-evening bands, and though the judges did their best to determine the proper finalists, the selections were by no means easy or fully appreciated by all. Few in the audience could imagine the give-and-take that went on in the stuffy student-manager's Fieldhouse office or the compromises that had to be made. Going against the grain in a number of cases, the eight finalists selected for the Saturday-night session that would stretch from 8–11 P.M. were the Brian Hardy Trio of Purdue University, the Modern Men of Dartmouth College, the Lettermen of Notre Dame, the Bob Pierson Quartet, the Dots Trio of Fairmont State College, West Virginia, the Northwestern Jazz Workshop Band, the Ohio State University Jazz Forum Big Band, and the North Texas State Lab Band.

Out of the roaring, crowd-jammed finals that evening emerged the triumphant winners, selected once again by the judging panel of Kenton, Suber, Conover, Holzfiend, and Share, who returned to the Fieldhouse world from their tiny cubicle after long minutes of discussion and several rounds of Irish coffee.[19] Surprising no one, North Texas State promptly snared both the Associated Booking trophy as Best Overall Group and the Detroit Jazz Festival summer engagement as Best Band. While challenged by the loose, freewheeling drive of Ohio State and Northwestern's fired-up finals play, the North Texas Lab Band's imaginative, complex arrangements, original compositions such as "Powell One" by trombonist Morgan Powell and rich, deep "Kenton-like" sound stole the show.[20]

Taking time to glance over at Stan Kenton during the Lab Band's finals set, judges' chairman Charles Suber noted the look on the bandleader's handsome, but ordinarily road-weary face as "transcendent." "He didn't look tired anymore," detailed Suber. "He could see a new crop of [Buddy] Childerses, [Maynard] Fergusons and [Conte] Candolis right before his eyes.[21]

Among the small groups, the Dots Trio, led by pompadoured, "Erroll Garner-like" pianist Tom Mustachio was selected as Best Combo.[22] An eighteen-year-old music major, Mustachio and his trio (bassist Frank Allevato, drummer Gene Piccalo) had refined their collective skills playing at college and fraternity dances in Fairmont, West Virginia (as well as at the local Three Dots Club from which they derived their name) and offered CJF audiences "cool" jazz versions of standards like "Misty" and "The Lady Is a Tramp."[23] "We wanted to give them a melody they knew," explained Mustachio, "something they could follow when we took off on our own."[24]

"They loved them," said Dots road manager Stanley Rote about the crowd. "The whole place went wild when they played," he continued, "They called for more when they were through and when they were chosen as the winners, the people just about tore down the auditorium."[25] Also named Best Pianist and Most Promising Soloist, triple-winner Mustachio received a Wurlitzer electric piano, a group engagement at the Blue Note in Chicago, and a scholarship to the upcoming summer National Stage Band Camp (by 1960, fast becoming known as the Stan Kenton Clinics). Still, upon learning that Associated Booking Corp. was eager to set up a cross-country tour for the trio, the pianist appeared to be somewhat perplexed by all the sudden attention.[26]

Trumpeter Marvin Stamm of North Texas State took honors as Outstanding Instrumentalist and Best Trumpet, and thereby pocketed a Berklee Scholarship as well as a new Conn trumpet, while Lois Nemser (best vocalist), Al Beutler (alto saxophone), Loren Binford (trombone), Bob Pierson (flute), and Dave Young (tenor saxophone) were also winners.[27] With these pronouncements and more, another festival was suddenly over, thanks to the efforts of chairman Jim Naughton (whose grade-point average dropped from 4.9—out of a possible 6—to 3.7 over the course of the year due to jazz-event demands).[28]

"This," exclaimed a tired-looking Stan Kenton (who had flown in from California on two hours' sleep, would stay up talking with student musicians until 5 A.M. Sunday morning, and then fly home), "has been the most magnificent, clean-cut, swinging affair I've ever attended."[29] Duly impressed with the potential of bands like North Texas State, Kenton then quipped, "If they ever turn professional, I know a lot of guys who aren't going to like it."[30]

Soon, however, Stan Kenton wasn't alone in his praise. Three weeks after the festival had shut down, *Time* magazine dubbed it "the hippest college bash of them all," and declared the music heard at Notre Dame to be some of "the finest and freshest jazz in the land."[31] The *Jazz Review* termed the proceedings "beautifully produced,"[32] while *down beat* predicted the CJF would probably "set a pattern for universities and colleges all over America in coming years."[33]

On yet another upbeat public-relations note, the American Federation of Musicians gave the green light for tapes of the festival to be broadcast on NBC's "Monitor."[34] Disappointingly, *The Saturday Evening Post*, which had inconvenienced festival participants by hustling them all out onto the Fieldhouse basketball floor early Saturday morning to take a large group color shot for their "Faces in America" series (incorrectly rumored by many to be a cover shot), never ran the photos at all.[35]

From Jim Naughton's point of view (*Saturday Evening Post* coverage or not), the festival had obviously done all it could have been expected to do. He had worked with a dream, a vision of jazz that previously had only taken a one-day shape. He had expanded festival horizons far beyond anything Tom Cahill or Bill Graham could have imagined and placed the event firmly before the national eye. He had set a new standard of excellence for festival organization and publicity and, as a result, could turn over to his successor a popular, exciting, and increasingly important event capable of showing a profit (over \$3,000 had come in from festival crowds, most of whom had had their fill of top collegiate jazz for the bargain basement price of \$1).[36]

Most of all, though, Jim Naughton had established a standard of tireless student dedication to an idea, an idea of jazz that went beyond the act of receiving and awarding valuable prizes or negotiating the media recognition and hype that a growing festival demanded. He had given the collegiate ranks a two-day celebration and shed a new light on a larger, as yet still-untapped, world of jazz.

1 9 6 1 There is a photo taken by the *South Bend Tribune* showing Stan Kenton as he strides across the 1960 Collegiate Jazz Festival stage, arm thrust out forcefully to clasp the hand of a somewhat awed Fr. George Wiskirchen. In the background, young high-school-band Melodons stare out into the crowd, as if stunned by the five-minute standing ovation that has just ended. The light of a camera flashbulb glares off a pair or two of awkward-looking, thick-frame eyeglasses. A heavy curtain blankets the back of the stage. Judges Charles Suber, Frank Holzfiend, and Robert Share mill about the foreground with enthusiastic grins in place. As if to signify the sports-oriented character of the Fieldhouse area caught in use, a rectangular basketball scoreboard of late fifties vintage peers out from an upper photo corner at the unusual jazz scene below.

It isn't a particularly noteworthy shot, but there is something extraordinarily powerful about the handshake itself—in the way Stan Kenton—the major name in jazz at the time—congratulates the director of this talented high-school band. It seems to signify a bond, a welding of two forces, a door opening up somewhere for a brand of jazz that had been given a larger life the past two years on the campus of the University of Notre Dame.

Just a photograph. Stan Kenton encouraging another aspiring bandleader, offering his appreciation of yet another yearning musical performance. It wouldn't mean a thing at all but for the firmness of

Kenton's handclasp and the confidence with which it says: "I listened, I appreciated, I want to help."

The words, of course, are imagined, but Kenton's conviction about college jazz was not. The popular bandleader made good on his handshake—not specifically then and there with Father Wiskirchen or anyone else connected with the 1960 festival that had opened his eyes to so much, but soon, within a few months at the second National Stage Band Camp, held at Indiana University in Bloomington, Indiana.

At the camp, Kenton crossed paths with the North Texas State Lab Band once more. Deeply impressed for the second time, he helped to book the band into Midwest music impresario Ken Morris's Leesburg, Indiana, Tippicanoe Gardens club for an August performance date and eventually flew in to direct the group personally and view the show.[1] Soon, North Texas State became a favorite Kenton project, and he continued to express public hopes for a recording session with the band in the near future.[2]

Profiting tremendously from the Kenton, Notre Dame, and Georgetown University Intercollegiate Jazz Festival (the band had managed a second-place finish at this new, Washington, D.C., event in May) stamps of approval, the North Texas State Lab Band under the direction of Leon Breeden continued to barrel along to distant stages across the nation in order to bring the collegiate-jazz message to life. Perhaps not unexpectedly, within the next few years, talented NTS personnel such as trumpeter Marvin Stamm, saxophonist Allan Beutler, tuba-man Dave Wheeler, and trombonists Dee Barton and Morgan Powell would all be off to join Stan Kenton's big band.

Besides the summer clinics and adviser aid selflessly provided to North Texas State, another, less heralded early-sixties Stan Kenton collegiate-jazz legacy was the growth of the newly instituted program of jazz studies at Indiana University. Run by former Kenton trombonist Edwin (Buddy) Baker, the program soon flourished amid the publicity brought to Bloomington by the popular, Kenton-dominated clinics.[3] The state of Indiana, so it seemed, couldn't get its fill of jazz. Taking the hint, the Collegiate Jazz Festival at the University of Notre Dame rolled on toward its third anniversary, in 1961.

By 1961, the college jazz movement and the youth that championed the cause had made an undeniable thrust into the nation's consciousness. Collegiate jazz festivals of note (more often than not deriving their format and organization from Notre Dame's example) had sprung up in 1960 at other universities such as Villanova and Georgetown, thus offering various regions of the country an opportunity to explore further and display indigenous jazz talent. With the rise of such festivals, it became increasingly common to find talented collegiate jazz bands or combos embarking on a jazz-festival "circuit" of sorts in the spring. After all, why limit visibility and the chance of obtaining professional advice, substantial awards, and coveted club engagements to a single event? Whether due to illness, jitters, equipment difficulties, or just an off day—one down performance could easily forfeit a group's festival prize shot. With these things in mind, however, there was little disagreement that, of those festivals on the "circuit," there was none more important than the one at Notre Dame. It was both the cornerstone and the trendsetter of the collegiate jazz movement.

To begin with, Notre Dame's religious affiliations gave the festival and the jazz education movement an instant (and curious) respect seldom encountered elsewhere. Admittedly, the yeoman's work had been done by Berklee and North Texas State, but there was something unaccountably potent and eye-catchingly paradoxical about jazz in this most peculiar of Midwest locales. In addition, there was an additional recognition factor granted by dint of Notre Dame's world-renowned sports exploits, National Gridiron Championships, immortal "Four Horsemen," and the like.

Still, despite the obvious gains, there were many (a number of whom were, oddly enough, professional jazz musicians) who remained unconvinced of the purpose and legitimacy of collegiate jazz in an academic setting. Once again, it fell to the collegiate jazz festivals in 1961— particularly Notre Dame's—to step forth and attempt to dispel the unfortunate skepticism surrounding jazz education.

Taking control of the festival this year from Jim Naughton (who had graduated) was yet another Notre Dame senior, Dave Sommer. A jazz-festival committee member in 1960, Sommer had originally caught the CJF bug as a result of his penchant for photography, which had led him to the striking musical subject matter on display at the inaugural Notre Dame jazz event in the spring of 1959. (After the '60 Collegiate Jazz Festival, Sommer had even achieved a unique celebrity-of-sorts status on campus when one of his '59 photos found its way into a brief, but important *Time* magazine piece on the second CJF.)

Launched as "the New Dimension in College Jazz," the 1961 CJF proposed to present "Jazz tailored in a bright new context."[4] "All the good things from the successful 1960 Collegiate Jazz Festival," explained a strikingly designed '61 publicity pamphlet (which came complete with enthusiastic Collegiate Jazz Festival quotes from Stan Kenton, Frank Holzfiend, *down beat, Time* magazine, and the *Jazz Review*), "will be even better this year: larger audiences, wider publicity, more and better prizes, better production."[5] Though the lines may have waxed a trifle idealistic, a look to festival preparations a few weeks before the spring event revealed some startling developments.

Beginning with a $6,500 prize list of instruments, National Band Camp/Berklee scholarships, trophies, and, for the overall top combo and band, respective engagements at the Indiana Jazz Festival and New York's Half Note Club, the third CJF seemed well primed for excitement. Groups from Illinois, Indiana, Michigan, Minnesota, Iowa, Ohio, Massachusetts, New Hampshire, New York, and Texas were set to attend. In addition, the already lengthy festival advisory-board list had been expanded to include the names of Stan Kenton and Leonard Bernstein, and there were tentative plans for Capitol Records to press albums of the '61 band/combo finalists.[6]

Lastly, five distinguished judges were scheduled to arrive in South Bend in late April: *down beat*'s Charles Suber, Berklee's Robert Share, noted composer/arranger Johnny Richards, composer/group leader/ theorist George Russell, and 31-year-old introspective jazz-piano pioneer Bill Evans[7] (a late replacement for composer/arranger Quincy Jones, who was unable to attend). Seeking to dispel previous judging-system complaints, chairman Dave Sommer made sure to include the Collegiate Jazz Festival category of "originality" on the standard Music Educators National Confederation judging form.[8]

Kicking off the Friday-afternoon preliminary round in the Old Fieldhouse once more was the Northwestern University Jazz Lab Band, appearing this year under the direction of graduate-student Ken Bartosz. Also performing that afternoon was a group from Miami University (Miami, Ohio), called the Colleagues, which featured a young guitarist named Cal Collins. Highlighting the evening session were performances by the 1960 Best Combo award-winning Dots Trio and Father Wiskirchen's Notre Dame High School Melodons (recent winners of a second consecutive Chicago-area high-school Stage Band contest), as well as a nine-piece North Texas State Jazztet (made up of pianist/ leader Lanny Steele, guitarist Don Gilliland, trumpeter Marvin Stamm, trombonist Morgan Powell, drummer Paul Guerrero, bassist Toby Guynn, and saxophonist Archie Wheeler) and an Amherst College Duo composed of pianist David Lahm and bassist John Brasher.

Originally scheduled to appear in a group called the Amherst College Five (which normally included student tenor-saxophonist Lew Tabackin), Lahm and Brasher had unfortunately found their number whittled down to two by performance time due to other unbreakable commitments. Gamely deciding to go on anyway, the duo's preliminary set was initially hampered by a malfunctioning microphone and, later, by an irritatingly inattentive crowd. For the judges fighting to make out the intricate, experimental music in the Fieldhouse din, this marring of one of the festival's truly original performances was simply too much to bear.

Storming out of his seat at one end of the basketball floor midway through the second number and moving quickly toward the stage, compassionate, outspoken judge Johnny Richards grabbed a microphone and—after apologies to the flabbergasted musicians—let the crowd have it with both barrels. "Ladies and gentlemen," he began in clearly angry, emotional tones. "You have come here to listen to performances by young artists. This young man came out here and he's in trouble! He was supposed to be playing with a . . . [Richards turned to Lahm for a moment for confirmation] quintet? Am I right? Now, the least you could do is have the courtesy to listen, or get out!"[9]

Letting loose an exasperated-yet-statesman-like "I thank you," Richards dismounted the stage and returned to his seat as the crowd applauded and subsequently settled down to more serious listening business. Onstage, a somewhat shaken duo paused for a moment, unsure of what to do. Finally, David Lahm moved back to the microphone to mention in a barely audible voice, "We'll do [John Lewis's] 'Django' again."[10] Battling back nerves and bizarre circumstances, the duo performed brilliantly and was a shoe-in for the Saturday-evening finals.

Appearing on the Saturday-afternoon preliminary agenda were several other aggregates-of-note, including the 1960 finalist Modern Men of Dartmouth College, the University of Detroit's perennial Bob Pierson Quartet entry, the University of Michigan's Omar Clay Trio (which harbored a talented young pianist named Bob James), the North Texas State Lab Band, and a Chicago-based group known as the Paul Winter Sextet.

Formed in early 1961 by Chicago-area college students under the leadership of Northwestern University saxophonist/student Paul Winter (who had spent his high school summer months traveling in Ringling Brothers Circus bands), the Sextet was unfortunately forced to play its preliminary set without the key services of trumpeter Dick Whitsell, who had been felled the previous day by a serious illness. Despite this difficulty, the band fired through dynamic material that featured the energetic, rough-and-ready Chicago-style baritone saxophone of group member Les Rout (also a last-minute substitute), as well as potent solos from pianist Warren Bernhardt and combo leader Paul Winter.

Out of the fierce finalist big band and combo competition between North Texas State, the Sam Houston State Teacher's College Houstonians (under the direction of Jerry Coker), and a hard-driving State University of New York Jazz Workshop band led by student arranger/ tenor saxophonist Don Menza, on the one hand, and the North Texas Jazztet, the Omar Clay Trio, and the Lahm-Brasher Duo, on the other, (the Paul Winter group had, somewhat surprisingly, been overlooked), the 1961 winners strode forth. Repeating its 1960 sweep of Finest Jazz Group and Best Big Band Awards, North Texas State also took in a number of individual soloist honors for Tom Wirtel (trumpet), Dee Barton (trombone), Toby Guynn (bass), Don Gilliland (guitar), Paul Guerrero (drums), and trombonist Morgan Powell (Most Promising Soloist).[11]

Edging in ahead of the talent-laden North Texas Jazztet as best combo was the Omar Clay Trio which reaped the New York/Half Note engagement as a proper award. Meanwhile, Don Menza's full-bodied tenor work earned him both the 1961 Collegiate Jazz Festival's Outstanding Instrumentalist award and a new saxophone,[12] David Lahm (whose mother, Dorothy Fields, was the composer of such well-known songs as "On the Sunny Side of the Street") lay claim to a Wurlitzer electric piano as Best Pianist, and Bob Pierson garnered yet another award as Most Promising Soloist, as did Northwestern's Jim Dipasquale (the latter also adding a Most Promising Arranger award to his Collegiate Jazz Festival prize haul).

Chosen Outstanding Soloist on baritone saxophone, Paul Winter Sextet-member Les Rout encountered more difficulty than most in receiving his award. Clambering onto the elevated stage excitedly to shake award-announcer Charles Suber's hand, a wide-eyed Rout held his saxophone prize gingerly for a moment before asking, "Can I keep it?" Somewhat taken aback, Suber (who was unaware that Rout was a substitute for program-listed Winter Sextet-member Jim Spaulding) quickly replied, "Of course, why did you ask?" No longer able to contain his confusion and enthusiasm, Rout looked up at Suber and blurted, "But I'm not Jim Spaulding!" Informed that the instrument was rightfully his since it was he who had been selected Best Baritonist—not Jim Spaulding—Rout departed with horn under arm and transcontinental jazz grin in place.[13]

"The New Dimension in College Jazz" had proven the worth of collegiate jazz once more, doing much to live up to the idealistic prefestival pamphlet which had predicted a music and movement "finally coming of age."[14] "If big band fans have lamented the demise of their favorite kind of jazz," previously skeptical *down beat* critic Don DeMicheal wrote enthusiastically, "they can back away from the wailing walls. Big bands are still very much with us—on college campuses

across the country. There are few bands traveling the road today that
have the fire, guts and originality of the bands heard at the festival.
. . . All the finalists . . . could compete on equal ground with Count
Basie, Stan Kenton or any other big band."[15]

"The Notre Dame Collegiate Festival exists," echoed *down beat's*
Charles Suber in a June 1961 editorial,

> only because there is a vast movement toward jazz in our colleges and
> universities. . . . The future is likely to see a broadening of the move-
> ment, for it is beginning to feel pressure from below, pressure from those
> youngsters now in high school bands who will soon be moving on to
> college. . . .
>
> There is another thing that is deeply significant about the Colle-
> giate Jazz Festival. It intimates how strong are the roots of jazz. These
> college musicians aren't playing jazz for money, to run up big record
> sales, or because it is the best way they know to make a living. They
> are playing it for the sheer wish to play it, for the appeal of jazz as an
> expressive medium.
>
> This in turn offers strong reassurance that, whatever the vicissi-
> tudes of the record business or nightclub operations or the antagonism
> of those who don't understand jazz, this music will go on in the fore-
> seeable future. It will go on because all over America, young musicians
> want it to go on.[16]

> We have never considered the Notre Dame Festival to
> be just another festival where a "program" is to be
> presented. We have felt that at Notre Dame the con-
> centration is aimed at providing the opportunity,
> available at no other place nationally, for the COLLEGE
> approach to jazz to be presented with emphasis on
> NEW things which could be heard ONLY at Notre
> Dame. — Leon Breeden

1
9   In May, 1961, barely a few weeks after the next Collegiate Jazz
6   Festival had begun the intricate process of gearing up for the
2   spring of 1962, a healthy and intact Paul Winter Sextet went on
       to the Intercollegiate Jazz Festival at Georgetown University in
       Washington, D.C. There, playing spiritedly before a panel of
       distinguished judges including trumpeter Dizzy Gillespie and
jazz-producer/impresario John Hammond, the Sextet won the Best Jazz

Combo award, while pianist Warren Bernhardt took Outstanding Musician honors overall. During the competition, Dizzy Gillespie leaned over to Hammond and exclaimed, "Man, there couldn't be any group better than this one!"[1] It was a comment John Hammond would soon take to heart.

Moving on to play at the Evansville (Indiana) Festival and the Saugatuck (Michigan) Festival (where the Sextet encountered and impressed pianist Dave Brubeck), the Winter-group members continued to make a name for themselves, led at all times by their ever-hustling salesman/leader Paul Winter.

In the summer of '61, Winter came across a copy of *down beat* magazine with a picture of guitarist Charlie Byrd on the cover. Byrd had just returned from South America on a U.S. State Department tour and was being greeted in the cover photograph by cultural-exchange-program-director Heath Bowman. Sensing a unique opportunity, Winter sent Bowman a three-page letter describing his group, its collegiate nature, and the sort of tour he had in mind (included with the letter were two possible travel itineraries—one for the Far East, the other for European communist-controlled countries—both constructed with the aid of two Northwestern University professors). Stressing the fact that the Sextet would include major universities in either of the proposed performance schedules, Winter waited patiently for a reply, believing that he actually had no more than a "two per-cent" chance at being selected for such a tour.[2]

By accident, of course, the group happened to be evenly integrated (Les Rout, drummer Harold Jones, and bassist Richard Evans—replacing Scotty Holt—were black; Winter, Dick Whitsell, and Warren Bernhardt were white). Additionally, each member had a college degree or was involved in obtaining one.[3] These qualifications (as well as sparkling letters of recommendation provided by Messrs. Gillespie, Hammond, and Brubeck), coupled with the State Department's early sixties desire to establish rapport with countries under communist control, resulted in State Department approval of a Winter Sextet tour—to Latin America.

Underway on the unprecedented six-month, 23-country, 27,000-mile tour, the group performed before vast crowds and invariably "communicated" with the restless youth of numerous nations in a way other groups just hadn't been able to do at all. (Along the way, the Sextet, it must be noted, also encountered its share of pro-communist hecklers, pointed questions about race, gas pellets, and more.)[4] Returning to the United States amid critical acclaim, the Winter combo (which had somehow convinced Columbia Records' Brazilian affiliate to record a bossa-

nova album with the group in Rio)[5] was of considerable help in convincing both the State Department and the public of the many positive
effects that could be reaped by sending young collegiate-jazz groups
on State Department-sponsored foreign tours. Because of the Sextet's
efforts (and those of other professional jazz groups such as Charlie
Byrd's as well), jazz now had the potential to become the new am-
bassador of the U.S.A., mainly because the rhythmic qualities inherent
in the music seemed to somehow bypass language barriers and American stereotypes, even in locations that had never encountered jazz
before.[6]

In what appeared to be the ultimate endorsement of the Sextet's
efforts and tour, news of an even more unprecedented jazz opportunity for the group soon filtered down: an invitation to play at the White
House. The first jazz unit ever to tred inside the hallowed Washington, D.C., halls, the precedence-shattering Paul Winter Sextet appeared
in the East Room of the White House in November 1962 as part of Jac-
queline Kennedy's series of musical programs by Young People for
Young People. After the final notes of the rousing concert of bebop,
bossa-nova, adapted Haitian folk material, and originals by Evans, Bernhardt, and Winter had faded away, Mrs. Kennedy applauded energetically, rose hurriedly from her chair, and moved to the bandstand.
Shaking hands with Paul Winter, she said enthusiastically, "Simply
magnificent. We never had anything here like this before. Thank you
very much." Turning around to the audience the First Lady then said,
"I liked that," an unexpected sign of approval that received front-page
news coverage throughout the country the next day.[7]

If there was a surge of enthusiasm toward youth and country in
the early sixties (perhaps due in part to the new vitality of the economy
and the relatively young, vigorous age of the new president as well
as his attractive, fashion-trend-setting wife), it certainly appeared to
be having a salubrious effect on collegiate jazz. Youth seemed suddenly to have a place all its own in Washington, D.C. eyes, with Peace
Corps, State Department tour, and other avenues of visibility, responsibility, and experience open wide. Without a doubt, of course, much
of the publicity and success of collegiate jazz during this period was
due to the Paul Winter Sextet, which had, in a sense, shaped its own
destiny in 1961–62. In the meantime, however, the 1962 Collegiate Jazz
Festival at Notre Dame was making some waves of its own.

Run this year by Notre Dame student Tom Eiff, the '62 Collegiate
Jazz Festival began to take on a shape that, to a certain degree, reflected
musical trends both within college ranks and in the professional jazz
world at large. Much more open to new forms and sounds, younger

musicians on college campuses were in fact often even willing now to explore areas of jazz as yet unaccepted by the rest of the jazz community. By 1962, one of these areas was, most definitely, the music of Ornette Coleman, a quiet, soft-spoken, onetime Los Angeles elevator operator with a plastic alto-saxophone and a "strange" set of musical ideas.

In contrast to standard, straight-ahead bebop or swing, Coleman had devised a method of allowing each of the members in his group (bassist Charlie Haden, trumpeter Don Cherry, drummers Billy Higgins, Ed Blackwell) to improvise, "freely," outside traditional jazz frameworks and notations. Group interaction, interplay, and feeling took precedence over more linear, structured forms and, quite naturally, garnered more controversy than critical praise. But to some collegiate musicians, who were listening simultaneously to "cool" fifties sounds, fading college Dixieland band beats, forties Charlie Parker-developed bebop, and earlier big-band swing, such new innovations and experiments had merit as well. Along this line of thought student Frank McConnell remarked in a perceptive *Scholastic* article two weeks before the April '62 CJF that "Perhaps this year's Collegiate Jazz Festival will reveal a generation of atonalistic, junior Ornette Colemans waiting to invade the recording labs and the night clubs."[8]

Selected to appear at the 1962 event were ten big bands from Arkansas, Wisconsin, Colorado, Pennsylvania, New Mexico, Virginia, New York, and Texas. In addition, twelve combos from Missouri, Indiana, Michigan, Massachusetts, and more would attend, as would two guest bands: the perennial high-school Melodons (directed by Father Wiskirchen) and an unusual a cappella Ripon College (Ripon, Wisconsin) vocal group, led by tenor Al Jarreau. Also appearing would be a local campus group of some repute, the Notre Dame Quartet, which consisted of drummer Jack Carr, multiple Collegiate Jazz Festival award-winner Bob Pierson on tenor sax, bassist Hayes Cavanaugh, trombonist Al Hermann, and pianist John Griffith.

Under Tom Eiff's firm chairmanship eye, the festival advisory board stretched its long limbs once more to include the names of Willis Conover and John Hammond. In addition, the winning overall collegiate jazz group in 1962 would receive a giant loving cup, while the best big band would garner a "tailor-made" Berklee arrangement as well as a number of National Stage Band Camp scholarships. As for the victorious jazz combo at the festival, there would be no less than a week-long engagement at the Jazz Gallery in New York. (On a somewhat odder note, the festival committee—no doubt hoping to avoid previous festival stage delays—made plans to speed up individual Collegiate Jazz Festival group sets by placing a red warning light on stage "conspicuous to performers"; three minutes before the allotted twenty-minute band/combo time limit was up, the light would flash and thereby keep musicians on schedule.)[9]

Presented as "The New Excellence in College Jazz," CJF '62 opened with five top-notch judges once again in tow. These included noted composer and arranger Henry Mancini (of '61–'62 hit song "Moon River" fame), Mercury Records arranger Quincy Jones, *down beat* editor Don DeMicheal, and panel regulars Charles Suber (now president of the American Foundation of Music and no longer with *down beat*), and Berklee administrator Robert Share (also an arranger in his own right).

As if this wasn't enough incentive to spark the Notre Dame student body to attend, door prizes of stereo systems and formal prom bids were also offered, as well as the thought-provoking chance to see the "famous Indigos" (with Al Jarreau) and to meet girls—the latter always an incentive at all-male Notre Dame. (Thoroughly emphasizing this last point, a student-body publicity release before the festival noted that girls from no less than "sixteen girls schools including two modelling schools and twenty-two sororities" would attend. Clearly, the 1962 festival committee was hard at work on all matters, large and small.)[10]

"Artistically the best yet," according to *Scholastic* student reviewer Frank McConnell, the festival produced an even higher quality of collegiate jazz than it had in previous years.[11] As expected, Father Wiskirchen's Melodons (who had recently taken the stage at Chicago's McCormick Place with top professional jazzmen such as Woody Herman and Ahmad Jamal) shut down the Friday-night session with a bang and garnered a third consecutive standing ovation. (Of particular note this year was the fact that Father Wiskirchen's pioneering work, *Developmental Techniques for the School Dance Band Musician*, written to fulfill master's-degree requirements at Northwestern University, had been published by the Berklee School of Music Press in 1961, thereby giving further impetus to the stage-band movement while offering extensive, professional insights into methods for teaching jazz to young musicians.)

In regard to other major collegiate advances of this period, the North Texas State Lab Band had further publicized its collegiate jazz cause in 1961 by recording an album for 90th Floor Records. Boosted by impressive reviews, the album was graced by Stan Kenton's enthusiastic liner notes which expressed the hope that "by calling attention to other colleges and universities to what has been achieved in

Denton, Texas," the recording could "inspire other colleges and universities to realize the importance of education in this form of American Music."[12]

Selected once more as a finalist, the North Texas State Lab Band juggernaut seemed, in 1962, to be in a class by itself. There were, however, other finalists selected, and these included the Henderson Collegians from Henderson State Teachers College in Arkadelphi, Arkansas, and Dr. Eugene Hall's Michigan State University Television Orchestra (formed barely eight months prior to the festival). In the combo division, the returning David Lahm/John Brasher duet made the final round as did a Jamey Aebersold-led Indiana University Jazz Combo and a startlingly inventive group from the University of Michigan known as the Bob James Trio. When the verdict was in—despite yet another dynamic North Texas State performance night—it was clearly the state of Michigan's day.

Over the somewhat Ornette Coleman-influenced play of tenor saxophonist Aebersold's Indiana aggregate and the expectedly intricate Lahm/Brasher interplay, the Bob James Trio stormed through an experimental finals set and walked away with practically every Collegiate Jazz Festival prize in the house. A member of the 1961 CJF award-winning Omar Clay Trio, pianist James was joined this year in his adventurous onstage musical game by bassist Ron Brooks and drummer Bob Pozar. Originally formed, according to Brooks, "to have some fun" playing together, the James Trio performed tightly and excitingly in both individualistic and collective ways.[13] Presenting two works by University of Michigan graduate student Roger Reynolds during the finals set, James and Pozar both exhilarated and baffled judges and crowd by producing sounds from " . . . a garbage can, an oil drum, tympani, various orthodox drums and cymbals, mallets on piano strings, glass and other sound-producing objects," while Brooks simultaneously tinkered with a tape recorder emitting "strange sounds."[14]

Despite these potentially pretentious forays into "electronic" music and theatrics, the trio's mastery of the jazz idiom and respective instruments was more than evident and, for their efforts, they came away with multiple awards as Finest Jazz Group, Best Combo, Best Pianist, Best Drummer, Best Bassist, and Most Promising Leader. Impressed by the performance, judge Quincy Jones remarked, "It's the only jazz group I've seen [at the festival] where the drummer watches the piano player," and then signed the trio to a Mercury Records recording contract.[15] Obviously, Jones's gesture was entirely appropriate for, as *Scholastic* reviewer Frank McConnell would note, within a few years the trio might well be able to "scare anybody on the continent."[16]

On the finals band side, North Texas State, as expected, played brilliantly once again, showcasing arrangements of "I Remember Clifford," as well as complex student originals such as Morgan Powell's "Volume XII" (voted the festival's Outstanding Composition) and the "at times nearly atonal" work, "David Taylor."[17] Unfortunately, the one thing the Lab Band hadn't counted on at Notre Dame was coming up against a band from Michigan State led by North Texas State Lab Band founder and former director Dr. Eugene Hall.

Deriving its peculiar name from the Michigan State University television station, WMSB (on which it occasionally performed), Dr. Hall's Michigan State University Television Orchestra tore into charts such as Nat Pierce's "Middleman" and clearly outdid the rest of the competition—North Texas State's musically complex offerings included. Honored with a standing ovation at performance end, the band made judging decisions close indeed. As it turned out, two-time Best Band-winner North Texas State had to settle in 1962 for a runner-up slot against the "grand, swinging orchestra" from Michigan State.[18] "The reasons for the results are, of course," remarked student reviewer Frank McConnell, "that nothing is more uncertain than one's use of the superlative."[19]

Beyond these two fine groups there were a few other 1962 individual winners of note. Duquesne University Stage Band trumpeter Paul Hubinon was named Outstanding Instrumentalist; Jim Depasquale of Northwestern was once again tabbed as Most Promising Tenor; Bob Pierson of Notre Dame (the first Notre Dame musician to receive a Collegiate Jazz Festival award) scored yet again as Most Promising Altoist; Don Gilliland of North Texas State took the Outstanding Guitar award for the second year in a row; Jamey Aebersold managed top honors as Best Alto-Saxophonist; and Bob Shurley, a former Little Rock, Arkansas postman now with the Henderson Collegians, took the top Tenor-Sax award. Finally, Northwestern's Loren Binford repeated as Best Trombonist, and out of an exciting, experimental piano/vocal duo that included eclectic pianist Ran Blake, singer Jeanne Lee emerged as Best Vocalist.

"The world looked cleaner somehow, the future brighter after the last note had sounded at the fourth annual Collegiate Jazz Festival," noted a *down beat* magazine review a few weeks after the festival.[20] "And the time has come for the efforts of college jazz groups to be given serious consideration and recognition for being the healthiest sign of continued vitality in the jazz world."[21] "The future of jazz," echoed Frank McConnell in the *Scholastic*, "and the future of the Collegiate Jazz Festival are, at least from the 1962 performances, very bright indeed."[22]

1 9 6 3 As if to stress the importance of collegiate jazz and the pressing need to distribute its message to musicians around the country, tapes of the 1962 Collegiate Jazz Festival finalist groups were sent to Silver Crest Records in New York, and a limited number of three-record albums (based on orders placed at the festival) were mastered and pressed. Although University of Notre Dame audio-visual instructor and sound-equipment-buff Everett Warren had recorded the festival in '59, '60, and '61, this was the first realized effort to put the Collegiate Jazz Festival on record in solid form. (Dave Sommer's tentative and somewhat idealistic '61 deal with Capitol Records, had, unfortunately, fallen through.) Placed alongside recently released North Texas State and Paul Winter Sextet albums, and the much-anticipated future Bob James Trio/Mercury Records release, the Collegiate Jazz Festival recording (although not commercially distributed) offered yet another way for the collegiate-jazz word to infiltrate the still largely unyielding academic ranks and get through to the young musicians themselves.

At the same time the Collegiate Jazz Festival was changing its year-to-year appearance, the Notre Dame campus was also undergoing an impressive series of alterations. By late 1962, the Navy Drill Hall had been razed to make room for a new $8 million, thirteen-story library, the construction of which was already underway. On a far northwest corner of the campus, apartment buildings designed to replace wooden "Vetville" married-student-housing huts (also razed for the library site) were taking shape. In addition, a stone's throw southeast of the Old Fieldhouse a $2.2 million radiation laboratory (funded in part by the U.S. Atomic Energy Commission) was nearing completion. Lastly, a $300,000 buff-brick-walled geodesic dome-topped structure for student activities, Stepan Center (named for Stepan Chemical mogul/ Notre Dame donor Alfred C. Stepan) was dedicated in May 1962. Able to hold upward of 3,000 people and deal with a multitude of concerts, meetings, functions, and dances, Stepan Center would serve in place of the now-extinct Drill Hall. For the moment, however, jazz would still be relegated to the poor acoustics of the Fieldhouse.

Termed the "New Stream in College Jazz," the fifth Collegiate Jazz Festival, scheduled for spring 1963, found itself able to select twenty-two participating bands from the largest pool of applicants yet.[1] Once again, a cross-section of schools from such far-flung locales as

Michigan, Florida, Colorado, Maryland, Pennsylvania, and many other states would serve to tap the collegiate-jazz pulse and see where the music was headed. (As usual, of course, Father Wiskirchen's Melodons—this year including trombonist James Pankow—would return to the CJF guest band slot.)

In order to expand the festival's ability to call into question the nature and direction of collegiate and professional jazz, as well as to provide the finest educational format for attending teachers and student musicians, '63 chairman Charlie Murphy expanded the CJF to include a Jazz Forum—an informal, open-to-the-public, Saturday-morning question-and-answer session with the judging panel slated to be held in the campus Law Auditorium. In addition, there would also be an official Collegiate Jazz Festival Jam Session (the first), downtown in the main ballroom of Robert's Supper Club on West Colfax Street after completion of the Friday-evening preliminary round. Set to include seasoned judging alumni Charles Suber and Robert Share, as well as composer/arranger Manny Albam, top vibraharpist Terry Gibbs, and internationally respected jazz critic Leonard Feather, the "Forum" would assuredly prove provocative and educationally worthwhile. As for the "exclusive Jam Session"[2] (set to feature Terry Gibbs and his quartet initially and various student musicians thereafter), it would allow for performance and interaction away from the competitive tension and Fieldhouse formalities.

By spring a new festival logo had also arrived to accompany the now-familiar abbreviated "CJF" heading. Humorously referred to as the " '63 splotch,"[3] the symbol—a Jackson Pollock-esque splash of rich purple ink complete with a Halley's comet-like purple tail—was described by executive festival chairman Dave Paliganoff in the '63 festival program as being representative of Collegiate Jazz Festival attempts to "move the college stream of jazz to streak onward to a greater horizon. . . . It [collegiate jazz] is streaking from the mainstream of jazz," he continued, ". . . . Like moving out in a more creative, educated, disciplined and vibrant but free flowing, dynamic, swingin' current. . . ."[4]

Although the Collegiate Jazz Festival had originated with few thoughts in mind other than lifting the ponderous college jazz stone and observing what lay beneath, subsequent years of criticism, expansion, and student effort had also allowed the festival committee to realize several unique things about the CJF. One, it had demonstrated that college students could become interested in and wholeheartedly support what Notre Dame music critic/student Frank McConnell described in a late March 1963 issue of the *Scholastic* as a "program distinguished for a standard far above that of many of the professional jazz festivals."[5] Two, the festival did, in general, seem to reveal pockets of major talent while offering hints as to what directions modern jazz might be taking.

Third, there was little pressure, financial or otherwise, to present music at the Collegiate Jazz Festival that pandered to the tastes of the masses. Those who came to the Collegiate Jazz Festival were fore-warned of the range and diversity of the voices to be heard—some stimulating, some divergent, some strident—but all part of the burgeon-ing "stream" of college jazz. Finally, realizing the importance of presen-tation in properly stating the collegiate-jazz case and thereby gaining its further acceptance, the Collegiate Jazz Festival committee took itself seriously enough to present a well-produced, professional package each year. Still, the idea of competition (despite the fact that it set the Col-legiate Jazz Festival and other such events apart from professional jazz festivals), healthy or not, festered. As it happened, however, there were other matters to worry about come festival time.

Two days before the 1963 Collegiate Jazz Festival, the United States Air Force Academy Quartet wired best wishes as well as regrets. Unable to obtain an anticipated flight to the Midwest from Colorado, the group was abruptly forced to cancel out. Next, barely two hours before the initial Friday-afternoon music session was set to begin, the Fieldhouse stage (this year equipped with an acoustics-aiding wooden-bandshell frame complete with a large, precariously perched cardboard CJF logo and attached purple "splotch") partially collapsed. Fortunately, Notre Dame's director of maintenance and the festival sound engineer were able to repair the damage a few minutes before show time and—somehow—despite the thunderous jazz sounds that followed, the jury-rigged stage survived.[6]

From the fine crop of twenty-one bands and combos, six finalist groups emerged. These included the Chicago-based Wright Junior Col-lege Stage Band (featuring trumpeter Oscar Brashear and trombonist Frank Tesinsky), the Roosevelt University of Chicago Institute of Jazz Studies Lab Band, the Denver University Stage Band, an experimen-tal "free jazz" Indiana University Jazz Sextet (led once more by Jamey Aebersold), the Jazzmen from Chicago's Crane Junior College (con-taining Earth, Wind, & Fire founder/drummer Maurice White and even-tual Earth, Wind, & Fire horn-section members, Don Myrick and Louis Satterfield), and the University of Michigan's Bob Pozar Trio.

As in 1962, it was once again Michigan's day. Selected for the second consecutive year as both Finest Jazz Group and Best Combo,

a University of Michigan group, the Bob ("Turk") Pozar Trio was little
short of spectacular, for individual group members Pozar, Ron Brooks,
and Mike Lang (replacing Bob James) also swept respective Drum, Bass,
and Piano Soloist awards. An "almost automatic choice"[7] as best small
group because of its adventurous interplay and solid rapport, the trio's
bragging rights to a prize windfall including New York Village Van-
guard and Chicago London House engagements were challenged during the finals only by the "frankly experimental"[8] Indiana Jazz Sextet,
which managed three individual awards for group leader Jamey Aebersold (Best Alto-Saxophone, Best Original Composition, Most Promising Leader) and one award apiece for soloist Warren Grimwood (Best
Tenor) and pianist Tom Hensley (Most Promising Soloist).

Trombonist Frank Tesinsky of Wright Junior College, a musician
whose talents were termed "extraordinary" by judge Leonard Feather,
took the Outstanding Instrumentalist award,[9] while band teammate
Oscar Brashear (whom Feather noted "already sounds strong enough
to play lead in any band in the country") took the prize as Best Trumpet.[10]
Other award winners included Michigan State University Television
Orchestra trumpeter Woody James (Most Promising Soloist) and Crane
Junior College alto-saxophonist Don Myrick and bassist Eugene McCarthy (both selected as Most Promising Instrumentalists). As far as the
big bands were concerned, it was Denver University's powerful, loose,
supple play that led the way and won.

"It was a brilliant festival," commented *down beat* magazine in a
postfestival review, "one that will stand as the turning point in college jazz."[11] Impressed by the overall strength of individual soloists
(a feature that had not been extensively noted at previous Collegiate
Jazz Festivals), the magazine went on to cite this development as well
as the fact that there was "little taint of amateurism left" among participating groups as a sure sign that "college jazz has come of age."[12]

Terming the festival one of his "most refreshing and invigorating
experiences in the past few years," critic Leonard Feather went on in
his liner notes for the second Collegiate Jazz Festival three-record
finalists' performance album (mastered and pressed, like its predecessor, by Crest Records in New York), to cite the "remarkable performance level of the bands and the combos at the Festival. . . . It was
a privilege to be a judge at the Festival," he continued, "My only regret
is that by selecting a few winners among so many first rate talents we
were obliged to bypass some who were clearly of potential importance.
But their chance, I'm sure, will arrive in due course. As long as there
are opportunities like the Festival to encourage them, the musicianship of this caliber cannot be held down."[13]

1
9
6
4

Though college jazz was spreading quickly throughout the nation by 1963 (via albums, festivals, and word-of-mouth), it was also still encountering stiff resistance from the old-guard academic institutions. Despite the success of jazz-education programs at Berklee and North Texas State, the majority of programs were, as *down beat* school-jazz columnist Fr. George Wiskirchen noted in an article late that year, ". . . student inspired or student demanded" things, recognized by the school but looked upon as "the poor stepchild of the music department. . . . While much progress has been made in selling jazz and in dissolving prejudice," continued Father Wiskirchen, "there is still much to be done to establish a solid philosophy of jazz in education. If the case can be presented logically and forcefully, jazz will be accepted."[1]

Seeking to present an even broader range of collegiate jazz, the 1964 Collegiate Jazz Festival run by student Sidney Gage retained the "New Stream" theme, as well as the purple Collegiate Jazz Festival trademark "splotch" and increased the number of participating bands to twenty-seven and the judging panel to six. In order to provide additional performance incentive, arrangements had been made for a three-man panel from the Cultural Presentations Office of the U.S. State Department to attend the '64 festival at Notre Dame. Headed by music critic John S. Wilson, the three-man team would select groups to represent the State Department on foreign "goodwill" tours.[2]

Unfortunately – State Department-tour lures notwithstanding – there were unforeseen developments in both American musical tastes and politics during late '63 and early '64 that would severely affect the perpetually precarious state of jazz and the ordinarily steady Collegiate Jazz Festival crowd-numbers. The most important of these events – one that shook the entire country to its very core – took place on November 22, 1963, in Dallas, Texas. With the assassination of President John F. Kennedy that fateful day, America's previously buoyant early-sixties mood gave way to sudden anger, dismay, and deep-rooted melancholia.

Lurching about in search of something refreshing and new that would reinvigorate its flagging spirit, America suddenly found its fancy taken by an odd, infectious brand of rock and roll emanating from an unlikely port in England. First hitting the States in early 1964 in the form of a record entitled, "I Want To Hold Your Hand," the music, created by a gangly four-man group of Liverpudlians known as "the Beatles," was both riveting, invigorating, and instantly popular – at least among American youth. On the basis of astounding early-1964 record sales (1.5 million copies alone of "I Want To Hold Your Hand" in a matter of weeks), a February American tour that would include an appearance on the well-known Ed Sullivan Show was arranged for the group. Landing in New York to tumultuous airport applause, the roar of the Beatles and their accompanying "mania" (as well as a new generation of rock-and-roll writer/performer) was on—much to the dismay of struggling jazz musicians. Needless to say, by spring and CJF '64, a number of previously supportive heads had been turned in other directions.

Faced with this new widespread surge of rock and roll and the upswing in folk-music consciousness that had occurred on campuses across the nation in the early sixties (a movement that resulted in March 1964, in the inaugural Notre Dame Stepan Center-held Collegiate Folk Festival or CFF),[3] the Collegiate Jazz Festival fought to hold onto its hard-won share of listeners with a $5,000 list of prizes that included Berklee Scholarships, various instruments, and a two-week Chicago Playboy Club engagement for the Best Female Vocalist. Just as impressive, of course, was the panel of judges CJF chairman Sidney Gage had managed to line up: Charles Suber, Robert Share, composer/arrangers Oliver Nelson, George Russell, and Gary McFarland, and, last but not least, widely-hailed alto-saxophonist/combo leader Cannonball Adderley (all of whom would take part in a Collegiate Jazz Festival symposium on Saturday morning; in addition Adderley, Russell, McFarland, and Nelson would take part in a jam session after the Friday-night preliminaries had ended).[4] Best of all, however, in deference to the perpetually date-starved Notre Dame male populace, girls from an unprecedented "81 Mid-Western Colleges" had been invited to a Saturday-afternoon festival "rally" at nearby Giuseppie's Restaurant.[5]

Although plagued by a noticeable drop in attendance, the sixth Collegiate Jazz Festival was again studded with stellar performances, thus making the judges' finalist decisions extremely difficult. Confronted with such a wealth of talent, the judges (after a stormy three-hour-long decision-making session)[6] emerged and presented finalist selections to four combos—instead of the traditional three. These included the Jamey Aebersold Septet of Indiana University, the Belcastro Trio of West Virginia University, the Jazz Interpreters of Chicago's Crane Junior College, and the Billy Harper Sextet of North Texas State (which included an original Harper composition entitled "Capra Black" in its preliminary set).

As far as the big bands were concerned, the finals would pit a twenty-piece brass-laden University of Illinois Jazz Band led by Walden String Quartet member/jazz program director John Garvey against yet another Michigan State University Television Orchestra (this year under the direction of graduate student/'59 Collegiate Jazz Festival Best Trombonist George West) and a Northwestern University Jazz Workshop Big Band directed, oddly enough, by Fr. George Wiskirchen, whose Melodons (appearing for the second consecutive year with trombonist James Pankow in tow)[7] were, as usual also appearing on the 1964 Collegiate Jazz Festival performance bill. Try as they might, Michigan State and the Good Father's swinging, Count Basie-like Northwestern entry (featuring trumpeters Mike Price and Ed Sheftel and alto-saxophonist David Sanborn), came up short in the finals, losing out to Illinois (which included a young trumpeter named Cecil Bridgewater).

If there was a particularly first-rate "original" group to be named at the festival, however, (the Illinois band's fine performance notwithstanding), it was the Jamey Aebersold Septet. Creating a unique, driving, freely conceived and rendered jazz sound, the group slashed its way through two original compositions in the finals with the aid of brilliant Collegiate Jazz Festival veteran/cellist Dave Baker.[8] Up against the brake-drum thumping exploits of Belcastro Trio drummer Guy Remonko (this, of course, while group leader/pianist Joe Belcastro took time to pound the insides of the nine-foot Steinway grand piano on stage with a set of xylophone mallets),[9] as well as the audience-favorite Crane Junior College Jazz Interpreters and the inventive, John Coltrane-esque touch of talented North Texas State tenor-saxophonist Billy Harper and his sextet, the Aebersold group edged itself ahead into both Finest Jazz Group and Best Combo awards, thereby earning the right to perform at the upcoming Ohio Valley Jazz Festival on the same night as Woody Herman, Stan Getz, and Thelonious Monk.[10] (To this prize list was also added the honor of performing along with the University of Illinois band at the next day's Indiana Musician's Ball in South Bend, held in the Pick-Oliver Hotel.)[11] "It was," wrote *Chicago Daily News* critic Buck Walmsley, "an obvious victory for those who feel that a college group should concern itself more with musical composition than what is called 'swinging.' "[12]

Other festival standouts included alto-saxophonist/sociology major Vernice "Bunky" Green of the Wright Junior College Big Band (who took home awards as Outstanding Instrumentalist and Best Alto-Saxophonist),[13] Billy Harper (Most Promising Instrumentalist), former Melodon-turned North Texas State vibes player Dick Sisto (Outstanding Miscellaneous Instrumentalist), Northwestern band drummer Gary Miller (Best Drums), DePaul University's Brian Trentham (Best Trombone), Michigan State University's Ron English (Best Guitar), and DePauw University bassist Brent McKesson (Best Bass). In addition, Aebersold Septet members Tom Hensley (Best Piano) and Dickie

Washburn (Most Promising Trumpet), and Jazz Interpreters Cleo Griffen (Best Trumpet), Cheryl Berdell (Best Vocalist), and Willie Collins
(Most Promising Drums) took home awards.

Reaping enthusiastic postfestival critical huzzahs once more, the
'64 Collegiate Jazz Festival soon released yet another three-record album
of finalist groups. Reviewing the album in *down beat* magazine in
September 1964, critic Bill Mathieu termed the quality of the Collegiate
Jazz Festival music captured on each of the records "astonishingly
high."[14]

"The CJF committee," elaborated '64 judge Gary McFarland in
a set of perceptive liner notes that graced the album's back side, "should
be extraordinarily proud of the progress they have made during the
past six years . . . . By maintaining absolute control the committee has
been able to first, insist upon incredibly high musical standards, second, thumb their noses at rank commercialism and, third, continue
to provide a main artery for jazz survival.[15]

"One of the healthiest aspects of this year's festival," continued
McFarland,

> was the free use of source materials, regardless of the vintage. One could
> hear the influence of Basie, Ellington, Herman, Kenton and Gil Evans
> in the big bands; Cannonball Adderley, Miles Davis, Art Blakey, Horace
> Silver in the small groups; and John Coltrane, Stan Getz, Clifford Brown,
> and a very obvious Bill Evans influence (thank heavens) among the
> soloists. With respect to the "new thing," I was very pleased and sur-
> prised to hear the Belcastro Trio's use of an extensive rhythmic and har-
> monic range (even to the inclusion of two sets of brake drums that are
> played with mallets—I presume that they are constructed from auto-
> mobile brake drums); the use of serial techniques by the University of
> Michigan band; and the use of the George Russell-Ornette Coleman small
> group concept. The exposure of the many influences heard at this year's
> Festival cannot help but to lay a stronger foundation upon which to build
> the jazz of tomorrow.[16]

1965 By early 1965, the sound of collegiate jazz was not only turning
American ears but those in other parts of the world as well. Due
to the tireless efforts of John S. Wilson and other government
representatives, the State Department had offered foreign tours
to a number of groups heard at collegiate jazz festivals across the
country, particularly those at Villanova and Notre Dame. In fact,
out of the 1964 Notre Dame Collegiate Jazz Festival alone, no less than

four bands and combos had been selected for globe-trotting jazz-performance duty by Secretary of State Dean Rusk's office.

Included among those groups chosen from the talent-laden Collegiate Jazz Festival '64 ranks was the University of Michigan Jazz Band (not even a '64 finalist, but obviously up to State Department sound, professionalism, and availability standards), which was slated to leave in late January 1965 for a four-month tour of thirteen Caribbean and Central American countries.[1] Expanded to a sextet with the addition of '64 CJF Outstanding Instrumentalist Bunky Green and others, the Modern Jazz Interpreters of West Virginia State University (also bypassed by judges for that year's finals) had already managed a summer 1964 North African tour that included a three-week engagement at the World Trade Fair's U.S. exhibition in Algeria.[2] Also on the State Department tour agenda was the University of Denver Stage Band ('63 CJF's Best Band) which had been selected for a three-month tour of the Far East (Honolulu, Tokyo, Okinawa, Korea, South Vietnam, Fiji, Australia, and New Zealand) scheduled to begin in early January 1965.[3] (Unfortunately for the fourth and final State Department-selected group, the Father Wiskirchen-led Northwestern University Jazz Workshop Band, the ugly head of jazz-disapproving academia reared itself once more, and the group was forced to cancel plans for a long-awaited goodwill trip to Latin America, primarily because the university refused to recognize the band's affiliation with the school.)[4]

On a less worldwide but even more caution-inducing note, the debacle of the first annual Oread Collegiate Jazz Festival (sponsored by the University of Kansas student government) in April of 1964 put many of those in the collegiate-jazz world on guard. A large-scale event modeled on the Notre Dame festival that boasted appearances by North Texas State and University of Denver bands as well as a judging panel made up of luminaries such as Woody Herman, Robert Share, Creed Taylor (of Verve Records), Matt Betton, and critic Martin Williams, the Oread festival was a complete, riveting success—that was, until several of the much publicized grand prizes fell through. Promised both a European tour and an engagement at the New York World Fair's Jazzland as part of its Best Group award, the Bill Farmer Quartet of North Texas State (which contained drummer Ed Soph) suddenly found itself a few months after the event with nothing to show for its Oread efforts as both prizes dissolved into thin air. Although attributable to inexperience on the novice student organizers' parts as well as multiple misunderstandings among travel agencies, World's Fair representatives, and European festival/club heads, the unfortunate occurrence sent shock waves through the collegiate-jazz world.

If all this were a rare case of college festival winners not getting their prizes [commented *down beat* critic Don DeMicheal], it would not merit much investigation or concern, as disappointing as it might have been to those involved. But, unfortunately what happened to the Bill Farmer Quartet is not rare; it happens all too frequently to festival winners. . . . College festivals are well enough established so that there should be no need to attract participants and press coverage by waving flags of tours and engagements when, in truth, such things have not been settled— something on paper, signed. . . . In sum, more responsibility on the part of their organizers is desperately needed at these festvals, for there should never again be such a botch as the Farmer-Oread affair.[5]

Following on the heels of the fifth annual Intercollegiate Jazz Festival at Villanova University, as well as the disturbing Oread incident, the seventh Notre Dame spring jazz rite run by chairman Daniel Ekkebus featured ten combos and eight big bands from the usual diverse range of locales. Talent scouts from the State Department and the National Student Association[6] were also on hand to look over the '65 college jazz crop, which was ably judged by flugelhornist/trumpeter Clark Terry, multi-instrumentalist Paul Horn, composer/arranger Arif Mardin, and "permanent" judges Charles Suber and Robert Share. (Noted Chicago/WCFL radio disc-jockey Sid McCoy ably emceed the Friday-evening preliminaries for the second year in a row.)

Both provocative (in terms of participating combos) and stirring but somewhat straightforward (in terms of participating big bands), the preliminary Collegiate Jazz Festival rounds whittled challengers down to four finalist bands including the Westchester State Criterions, Father Wiskirchen's Northwestern University Jazz Workshop Band, the University of Indiana Jazz Ensemble led by Jerry Coker, and John Garvey's twenty-piece University of Illinois Big Band. Out of the combo ranks, the University of West Virginia Joe Belcastro Trio, the Brian Trentham Quartet of Columbia University, and the Jerry Green Sextet of Indiana University were also selected for the finals. (Passed by for the finals in the stiff combo competition area were the West Virginia State Modern Jazz Interpreters, who had returned to Collegiate Jazz Festival '65 decked out in colorful tribal robes acquired on the group's North African tour in the summer of '64; as consolation, Interpreters' pianist Robert Thompson and bassist Reggie Minor would take home outstanding soloist awards.)[7]

Vying for the usual scholarships, club engagements, and assorted other prizes, the finalists battled it out in the Saturday-evening Fieldhouse session, which strained the patience of the Collegiate Jazz Festival crowd (due to the extra finalist big band) with an unusual hour-behind schedule pace. Although a new guest group, the Blue Diamonds (a group made up of musicians from Bloomington, Minnesota's Senior High School and the University of Minnesota) had performed earlier in the day at the end of the Saturday-afternoon music session, Father Wiskirchen's Notre Dame High School Melodons returned once more at festival's end to captivate listeners while the judges conferred to select the winners.

Returning to the center of the Fieldhouse basketball floor, the judges announced that the Belcastro Trio had been chosen as Best Combo. Composed of drummer Guy Remonko (Best Drummer), pianist/leader Joe Belcastro (Best Composer for the work "Phrenetic"), bassist Robert Hackett, and high-coiffed junior journalism major/vocalist Joyce Breech (Best Vocalist), the group—which had been performing in one form or another at the Collegiate Jazz Festival since 1960—finally captured its long-sought-after prize. Left behind in the Belcastro Trio dust, trombonist Brian Trentham's experimental "free jazz" Columbia University Combo had to content itself with bassist Cameron Brown's Most Promising Rhythm Man award; meanwhile the "avant-garde inflected" Jerry Green Sextet from Indiana University managed individual awards for alto-saxophonist/leader Green and "strong but sometimes verbose" trumpeter Randy Brecker.[8]

Coming up short for the second year in a row, Father Wiskirchen's Northwestern aggregate and the other finalist bands were eclipsed by the unbeatable "sheen and power" of Indiana University's Ensemble.[9] (As some salve for their loss, however, talented Northwestern alto-saxophonist David Sanborn and former Melodon flautist James Gillespie received respective Most Promising Soloist and Best Flute awards.) Other award winners included Notre Dame Jazz Quartet and big-band Lettermen member Larry Dwyer (Outstanding Trombone) and University of Illinois soloist Wallace Rave (Outstanding Guitar). Named Outstanding Big Band Composer for his "Variations On a Theme Called Whiffenpoof," Ohio State University Big-Band student director Ladd McIntosh added an offbeat note to festival history by stalking self-righteously up to the onstage microphone to "refuse his award."[10]

(Late Friday night after the preliminary session had ended, a jam session that included both judges and Collegiate Jazz Festival student performers at Robert's Supper Club on Colfax Street in downtown South Bend produced similar offbeat results, as one young musician in particular leapt off stage after taking his solo turn, ran hurriedly the length of the room to a pay phone at the back and called home to shout, "I just played with Clark Terry!")[11]

1
9
6
6
Mastered and pressed by Crest Records, the fourth Collegiate Jazz Festival three-record album emerged in mid-1965 with a striking yellow cardboard cover adorned by only a black CJF logo, festival locale, and finals session date. Yet another encapsulation of mid-sixties collegiate-jazz progress and diversity, the album did little, however, to assuage serious doubts about the festival's future. Faced with dwindling attendance figures and a progressively flawed festival organizational mechanism that passed from student chairman to student chairman each year (all of whom, it seemed, had to learn the event's inner workings and procedures on the run), the CJF—for all its collegiate-jazz contributions and history—was beginning to show signs of age.

In addition, there were new, radical developments taking place in both music and the world at large. Rock—now the dominant music God—was embarking on a rebellious, psychedelic sixties phase that would further siphon jazz audiences and, as a result, continue to threaten the livelihoods of many professional jazzmen and women. Blacks were finding a new self-awareness in everyday life through the words and efforts of influential leaders such as Malcolm X and Martin Luther King, Jr. In jazz, the "new" sounds championed by Ornette Coleman in the early years of the decade had given way to spiritual, "freedom-oriented" explorations by John Coltrane, Albert Ayler, Archie Shepp, and others. It was a time of uprising and change in music, culture, and campus ideals. In a similar way, though preparations for the eighth Collegiate Jazz Festival at Notre Dame proceeded wearily along as they had in previous years, this would also be a time that marked the beginning of the end of the CJF's first period of growth.

These matters, of course, did not filter down all at once to '66 Collegiate Jazz Festival personnel. Led by chairmen Tony Andrea and Tony Rivizzigno, the '66 CJF committee had its hands full with mere festival organization, as well as the puzzlingly jazz-unresponsive-of-late Notre Dame campus crowd. "The academic perspective [of the performances] implies an interaction between artist and audience," explained co-chairman Andrea in a prefestival *Scholastic* attempt to inspire greater jazz interest among Notre Dame student body members. " . . . The sensitive and enthusiastic listeners are as important to the performance of the musicians as the creatively imaginative and distinctive performance of the musicians is to the response of the audience. This dialogue of creativity and response is what made Notre Dame's College Jazz Festival great."[1]

Once again at spring-festival time, the scent of State Department foreign tours lay heavy in the air, as talk of the CJF-instigated late-fall

1965 Belcastro Trio Latin American tour and the almost-completed fifteen-week Indiana University Jazz Ensemble jaunt to India, Pakistan, Syria, Iran, Iraq, Jordan, Lebanon, Greece, Egypt, Cyprus, and Turkey floated back and forth inside the worn, white brick Fieldhouse walls.[2] Perhaps due to this added foreign-tour lure, schools from as far away as California, Arkansas, and Massachusetts were in attendance at the 1966 college-jazz gathering in South Bend, which, given the poor acoustics and increasing seating difficulties inherent in the performance locale (and the new Stepan Center/CJF negotiations underway) was most likely destined to be the last Collegiate Jazz Festival the Old Fieldhouse would entertain.

Presenting the usual wide range of influences, the ten big bands and nine combos in attendance at the eighth Collegiate Jazz Festival were sifted down over the preliminary periods to seven by judges Billy Taylor, Quincy Jones,[3] Don DeMicheal, Charles Suber, and (subbing for an unable-to-attend Robert Share) Fr. George Wiskirchen. These finalist groups included the University of Illinois Jazz Band and Quintet, the big-band Criterions of Pennsylvania's West Chester State, the (former North Texas State/CJF award-winning trumpeter) Tom Wirtel-led Indiana University Jazz Ensemble II, a West Chester State Quintet, Northwestern University's Ed Sheftel Combo, and a group from the host school, the Notre Dame Jazz Sextet.

Playing but one extended composition, "It Was a Very Good Year," for both the preliminary and finals sessions, trumpeter Ed Sheftel and his four-man Northwestern University combo crew (pianist Paul Libman, bassist Dennis Gardino, drummer Julio Coronado, and flautist/recorder player David Starr) scored well with their collective free-form playing, overall artistry, and poise and quickly knocked off the dazzlingly experimental Illinois Jazz Quintet led by trombonist Morgan Powell as well as the fast, professional-sounding Quintet from West Chester State and the spirited Notre Dame Sextet for the Best Combo award.

Consisting of two basses, trumpet, trombone, and drums, the Illinois combo, however, was perhaps the most daring and offbeat finals group, offering judging panel and audience humorous drumwork, scrambled noise effects, and dissonant, interconnected versions of songs such as "Bittersweet, Knocking," and Ornette Coleman's "Lonely Woman."[4] (In the middle of one selection, the Illinois musicians reduced their individual instrument outputs to a nonexistent level, only to continue to work their respective instruments vigorously in improvisational pantomime before completing the number by flailing confetti and rice at each other on stage—to the crowd's surprise and delight.)[5]

As far as the Notre Dame Jazz Sextet was concerned, of course, making the finals for only the second time in Collegiate Jazz Festival history (a Lettermen combo in 1960 held the honor of being the first) was an event in itself. Made up of trombonist Larry Dwyer, guitarist Paul Leavis, tenor-saxophonist Mike Turre, drummer Kevin Doherty, bassist Jim Szabo, and freshman alto-saxophone-sensation Bill Hurd (also a budding track star who would go on to set a U.S. record in the 300-yard dash in the Old Fieldhouse while at Notre Dame in 1968), the group was clearly the finest Notre Dame jazz entry yet and managed to snare individual awards for Best Guitar (Leavis), Trombone (Dwyer), and Most Promising Reed Player (Bill Hurd) at festival's end.

For the second year in a row, a big band from Indiana outplayed other finalists to take the Best Band award—despite the fact that in 1966 it was the school's second string band![6] (The top Indiana ensemble was, of course, still on a CJF 1965-inspired foreign tour at festival time.) Even more curious about the Indiana aggregate's surprising win, however, was the fact that the judges had almost eliminated the band from finalist consideration after a sluggish preliminaries performance and selected the equally impressive University of Iowa Jazz Lab Ensemble (featuring the "virile alto solos" of Outstanding Reed Soloist David Sanborn)[7] instead.

"Being named among the finalists must have acted as an elixir," noted *down beat* magazine's Don DeMicheal a few weeks after the event,

> for when the Hoosiers hit at the wind-up concert, they were like different men—everything fell beautifully in place, and neither of the other bands, as good as they were, approached the inspired level of Indiana. . . .
>
> The quality of the best college jazz groups is high. The amateurish small groups are about gone, and so are the pretentious and bombastic big bands cast in the likeness of Stan Kenton at his most postured. Not completely gone, however; there are still big band directors who evidently believe that labored composition is what jazz is all about, while a few soloists just as obviously are convinced the music is meant for open field chord and scale running. But the misled are very much in the minority—at least at the Collegiate Jazz Festival, the first and still foremost of the collegiate competitions.[8]

Fine, stirring words from a respected columnist. Unfortunately, despite the encouraging, postfestival arrival of the fifth CJF finalist album, another voice, contained in the Notre Dame yearbook, the *Dome*, which appeared a month after the festival had ended, was much less optimistic in a short piece that accompanied several Collegiate Jazz Festival photos.

After two anemic years, Notre Dame's folk festival rolled over quietly and expired. Next year, or the year after, or the year after that the CJF will probably do the same. . . . Despite the fact that the judges included names like Quincy Jones and Billy Taylor . . . student attendance was disappointing at the last session and minimal during the preliminaries. This lack of interest was mirrored in the lack of a post-performance jazz [jam] session. There is a good chance that it will soon be mirrored in the absence of CJF.[9]

Whatever the reasons for this audience decline—the advent of rock; disturbing trends in jazz experimentation and accompanying listener fears of being "left out"; an overwhelmingly successful Notre Dame sports year that included young football-coach Ara Parseghian's first National Championship, or just the usual low-budget CJF publicity difficulties—they were definitely beginning to take their toll. In fact, with mounting financial losses and diminishing student interest, there was an almost certain chance the CJF would soon be canceled. Something would obviously have to change to salvage the event. And it would have to happen fast. For the 1967 Collegiate Jazz Festival would find itself confronted not only by this interior student-audience problem but with its most formidable outside challenge yet as well: a national intercollegiate jazz festival set up with regional feeder festivals across the entire country.

If commercialism could hit collegiate jazz with greater glitter and lure than in the past, it would do so in the upcoming year. And, in the process, an already floundering, soon-to-be erased from student-event schedules Collegiate Jazz Festival—if it survived at all—would suddenly find itself in the unusual position of being backed against the wall.

A Change of CJF Gears

1
9
6
7

In April of 1966, a new collegiate jazz festival made its debut in—of all places—Mobile, Alabama. Known for its intense recent racial history, the state could hardly have been a more challenging choice for the presentation of a black-originated form of artistic expression, but somehow a young, creative public-relations man and promoter with plenty of ideas named Bob Yde brought it off—to the amazement of many. Packing the judges panel with jazz-recording and education names such as John Hammond, *down beat*'s Dan Morgenstern, critic Stanley Dance, and Fr. George Wiskirchen, Yde's hurriedly constructed dream served to move large-scale collegiate jazz not only into the South but into a somewhat disturbing commercial arena as well. From the start, it was evident this was no ordinary festival maker; rather, this was a high-rolling jazz gambler willing to take the big risk.

Sponsored by a group of Mobile businessmen (as opposed to university funding at Notre Dame, Villanova, and Oread), the festival found able hosts in the University of Alabama and Spring Hill College and subsequently emerged with excellent all-around marks. ABC's radio network carried festival music highlights; the winning Florida Jazz Quintet received a Columbia Records contract and a Newport Jazz Festival performance slot (as well as a stint at Al Hirt's New Orleans club); NBC-TV was even considering other Mobile winners for an upcoming television special entitled "Class of '67." (Representatives of the State Department, ever eager for a foreign tour goodwill group, had, of course, also been on hand.) "Phenomenally successful for a first-year venture," concluded attending critic James L. Collier, "Mobile is a good model of the strengths and weaknesses of college competitions."[1]

Thoroughly (and rightly) proud of his product, Bob Yde, however, wasted little time in going for the collegiate jazz jugular. Reaching out for that grandiose scheme that separates the small festival heads from the "men of vision," he soon set out to convince the business and collegiate jazz worlds that a national competition of some sort was presently necessary. Eventually three sponsors (TWA, the Sero-Shirt company, and the City of Miami) turned an ear to Yde's proposal. In short order, Yde was made president of what was, at first, termed the "Intercollegiate Jazz Festival." (Because of sponsor fears, the event's name would be changed in early 1967 to the "Intercollegiate *Music* Festival.")[2]

As 1967 approached, the regional roster of festivals that would feed into the Miami superfestival included Villanova (March 24-25), the Cerritos Jazz Festival (Norwalk, California; March 3-4), the Midwest College Jazz Festival (Northwestern University, Evanston, Illinois; March 10-11), the Little Rock Jazz Festival (Little Rock, Arkansas; March 24-25), the Mobile Jazz Festival (April 7-8), and the Intermountain Collegiate Jazz Festival (April 7-8).[3] Viewed in its entirety, the event's structure appeared surprisingly sound—particularly after such a whirlwind creation.

Regional winners from the feeder festivals would arrive in Miami to play before a group of adjudicators that included Fr. Norman O'Connor, Oliver Nelson, Robert Share, Gary McFarland, Phil Woods, and the ubiquitous Charles Suber. In addition, Voice of America jazz broadcaster Willis Conover would appear as emcee. Trophies and attention would be plentiful. (As an added attraction, Miss Miami Beach, Juanita Jones, was even scheduled to be present on stage to congratulate eventual award winners.) In fact, the event was so well organized, exciting, and inevitably going to happen that few of those who had hurriedly hopped aboard the red, white, and blue Intercollegiate Jazz Festival bandwagon headed for Miami even took notice of the somewhat curious fact that the Notre Dame Collegiate Jazz Festival—the foremost such festival in the land—had no part in the extensive hoopla at all. Taking a high-rolling risk of its own, the 1967 Notre Dame event had decided to go on alone.

With respect to Notre Dame's philosophy concerning the Miami event and the decision to stay away, a CJF release of November 1966 seemed to get to the heart of the matter. "One thing that must be made clear," read the release's closing lines, "is that the Notre Dame Collegiate Jazz Festival has absolutely no affiliation with the Inter-Collegiate Music Festival of Miami. We refused to be one of its regional festivals because we felt that our own interests as well as those of our participants would best be served by remaining an independent leader in collegiate jazz."[4]

Behind such clearheaded resolve, however, also lay some other extremely disturbing Notre Dame jazz-festival facts. At the same time in mid-1966 that Bob Yde was making initial contact with '67 CJF Chairman Paul Schlaver in order to lure the famed CJF into his Miami fold, Schlaver was struggling against enormous odds to stave off university cancellation of the festival. Selected by default to be '67 chairman, Schlaver met with the Vice President for Student Affairs in late spring after the '66 CJF had closed its Fieldhouse doors, totaled up losses on program and ticket sales, and licked its dwindling audience/Notre Dame student-participation wounds once more.

Sitting down that day with Rev. Charles McCarragher (an Irishman noted for his stern ability to lay down the Notre Dame undergraduate law), Paul Schlaver quickly determined that—much to his surprise—the administration could no longer finance the festival. Faced with mounting losses, the administration had concluded that the event would either have to be cut back drastically or ended and there was nothing more to be said. Shaken, Schlaver left McCarragher's office but soon began pondering mad, desperate festival-saving schemes with Co-Chairman John Noel, a Notre Dame junior who also was in charge of putting together the '67 festival program. Convinced that one mind was clearly not enough to meet the challenge posed by Father McCarragher, Schlaver and Noel soon became a wildly creative CJF team.

First mad scheme on the agenda: find the struggling CJF a new funding source.[5]

After some additional creative thought, Schlaver and Noel (both
of whom happened to live in the Chicago area during collegiate sum-
mers) decided to approach longtime CJF advisor and friend *down beat*
magazine. Desperate, energetic, and exuding the paradoxical panache
of men who have absolutely nothing to lose, the two took several runs
down to Hinsdale, Illinois (a southwest Chicago suburb) in the summer of 1966 to tell their sad CJF tale to John Maher, wealthy publisher
of *down beat* and various other magazines. Encountering Maher within
the comfortable confines of his immense Hinsdale estate, the two Notre
Dame students somehow convinced him to jump aboard the sinking
CJF ship and salvage the festival outright with a firm promise to cover
any festival losses in 1967 and to sponsor various festival parts as well.

Racing back to Father McCarragher's office at Notre Dame with
this good news, Schlaver and Noel were able to buy the festival a be-
grudged stay of execution. In addition, in order to ensure a successful
festival, they requested that Father McCarragher allow them some sort
of office space within the student-government complex in LaFortune
Student Center. Surprisingly, they got it. In return for these conces-
sions (and, of course, a stay of CJF-execution), however, Father McCarragher made plain the fact that the festival could no longer be considered an event outside of student-government domain; in the future
it would instead be placed under the jurisdiction of the Social Commissioner's wing of the Notre Dame Student Government. Lastly,
McCarragher made Schlaver and Noel promise to locate a faculty advisor of some sort at Notre Dame in the next year who would take
responsibility for guiding the event and thereby placate his understandable fiscal and organizational fears.

If Notre Dame was "bold" enough to make this move away from
Miami and Yde's Intercollegiate Jazz Festival dream at such a time of
crisis (there were, to be sure, many who thought the CJF foolhardy
to pass up such a potentially far-reaching affiliation at the time), the
decision did, in a way, offer the CJF a certain, intangible incentive that
had been lacking in the past few years. Even more importantly, the
move gave the festival a new goal and a renewed sense of purpose
that allowed student organizers to realize that numerous areas of
festival operation and procedure were in definite need of change.

To this effect, CJF '67 Chairman Schlaver and Co-Chairman Noel
decided to push ahead with plans to move from the "archaic N.D.
Fieldhouse" to the refreshing geodesic grandeur of nearby Stepan Center
on the northeast corner of the University of Notre Dame campus.[6] By

1966–67, the Fieldhouse had begun to fade as a year-round activity center on campus. In addition, its worn, ancient look did little to contribute to the image of a jazz festival in tune with the times. Stepan Center was simply better equipped, better lit and less medieval in mood. Though it would not be easy to leave the storied Fieldhouse dust and basketball-floor stage with all the many CJF memories behind, the oldest collegiate jazz festival extant definitely needed to update its milieu in order to reestablish its preeminence once more.

In the same November, 1966 press release Schlaver and Noel also made known the '67 festival's intent to emphasize "the educational and cultural aspects of jazz with three innovations."[7] The first of these innovations, a "concert-lecture series aimed at explaining the uniqueness of jazz in relation to other forms of music,"[8] took place in Washington Hall on February 12, a month prior to the '67 March CJF. Co-sponsored by the Notre Dame music department, the concert featured the Jamey Aebersold Sextet (Aebersold, alto sax; Alan Kiger, trumpet; David Lahm, piano; Stan Gage, drums; bassist Brent McKesson; Keith Spring, tenor sax) in a "history of jazz from Bebop to Avant-garde" that "allowed the audience to better understand the fundamental mechanics of jazz."[9]

Second on the CJF expansion list was the initiation of an annual two-day, three-session symposium preceding the festival itself which would make use of the attending CJF judges. Exploring "The Current State of Jazz," the symposium was held on March 2 and 3 in Notre Dame's new Kellogg Center for Continuing Education, or "CCE," just across from the Morris Inn on the southern-most side of the campus.

Taking its cue from the more informal '63, '64, and '66 judging-panel discussions,[10] this 1967 meeting of professional/educational jazz minds which included judging-panel members Robert Share, pianist Herbie Hancock, composer William Russo, trumpeter Donald Byrd, *down beat* editor Don DeMicheal, and Notre Dame music-department head Fr. Carl Hager did much to expand festival relationships with the academic community at large, and helped to keep the educators, musicians, and students in attendance up-to-date on the state of jazz. "Hopefully," explained festival organizers in the CJF '67 program, "this will blossom into a yearly discussion on pertinent developments and components of modern trends in music. . . . For too long a time have the majority of educators and cultural minded people entertained erroneous concepts about the legitimacy and value of jazz as a powerful art form. By establishing the symposium, the CJF hopes to do its part in fostering understanding, open mindedness and development in modern music."[11]

Lastly, the two CJF student innovators broadened festival bases by instituting in Washington Hall a high-school jazz-band competition cosponsored by H. & A. Selmer, Inc., the large Elkhart, Indiana-based instrument manufacturer and major CJF patron since 1959. Judged by Fr. George Wiskirchen, professional saxophonist/band leader Leonard Druss, and Kenneth Bartosz, (Director of Instrumental Music at Chicago's Loyola Academy), and limited to Indiana high-school groups, the contest accommodated nineteen bands from Indianapolis, Vincennes, Fort Wayne, Hammond, Bloomington, and Elkhart on Saturday morning, March 3, finishing a few hours before the CJF finals. Winners received valuable advice, Selmer trophies and plaques, and the much coveted chance to play at the CJF finals that night after the college band session had ended.

On another note of change, the CJF '67 jazz committee decided to offer cash awards of $500 and $300 to winning bands and combos and soloist award trophies instead of the usual instrument prizes. In addition, Paul Schlaver and John Noel took pains to reinstitute the popular postfestival jam session of past years and induced judges Herbie Hancock, Donald Byrd, and Don DeMicheal (an excellent vibist and drummer) to play. Held up the road on U.S. 31 in Christ the King Hall on Friday night after the preliminary round, the jam allowed for additional contact between students and judges and provided a more·informal place in which musicians could let loose.[12]

Eighteen collegiate groups from California, Massachusetts, and a healthy number of Midwest states assembled March 3 and 4 in Stepan Center to kick off the ninth annual Notre Dame jazz event. Ranging from a drum/piano duo to the massive twenty-five-piece University of Illinois ensemble, it appeared to be the usual diverse slice of college jazz, except for the fact that, for only the second time in festival history, Notre Dame itself was not represented by a musical group.

On a more upbeat note, one particularly significant development at CJF '67 was the appearance of the Indiana University Jazz Ensemble under Dave Baker, the first and (in 1967) only black college-jazz-band director in the country.[13] A potent past CJF student musician/leader, Baker had taken over his alma mater's jazz teaching spot after director Jerry Coker had been wooed away in 1966 to head up a new degree-granting jazz program at the University of Miami in Florida.[14]

Opening the '67 event was one of the most unusual CJF groups yet, a Santa Rosa Jr. College (Calif.) duo made up of pianist Jack Tolson and drummer Michael Brandenburg that went by the abstract name of 1/1=One. Attired in a suit jacket and flowing neckerchief, Tolson dominated the duo's preliminary set (which included his own mysteriously titled song, "W.N.I.A.B.C.") with impressive control, alternate plucking and pounding of piano strings with hands or mallets, and an extensive keyboard improvisational technique not unlike that of avant-garde pianist Cecil Taylor.[15]

"To some," wrote *South Bend Tribune* reporter Glenn Reitze in a festival analysis the next day, "what Tolson has written will—at very best—be puzzling. But to listeners reasonably sympathetic with 20th century 'serious' European and American composition, there is only one verdict on Tolson's works: they are beautiful."[16] Also included on the Friday-afternoon preliminaries performance agenda was a tight, swinging, vibes-oriented group from the University of California at Berkeley, the Leon Schipper Quintet, which turned judges' heads around with complex original compositions and loose, exciting musician interplay.

By Friday evening, Stepan Center was packed and waiting for the powerhouse big bands and combos. Ladd McIntosh's Ohio State University Jazz Workshop led off the charged-up night, and before things had wound down four or five hours later, a University of Illinois septet (with Notre Dame graduate/trombonist Larry Dwyer in tow), John Garvey's gargantuan Illinois band, an Indiana University Jazz Quintet (led by alto saxophonist Jerry Green and trumpeter Randy Sandke), and a fine Duquesne University Ensemble (featuring baritone saxophonist Paul McCandless) had appeared. As usual, the evening's surfeit of college jazz was capped off with a guest appearance by Father Wiskirchen's[17] twenty-two piece high-school Melodons (featuring—as had been the case in 1966—pianist Jim McNeely) for the eighth straight year.[18]

Saturday afternoon found several more jazz performance nuggets on display including those created by Dave Baker's Indiana Jazz Ensemble I, a Julliard School of Music quintet, and, back for the second consecutive year, a Herb Pomeroy-led Massachusetts Institute of Technology Concert Jazz Band made up entirely of science and engineering students (as the Institute had no music school at all). On a somewhat more offbeat note, the session also featured the courageous improvisational work of two handicapped musicians, South Bend native Richard Ecteau (who managed to remove his cast-encased left arm from a sling to play trombone with Indiana's big band) and MIT band/sextet cornetist Sam Alongi (who, due to a recent accident, found himself forced to play on a pair of crutches).[19]

Named to the evening's finals were top-notch big bands from Indiana and Illinois as well as a surprising Washington University Concert Jazz Orchestra from St. Louis, Missouri. Combos represented in the finals included the MIT sextet, the offbeat Californian 1/1=One duo, the Leon Schipper Quintet from Berkeley, and the Indiana University Jazz Sextet (proclaimed the day before by *South Bend Tribune* critic Glenn Reitze to be "one of the best combos playing in the United States today").[20]

Once into the finals, it soon became apparent that the Indiana/ Illinois struggle would top all other attractions. Under the driving leadership of Dave Baker (certainly no stranger to CJF atmospherics), Indiana's exceptional soloists Jerry Green (alto-saxophone) and Randy Sandke (trumpet) powered the band through a set of Baker originals and arrangements such as "4–5–6," "The Screemin' Meemies," and "The Professor."[21] Definitely an onstage juggernaut, Indiana roused the CJF crowd sufficiently but suffered a bit in the judges' eyes because of the overall similarity of the Baker works.[22]

Illinois on the other hand, made sure to diversify its set and even managed to surpass itself with what was perhaps the CJF's most blatant, theatrical, and bizarre music display yet. Starting off with fairly straight renditions of "Love Walked In" and Tadd Dameron's "Lady-Bird," the unpredictable John Garvey-led aggregate took a moment to dig into its sly bag of tricks before bringing forth a final composition that was announced simply as "They Just . . ." (as in the phrase "Old soldiers never die, they just fade away"). As far as the University of Illinois was concerned, it was the last moment the song was in touch with reality. Stationing two-thirds of the massive Illinois band onstage for the number in order to play a fragmented portion of "far-out" music that served to both enliven and baffle the Stepan Center/CJF crowd, Garvey suddenly bade a second, much smaller Illinois contingent to appear at the back of the geodesic-domed arena whereupon it began to march up the center aisle playing in the raucous, cacophonous way of a lurching Salvation Army Band, before finally finding a way to the stage in order to wage slam-bang improvisational battle with the totally incongruous sounds of the already onstage band.[23]

As if that wasn't enough, the larger onstage group just as abruptly stopped playing altogether and began to pantomime fierce improvisations on respective instruments, flailing the air in this mysterious collective effort before finally departing the stage one by one until only bearded Illinois drummer, Chuck Braugham, remained behind. Not to be upstaged, Braugham began to thrash the air with his drumsticks, before pounding the backstage curtain with abandon until he had managed to "play" himself out of sight.[24] Stunned into profound silence for a moment, the crowd suddenly roared in delight at the psychedelic "jazz happening" treat. Entirely unexpected, outrageously funny, and devastatingly entertaining, it was the CJF once again in the unadulterated, totally spontaneous flesh.

For the judges, however, this unusual finals display proved troublesome indeed. Many of the panel members were immediately repulsed by the band's theatricality which had so thoroughly disrupted the seriousness of the event. Obviously, it was creative, wild, and crowd pleasing, but, was it music? And where on the scoring sheet was there a space for musicians who pantomime instead of play? Trudging puzzledly to the back room at the north end of Stepan Center and shutting the door, judges Hancock, Byrd, Russo, Share, DeMicheal and composer Lalo Schifrin (a late arrival) knew well what sort of discussion fireworks would fly, and, as expected, they did. Fortunately, to cover the storminess of the session, the first annual CJF high-school-band festival winner, the "Variations" of Lincoln High School, Vincennes, Indiana (directed by Walter Anslinger), was soon onstage to offer the audience a tight, crisp, invigorating set of high-quality jazz.

To the surprise and dismay of Dave Baker and his fine Indiana aggregate, the judges returned with a verdict tabbing Illinois as the best big band. On top of that, the potent Indiana combo was passed over in favor of the complex, stimulating Leon Schipper Quintet which, in addition to the combo award, went on to pile up astounding individual honors for each quintet member, including multi-instrumentalist Bob Claire (Most Promising Reed Man), guitarist Bob Strizich (Best Guitar), drummer Tom Aubrey (Best Drums), and vibist/physics-music major Schipper (Best Miscellaneous Instrument).[25] As some consolation, Indiana's Randy Sandke (Best Trumpet), Jerry Green (Best Alto-Sax and Best Arranger) and David Luell (Best Baritone Saxophone) took home awards.

Out of the ashes of the CJF finals also emerged a new breed of outstanding CJF instrumentalist in pianist Jack Tolson, whose unique ability to distort and restructure melodies was amply displayed in selections such as "Linear Exposition" as well as in a melancholic, moving exploration of Tchaikovsky's ballet music entitled "Swan Lake Recapitulations."[26] As for the festival's courageous walking wounded, M.I.T. trumpeter Sam Alongi copped a Most-Promising trophy, while healthy and intact Ball State musician Dave Pavolka took Best Trombonist honors.

Against numerous odds, the 1967 CJF had once again proved the worth of a festival devoted to collegiate jazz at Notre Dame. Due to the efforts of students Paul Schlaver and John Noel, the festival had also undergone much-needed reevaluation and restructure and benefited greatly from a bevy of jazz consciousness-expanding festival ideas.

Perhaps even more importantly, the 1967 CJF had found a heightened pride and purpose by refusing to become a part of Bob Yde's Miami Intercollegiate Jazz Festival master plan.

In effect, Paul Schlaver had revived a dying event through a combination of wile, wit, crazed creativity, and fortunate outside funding. Together with John Noel, he had attempted to set up numerous educational possibilities for the festival and put together a 34-page CJF program that seemed to reflect all the seriousness, dignity, dedication, and effort the year and festival rightly deserved.[27] In terms of continuity, Paul Schlaver had also greatly aided the CJF by selecting and "training" cochairman John Noel as 1968 "chairman-to-be" the entire year.

Finally, Schlaver's last act was to fulfill the final promise made to Father McCarragher and find a faculty advisor for the festival, someone the CJF could turn to for help in battling administrative red tape or for needed advice in crisis situations such as the Bob Yde/IMF-Miami affair. Such an advisor would provide a stabilizing force that could give the event an added luster, as well as the confidence to pursue new ideas. Sifting through numerous prospects and suggestions, Paul Schlaver and John Noel soon turned up a promising lead: a young English professor at Notre Dame named Richard Bizot.

The Great Schlitz Beer Caper

> I've never experienced anything like the festivals. All your marbles are on the table. You play for the untouchables—the worshipped men of jazz—and you give them the best you have to offer. —Ladd McIntosh, *down beat*, September 8, 1968

1968 In the aftermath of CJF '67, several important festival criticisms came to light. Certainly, all those in attendance agreed the musical-talent level was high. *down beat*'s Don DeMicheal would soon point to this fact in print, stating that "if all the music played at the CJF this year could be averaged out, the median quality would be somewhere near very good, much higher than it would have been, say, five years ago."[1] Unfortunately, cautioned DeMicheal, "college jazz, even as good as that heard at this festival, remains on the plateau it reached three or four years ago when it developed able soloists. It's a high plateau, but not the highest." The experimentation of the early sixties which placed the CJF's musical presentations momentarily on a par with or ahead of developments in professional jazz had, it seemed, given way to a developmental "limbo" of sorts. Or so the critics would believe until an unusually startling occurrence at CJF '68.

Compared with its major full-blown 1967 rival, the Intercollegiate Music Festival in Miami, the CJF, though perhaps losing out in overall glitter and flash, managed to hold its own. At Miami, in a major upset, Ladd McIntosh's Ohio State Jazz Workshop Band (which hadn't made the finals at CJF '67) nudged out San Fernando Valley State's Studio Band and Leon Breeden's powerhouse North Texas State Lab Band to win the Duke Ellington Award (presented by no less than Duke Ellington himself). Other awards at the IMF were presented by John Coltrane (barely a few months before his untimely death), singer Tony Bennett, and ever-generous, concerned bandleader, Stan Kenton. In addition, there was extensive media coverage of the event and even a live album (produced by Impulse's Bob Thiele) that captured the winning groups in fine full-throttle form. Despite these successes, however, the IMF would forsake the sand and sun of Miami in 1968 for the presummer heat and glistening, high arch of St. Louis.

For Richard Bizot, a Notre Dame English professor who had attended the '66 and '67 CJF's, there was much to wonder about beyond the now somewhat more distant threat of Miami. Specifically, he was wondering how he had been convinced by an enthusiastic two-man team of Notre Dame students by the names of Schlaver and Noel to accept a role as CJF faculty adviser; how much that task would entail; what sort of administrative clashes might thereby arise; and what it actually was that a jazz festival faculty adviser was supposed to do over the course of a year. Unfortunately, there was little he could infer about the difficulties and enjoyments this first festival-adviser year would contain. In fact, if someone were even to have suggested to him in the slightest way in the fall of 1967 that the festival might possibly be supported in 1968 by a major beer company, he would have most likely brushed aside the idea with a hurried laugh. But, as Bizot soon came to realize, you could never quite predict what outrageous idea John Noel would come up with next and—what was even more frightening—eventually put into action.

With Bizot's sturdy faculty advice and support on his side, John Noel found himself emboldened to attempt a difficult range of festival tasks, the first of which was the updating of the festival's acceptance policy for collegiate jazz groups as well as the CJF's overall audience approach. With the increasing student awareness of musical and world events, a distaste for the escalating war in Vietnam, English pop-culture trends, and experimental, conceptual rock sounds that seemed to touch on so many of these other developments, even the somewhat South Bend, Indiana-isolated Notre Dame student body was beginning (however slowly) to alter its listening, dressing, and behavioral habits. To continue on without readjusting festival rules and content to accommodate some of these changes, Noel rightly realized, would only serve once again to push away the audience CJF '67 had worked so hard to reclaim. For this reason, as well as an understandable ever-present desire to keep to the leading, inventive course set in 1967 in the face of stiff competition from the Miami IMF, a brief addendum to the fall CJF application form made a new, somewhat startling policy clear:

> Electronic Music:
>
> The CJF has recently received a number of requests for information regarding our policy on electronic music. Because electronic music is becoming more and more a part of modern music, the CJF does not restrict nor discourage its use in festival competition. However, contestants must keep in mind that electronic devices are to be used only as a complement to, and not as a substitute for, musical talent. Its use, therefore, must not jeopardize the integrity of true creative jazz.[2]

This move, of course, takes on greater meaning when placed in the context of jazz's relation to rock and pop music at a time when once-clear distinctions between them were blurring with startling and often raw rapidity. In the process new audiences were being discovered. Some jazzmen such as vibist Gary Burton and saxophonist Charles Lloyd were fortunate enough to take advantage of this sudden chance for larger acceptance, while others (most notably the John Coltrane-inspired group of avant-garde experimenters that included saxophonists Archie Shepp, Albert Ayler, and others) held to their previous, more appeal-limited directions and spiritual ground.

In other areas, fascination with other cultures (much of it inspired by the Beatles) brought about a new diversity in instrumentation and sound as well as a cross-fertilization of music histories and influences that further served to confuse the era's musical/listening situation. On top of this, pop-art trends had brought about a new, heightened awareness of culture, while 1950-ish Allan Kaprowesque "happenings" seemed to be occurring with increasing frequency in the rock-music realm.

Obviously, neither jazz nor an event known as the Collegiate Jazz Festival could hope to reflect any more than a few of these new developments. Despite this fact, however, gatherings such as the CJF were, by 1968, without a doubt platforms upon which youth could express itself as it saw fit. Music, it seemed, was an outlet for an angered age, and the fact that John Noel recognized—if only in a small way—that such needs had to be expressed in a multitude of forms and instrumentations beyond those traditionally accepted was indeed an important step.

Responding to these various stimuli and influences, John Noel continued to go about the complex jazz-festival maneuvers that he hoped would attempt to capture a bit of all that was spinning so madly in the late-sixties air. Nodding to the jazz/pop controversy as well as the festival's reemphasized education bent, the '68 CJF Symposium entitled "The Current State of Jazz: Part II" would include a session devoted to the question, "Pop and Jazz: Fission or Fusion?" To augment symposium discussions with a tangible music presentation (and to continue the '67 CJF tradition of presenting an educational prefestival lecture-concert), Chicago composer/'67 CJF judge William Russo and his Chicago Fire group were invited to appear at Notre Dame in Stepan Center a week before the 1968 CJF.

Both a noted classical and jazz composer and a one-time Stan Kenton band trombonist/arranger, Russo, the director of Chicago's Center for New Music at Columbia College, eventually treated Stepan Center audiences to a lecture interspersed with "improvisations in jazz, blues and rock," provided by his eight-man ensemble.[3] Aiming to simultaneously please avant-garde, jazz, and rock buffs, Russo's performing group included no less than three amplified guitars (all guitarists, of course, doubling as vocalists), percussion, an electrically amplified cello and flute, and an electric organ, as well as group-leader Russo himself operating an onstage tape recorder.[4] Presenting several of the leader's "cantatas," the concert also featured a major Russo composition, "The Civil War," and the psychedelic light show of "Captain Electric."[5]

Continuing his expanded educational efforts, Noel set additional plans in motion for a Jazz Mass to take place in Notre Dame's Sacred Heart Church under Fr. George Wiskirchen's supervision and direction during the '68 festival weekend (unfortunately, the Mass plans would not reach fruition that year). In addition, he began extensive negotiations with both Dr. Pepper and a local cola bottler in order to sponsor a trip to the festival by the Leon Breeden-led North Texas State Lab Band, and corralled both the top bass man, Ray Brown, and (hot on the heels of pianist Herbie Hancock's '67 judging stint) another member of trumpeter Miles Davis's trend-setting late-sixties quintet, tenor saxophonist Wayne Shorter, to attend as judges.[6] (Other developments involved taking a wild shot at convincing Leonard Bernstein to be a '68 judge, and negotiating with the Bell Telephone Company to consider sponsoring a national television broadcast of the festival.) These evolutions aside, however, John Noel finally took the Notre Dame administration bull by the horns in late 1967 by making early overtures to the Joseph Schlitz Brewing Company, a well-known beer manufacturer and distributor, for festival funding and support.

Encouraged by *down beat* editor Don DeMicheal (who had admittedly grown to be a great fan and backer of the CJF over the years), Noel made contact with the Schlitz Foundation, a Schlitz organizational branch set up to help fund worthy causes in the arts.[7] In charge of the area of Modern Art was a man by the name of Robert Trent Jones. To his surprise, Mr. Jones suddenly found himself in 1967–68 to be the target of an all-out John Noel/CJF public-relations campaign.

Correspondence between Noel and Jones soon began to accumulate as 1967 rolled along and '68 approached. Finally, after exhausting every avenue and approach, Noel received a letter from Schlitz, admitting that the CJF was indeed an artistic event worthy enough to warrant foundation assistance. Much like the aid offered by *down beat* publisher John Maher in '67, Schlitz offered to cover any festival losses incurred in '68. In addition, for the '68 CJF "grand prize," Schlitz agreed to pick up a considerable amount of the tab involved in transporting the overall '68 festival group winner to the professional Newport Jazz Festival in Newport, Rhode Island in July.[8]

Ever in touch with those in high places (and hoping quite naturally to extend Schlitz goodwill further throughout the college ranks and the world at large) the Schlitz Foundation also soon contacted the U.S. Department of State Cultural Presentations, which in turn rapidly decided to send three delegates to the '68 CJF in order to select a collegiate band for a European tour that would include Soviet satellite nations such as Yugoslavia and Czechoslovakia. With a few bold strokes and plenty of luck it seemed the CJF had shrugged off its festival competition and reasserted its position as a leader in college jazz. Unfortunately, as John Noel soon came to realize, it was possible to be both an innovator in college jazz and a frustrated young man trying hard to convince Notre Dame administrative officials of the merits of his ideas at the same time.

Once again, the Vice President for Student Affairs, Father McCarragher, became the greatest obstacle between Noel and his not-a-little radical Schlitz festival-funding plan. Weighing heavily in McCarragher's favor was the fact that alcoholic beverages had never been served at Notre Dame cultural or sports events. In addition, an alcoholic-beverage ad had never been printed in a program for a campus event. For these reasons and others, the subject John Noel now broached with administrative brass could hardly have been a thornier one. Despite the obvious impasse, however, McCarragher had been fairly impressed with Noel's work on the previous year's festival and eventually—after many, many long counseling sessions—he consented, with deep reservations, to the Schlitz funding plan as well as to a tasteful, tactful presentation of the Schlitz Foundation's sponsorship of the 1968 CJF.[9]

As for other festival matters, Noel was encountering unqualified success. By February 1968, he had amassed a prize list of instruments, scholarships, club dates, and cash awards totaling $7,000—more than in any other CJF year. Groups scheduled to attend in 1968 would include 1967's finest CJF group, the University of Illinois Big Band, Ladd McIntosh's IMF-winning, four-french-horn-equipped Ohio State Big Band, Charlie Mariano's Tufts University Concert Jazz Band, and top bands and combos from Oregon, Texas, Tennessee, Pennsylvania, Massachusetts, Michigan, and Florida. One participating group—the University of Illinois Dominic James Combo—would even be making use of a tape recorder for "humorous effect" during its CJF performance.[10]

Judging the 1968 CJF talent would be a panel made up of arranger-composer Oliver Nelson, renowned bassist Ray Brown, Berklee music administrative director Robert Share, scarlet-lined, houndstooth-cape-outfitted arranger/composer Gerald Wilson, and critic Dan Morgenstern, who had assumed the mantle of *down beat* editorialship from Don DeMicheal in June, 1967. (Although listed in the program, trumpeter Freddie Hubbard would be unable to attend at the last minute; early in the year, tenor-saxophonist Wayne Shorter had also withdrawn.) Back for the first time since 1960, Willis Conover—the best-known jazz broadcasting personality in the world—would be the festival's master of ceremonies.

Friday evening's CJF music session turned surprisingly electric with the appearance of the Paul Zipkin Trio from Reed College in Portland, Oregon. Made up of tenor-saxophonist Paul Zipkin, pianist Larry Karush, and electric-keyboard bassist Laura Fisher, the unusual trio led off the night and presented experimental, challenging renditions of pop standards such as Jimmy Webb's "Sunny" (complete with a "nightmarish" electric-bass quality).[11] Leaving the audience more than a little baffled, the Zipkin bunch gave way to the surreal antics of the University of Illinois/Dominic James Quartet led by tenor/soprano saxophonist James Cuomo.

After a sprightly piece entitled "Hey, What Day is This?" the Cuomo quartet delved into a somewhat bizarre digital-computer-aided work simply titled "Those Old Stock Pavilion Blues, or Will The Big

Bands Ever Feed Back?, for five prepared jazzmen and 2 channeled tape, in 3 movements, played without interruption: Allegro, Collage and Tango."[12] While the two-channel reel-to-reel tape machine moaned, beeped, bleeped, booped, and shrieked out of sound speakers humorously nicknamed "Dominic" and "James," curved soprano-sax-toting Cuomo and rotary-valve flugelhornist Jim Knapp soloed vibrantly, to the surprise and delight of both crowds and judges.[13]

Still on a roll from the previous year's victory at Miami, the Ladd McIntosh-led Ohio State University Jazz Orchestra was up next. Thrown a bit offstride by performance delays brought about by band compositions accidentally locked in a bus, the twenty-six-piece group finally got it all together and soared through an all-McIntosh songbook including a number by the name of "Grooveness."[14] (Filling in the time gaps with favorable comments about Ohio State, emcee Willis Conover was eventually hissed by the audience for what was interpreted as his "partiality.")[15]

Appearing in the last collegiate-group slot of the blockbuster Friday-evening session was none other than John Garvey's twenty-eight-piece University of Illinois Jazz Band. Featuring tenor saxophonist Ron Dewar, trumpeters Cecil Bridgewater and Jim Knapp, multireedman James Cuomo, and vocalist Don Smith (a brother of professional jazz keyboardist Lonnie Liston Smith), the Illinois aggregate ripped through "Where's Charley?," a somewhat atonal "Yesterdays," "Three Shades of Blue," and a surging jazz-rock-blues vocal number entitled "Gotta Get My Mojo Working" which took the audience by storm.[16] Present and accounted for at the CJF for the ninth consecutive year, Father Wiskirchen's high-school Melodons closed down the Friday session once more.

Saturday afternoon featured well-known jazz musician Charlie Mariano's Tufts University Concert Jazz Band (containing a young pianist named Don Grolnick), as well as the swinging Memphis State Statesmen led by bright-red-coat-attired Thomas Ferguson, and the Michigan State University Jazz Ensemble, sparked by alto-saxophonist Andy Goodrich and led by George West. As for the festival's combos, the Mark Gridley Quartet (led by flautist Mark Gridley) scored well as did a last-minute group-addition from Indiana University not even listed in the program, the Randy Sandke Sound Band, featuring '67 CJF trumpet soloist-winner Randy Sandke and tenor-saxophonist Michael Brecker. In fact, the Sandke band delved so brilliantly into a jazz bag both avant-garde and entirely all-together in the semifinals, they were thought by most to be a shoe-in as Best Combo.

As expected, Saturday-evening finalists included the Sandke Sound Band, the Mark Gridley Quartet, the Dominic James Quartet, and big bands from the University of Illinois, Ohio State, and Michigan State (the latter of which just edged out Tom Ferguson's youthful, talented Memphis State group). In the finals, the five-man Dominic James combo presented a fine, bebop-oriented "Donna Lee," but seemed to wander a bit on subsequent originals and individual solo turns. Mark Gridley and his Michigan State combo crew took the spotlight next and offered intriguing music on Gridley's own "Kaleidoscope" and "Convolutions" but, puzzlingly, also seemed to fall short of the expectations that had been raised by the group's semifinals performance.

Enter Randy Sandke, Mike Brecker & Co., who, it seemed, merely had to run through a few basic scales and tunes to snare the combo prize. Jumping into a fairly straight but out-of-tempo rendition of Duke Ellington's stylish "Warm Valley," the group abruptly allowed the song to metamorphose into a percussive statement (complete with tambourine and cowbell) extended to the limits of audience endurance. Taking the performance to its extreme, the group then suddenly spun the song into a musical "freak out" on electronic and percussive instruments that, at times, seemed to be attempting to burst through the geodesic Stepan Center dome overhead. Capable of remarkable upper-register horn control, tenor-saxophonist Michael Brecker took center stage at this point and screamed away on his instrument along with #2 tenor-man Bruce Nifong over a howling electronic din sustained on combo organ, guitar, drums, and bass.[17]

As abruptly as the piece had burst into a rock-tinged affair, it suddenly ended, and the group left the stage—with eight minutes of performing time remaining in the set! Flabbergasted by the unexpected display (and perhaps a little perturbed by the group's unusual onstage bravado), the judges sat in their seats, stunned and unsure of what to do. Fortunately, there remained three big-band bouts to restore jazz sensibilities.

Opening the final portion of the finals program, dynamic Ladd McIntosh and Ohio State (set once again lengthily delayed—this time by preperformance amplifier feedback)[18] launched with remarkable precision and musicianship into McIntosh's upbeat "Variations on a Rock Tune," and "Goin' Out of My Head," as well as the more complex "Of Heroes, Gods and Demons"—all dramatically rendered by an on-its-feet aggregate (band member chairs having been removed from the stage to achieve this effect before the set).[19]

Unpredictable John Garvey and his Illinois gang took the stage next and gave fair warning to all present with a set-opening number entitled "Good, Big, Firm But Patient Aardvark," which featured trumpet/flugelhorn crowd favorite Cecil Bridgewater and alto-saxophonist Howard Smith. With group brilliance clearly evident in every way, the

Illinois band continued to dazzle the audience with Jim Knapp's "Medley," a bluesish bash with vocalist Don Smith termed "Muddy Water," and, in what was clearly the high point of the band's finals set, talented professional bassist George Duvivier's "The Lunceford Touch," complete with 1930s 2/4-time drumbeats and brass hat wafting.[20] Bringing up the rear, Michigan State's band performed valiantly but simply couldn't muster up enough of the right musical stuff.

Retiring to the Stepan Center back room as the CJF high-school contest winner Variations of Lincoln High School (Vincennes, Indiana) took the stage for the second consecutive year, the judges realized their work was cut out for them. What was to be done about the Sandke group that had caused such a display? Did they merit the Combo award? Was their music jazz at all? Hashing it out back and forth heatedly for over an hour, judges Share, Morgenstern, Nelson, Wilson, and Brown returned to the anxiously waiting student musician and avid jazz-listener crowd with a shocking CJF decision: there would be no Combo award in 1968 at all!

Somewhat stunned by the judgment (the Sandke group had, after all, been thought by attending critics and musicians alike to be far and away the best group), the student musicians waited for an explanation, but found none forthcoming. While the smoke cleared and the controversial combo decision fallout dust began to settle, the University of Illinois band took top honors as Best Band and Best Overall Jazz Group, thereby snaring the coveted trip to the Newport Jazz Festival. As for individual award winners, Ohio State's Ladd McIntosh took honors as arranger/composer, while three members of the controversial Sandke Sound Band managed awards: Michael Brecker (Outstanding Instrumentalist), Randy Sandke (Trumpet), and James Nelson (Drums). Elsewhere, Dave Pavolka notched another Best Trombone award, Andy Goodrich of Michigan State University took Best Alto-Sax honors, and Illinois' Ron Dewar pinned down the Tenor-Sax award spot, while Mark Gridley (Flute) and Tufts band member Don Grolnick (Piano) also took awards.

Within the next week, several noted jazz columnists offered explanations for the strange Sandke combo decision, which had, quite naturally, become the hot postfestival topic (and, perhaps, in no small way, a symbolic head-on clash of 1968 rock and jazz mentalities). Summarizing the situation more succinctly than most, *Chicago Daily News* music critic Buck Walmsley remarked, "The best group at the 10th annual collegiate jazz festival held Friday and Saturday at Notre Dame University in South Bend, Indiana didn't win. But it didn't lose either."[21]

Noting that the Randy Sandke septet "sounded much much bet-

ter than any of the seven other combos entered in the competition,"
and "more exciting and inventive than any of the nine big bands competing too," Walmsley went on to note that the group's decision to
"break out of the jazz idiom" in the finals was the straw that broke
the camel's back and brought on the judging difficulties.[22] "As rock,"
continued the critic of the septet's finals version of Duke Ellington's
"Warm Valley," "it sounded great. As jazz, it didn't meet the judges'
standards; so they decided that the group had not performed in the
finals to the extent of its abilities. Nor had the other two combo finalists.
To give the award to Sandke's men would be to set a precedent in
rewarding rock music in a jazz festival, the judges said. To give the
prize to one of the other two finalists would be, in effect, rewarding
mediocrity, they said. So there was no award."[23]

Another noted music scribe, John S. Wilson of the New York Times
(in attendance at the CJF to check out groups for State Department
tours for yet another year) remarked that "the judges' decision, which
was unanimous, was announced without explanation. It was learned
that the judges felt that none of the groups had performed as well in
the finals as it had in the preliminaries. One judge said privately that
to give an award under these circumstances 'would encourage a kind
of levity not in the best interest of the festival.' "[24]

Eventually, a third critical voice—this one belonging to '68 judge
Dan Morgenstern—was heard on the subject. Writing in the May 2,
1968, issue of down beat, Morgenstern agreed that in the semi-finals
the Sandke group "had given a remarkable performance, by all odds
the most original, creative and stimulating combo jazz heard at the
festival, avant-garde but together" and even conceded that though the
finals set was indeed "startling," it was also "not without merit."[25] Confronted with the diverse performances of the three finalist combo groups,
however, Morgenstern admitted candidly that the "judging became
a dilemma."

> Some of the judges [he continued] . . . wanted to give first place to the
> Sandke group on the basis of the afternoon (preliminary) performance,
> but since the award was to be given specifically on the basis of the finals,
> this was overruled by others who felt that a poor precedent would be
> set by rewarding an essentially non-jazz performance at a jazz festival.
>   On the other hand, there was no real basis for giving the award
> to either of the other groups, as judged in the finals. And so—no combo
> prize. (In later discussion—very friendly by the way—some judges were
> made to realize it was inexperience, not bravado, that was behind the
> Sandke experiment, along with imperfect understanding of the fact that
> they were to be judged as a group on the final performance only.)[26]

Though the judges' position was clarified, the end result nonetheless pointed up in a startling way the problems confronting the jazz world, or as Morgenstern went on to note in general, "the increasing difficulty of categorizing music."

For the tenth-anniversary CJF, new policies, precedents, and directions had been set, not the least of which had been the inclusion in 1968 of electric instruments, techniques, and sounds. "In addition to the now customary electric guitar and electric string bass," wrote John S. Wilson on this CJF subject, "an electric piano, amplified cellos and an electric keyboard bass were heard."[27] All, of course, in part attributable (at least in theory) to a small electronic-music addendum to a CJF press release many months before.

Heading out beyond 1968 toward 1969, the CJF high-school contest, prefestival concert, and symposium concepts were all intact. New connections with media personnel in the outside world had been established, and a number of hair-raisingly creative ideas had been attempted—many of them successful. Most importantly, a path toward the seventies had been struck with a diverse, if not occasionally startling overall festival sound and look. If there was musical controversy at CJF '68, it was perhaps fortunate, for, in all-knowing, all-seeing University of Notre Dame administrative eyes, it did a great deal to keep one bothersome item out of postfestival headlines: the fact that a beer company had helped to sponsor a Notre Dame student event.

> The most impressive thing about the CJF for the listener will be an overwhelming sense of communication. In 1963, when I was fifteen and attending my first CJF, I was still a relative newcomer to jazz and I didn't understand a great deal of what was going on. But as I sat and listened and watched, there was one thing I was sure of. These people were reaching me, as they've been reaching me and many others every year since then. — 1969 CJF Chairman Greg Mullen

1
9
6
9
In keeping with the tradition set in 1967, the 39-page '68 CJF-printed program attempted, in a small way, to be a barometer of changing jazz and music times. Included were articles on collegiate jazz by Dan Morgenstern and the jazz/pop/rock loggerhead by Don Heckman (reprinted from *down beat*'s 1968 *Music Yearbook*), two pieces on the history of the CJF by '68 chairman John Noel, updates on the high-school festival and guest-band Melodons, and

recaps of both the '68 CJF symposium and the prefestival concert in Stepan Center with William Russo's Chicago Fire. This, of course, was all in addition to the usual festival bios and photos, prize lists, and full-page ads from Blue Note Records, Martin Instruments, the Joseph Schlitz Brewing Co., ASCAP, Columbia Records, BMI, Fender Musical Instruments, Coca Cola, Goya Music, Selmer, and local South Bend car dealer, Gates Chevrolet (which—under John Noel's resistance-withering CJF duress—consented to donate a car for transporting judges to and from the festival and Morris Inn in 1968).[1] As usual, plaques, scholarships, compositions, and instruments had been donated courtesy of Selmer, Getzen, Artley, Reynolds, Willard Alexander, King, Gibson, Kay, Ludwig, Zildjian, and Conn.

By 1968, as Noel's historical CJF program compilations revealed, the decade-old CJF had played host to nearly two hundred groups from twenty-five states (California to Massachusetts, Texas to Oregon) and the District of Columbia, each year striving—and succeeding—to uphold the national character of the event. Analyzing the event's direction and history in the '68 CJF program, Noel pointed up two important factors in the CJF's longevity and success. "First," he wrote, "the CJF is committed to the belief that the future of jazz, the one truly American artform, will be influenced by educated American Artists. The collegiate jazz scene of today will have a great import on the whole future development of jazz. The CJF strives to foster this development by presenting the future jazzmen of America and their music to a large audience and by giving them the critical evaluation of the most respected jazz authorities . . . the second factor . . . is the vital support it [the CJF] has received from many sources."[2]

Unfortunately, despite the overall success of CJF '68, there were several important things to be considered, the most pressing of which involved the event's ongoing competitive stance. Over the past two years, the CJF had tried to emphasize the educational aspects of the event instead of the competitive side of its organization and character. This competitive side was, however, difficult to deny as an active ingredient in the success of any collegiate or high-school band festival—including the CJF. In a piece written for the '68 CJF program, *down beat* editor Dan Morgenstern (who had been attending college jazz events since 1964) attempted a thoughtful assessment of this ticklish point.

> A collegiate jazz festival is of course a highly competitive exercise. In a way, the competitive framework appears out of context in what, after all, is a creative artistic endeavor. But the competitive system is built in and without it, it would very probably be difficult—perhaps impossible—to hold these music festivals.

I mention this because, invariably, at each event I have attended, some (if not most) of the non-winners are bitterly disappointed. This is disheartening to the judges, who just as invariably have done their level best to listen carefully and judge fairly.

Music competitions—unlike athletic events—have no fixed and firm rules and regulations for selecting winners. No matter how scrupulously fair, judgements in the realm of esthetics are, to some extent, arbitrary and personal. Technical factors and comparative skills being equal, a choice between two excellent tenor saxophonists, for example, will be decided by the collective tastes of the judges. So, if you don't win, don't get bitter. The decisions are not absolute or made for all time.

Besides, winning is not (or should not be) the most important thing. Learning—from others, from new experiences in performing, from suggestions and criticisms—is far more valuable than walking away with a prize.[3]

For all Dan Morgenstern's insights, however, the fact remained that competition—important though it might be—would have to be closely examined in relation to future CJF's. In addition, a strident, penetrating voice in the Notre Dame *Scholastic* pointed out another fact that seemed to be disturbingly true. Writing a week after the '68 festival, Notre Dame student Marty McNamara (previously unknown as a music critic in *Scholastic* pages) remarked that the present semifinals/finals structure of the CJF created, in effect, a standardized listening product.

Much of the problem lies in the fact that, whereas, the individual awards are given for performance in the semifinals, the group trophies hinge only on Saturday night's twenty-minute spot. So it is not by accident that the semifinals see more outstanding solos and the finals more team or section melodies. This means the large crowd on Saturday night sees considerably less improvisatory work and more standardized numbers.

And since any demonstration of versatility must come in this very short period, we have the situation where a band will do as many as five numbers. . . . Exploration is what jazz is all about and to sacrifice this for the sake of diversity is to be a jack-of-all-trades and better carpenter than musician.[4]

Prodded by such charges, as well as by the controversies and disappointments created by past band award decisions, the slowly moving wheel of CJF change began to rumble to life.

After the 1968 CJF, it was also becoming apparent just how important the decision to stay clear of Bob Yde's Intercollegiate Music Festival had been. Comparing notes on the 1968 versions of the two oldest and most respected collegiate-jazz festivals in the nation held at Villanova University (February 23–24) and Notre Dame (March 13–14), Dan Morgenstern (who had the good fortune to be invited that year to judge both events) had a number of things to report.

> Since last year, Villanova has been one of several regional festivals associated with the IJF. On the basis of this year's showing, this has had both positive and negative results. On the plus side is the fact that the winning big band, combo and vocal group . . . will be competing in St. Louis; and that the entire finals (all three hours of 'em) were televised by 13 educational stations in the east.
>
> On the debit side were the restrictions resulting from the regional structuring of the IJF festivals. In former years, Villanova has played host to some of the best groups from all over the country. Now it can only draw from the East and there can be no question that this has resulted in less interesting lineups.
>
> Notre Dame, on the other hand, has retained its independence, and in terms of musical variety and level of performance, this paid off. Also, the IJF festivals give only first place awards to groups and no prizes to individual talent, while Notre Dame had quite an abundance of such awards.[5]

Morgenstern went on to mention that the Villanova proceedings ". . . were almost antiseptically professional," while at the Notre Dame event, "the pace was more relaxed. Stage waits sometimes seemed very long . . . but this was partly due to the privilege granted each big band of setting up the way it preferred. . . . The stage waits were serenely passed in the company of emcee Willis Conover, a past master at handling such chores."[6] (One band that turned up at both festivals, the Herb Pomeroy-led MIT Concert Jazz Band, even managed to get a humorous nod from the *down beat* editor for being ". . . visually distinguished by the greatest variety of hair styles and sartorial fashions displayed by any band at either festival—as befits scientists, mad or otherwise.")[7] In closing, Morgenstern (already a CJF festival adviser and friend in the *down beat* tradition established by Charles Suber and Don DeMicheal) patted the CJF warmly on the back, noting that "it was indicative of the overall excellence of Notre Dame's tenth that even the failures were interesting."[8] Obviously, collegiate jazz was still not without its flaws. And, on a more serious note in '68, neither was American society.

On April 4, 1968, civil-rights activist Dr. Martin Luther King, Jr., was gunned down in Atlanta, only to be followed in similar brutal manner a scant two months later by popular presidential aspirant, Robert

F. Kennedy. Coming on the heels of a four-year period during which the country had been increasingly torn apart by a senseless war in Vietnam, the assassination of a president, and the uprising of a new musical idiom and a new youth life-style (the latter just beginning to flex antiestablishment muscle on the nation's campuses), these shootings catalyzed a unified national outrage.

For blacks, the brutal loss of King sparked some to a more militant civil-rights stance and a fierce, renewed search for a black pride amid the social mess. For youth in general, the loss of Kennedy—a young, outspoken politician with a flare for dash and drama who had held to a staunch antiwar stance—snatched away the one hopeful figure on the political scene. For many, the only answer to such violence and swelling world idiocy involved a push against the "established" walls with the tools at hand: namely, people, purpose, music, politics, and dress. In the United States this head-on clash with authority manifested itself visibly nowhere more than on the college campus. For once, it seemed reality might actually creep into the framework of advanced education. Perhaps it would even go so far as to rip the entire framework of academia apart. For the violence of the late sixties had just begun to flourish and would soon reach an early peak at the Chicago Democratic National Convention (ruled by Mayor Richard J. Daley's iron hand) in the fall.

In the meantime, of course, jazz continued to move on. A somewhat forgotten commodity amid the combined political, artistic, and rock-music din, it fell into public disfavor once more but somehow managed to hold on—perhaps due in large part to the existence of collegiate jazz. With increasing frequency, jazz musicians encountering difficulty in obtaining club dates were turning up at collegiate and high-school jazz clinics or festivals, of which there were now quite a few. Some jazzmen such as Jerry Coker, Dave Baker, Herb Pomeroy, Charlie Mariano, Frank Tesinsky, and John Handy had even begun to teach on a full- or part-time basis, in turn, again, making use of the college circuit, which seemed to buffet professional jazz during these hard times while schooling aspiring younger musicians[9]—all of which, of course, took place in the face of still-strong opposition to jazz curriculums and jazz-band performances at universities across the nation. Still, despite this resistance, some important late-sixties strides toward increased academic acceptance had gradually been made.

One of the first big hurdles to be cleared by collegiate jazz occurred in 1968 at the March 14–19 biennial Music Educator's National Conference (MENC) convention in Seattle, Washington. There, for the first time, the 54,000-strong group (5,000 of whom were in attendance) held a Jazz Night at the Seattle Opera House in order to celebrate the conference's landmark organization and official recognition of the National Association of Jazz Educators (NAJE).[10] Included on the evening's performance bill were bands from Fort Vancouver (Washington) High School and Olympic College (Bremerton, Washington), as well as the Collegiate Neophonic Orchestra of Cerritos College, California (conducted by Stan Kenton) and—as might be expected—the North Texas State University Lab Band under Leon Breeden. As usual, North Texas State closed down the eye-opening evening and left the audience "clamoring for more."[11]

Meeting for the first time on March 15, the National Association of Jazz Educators quickly elected their first board officers: M. E. Hall (president), John Roberts (president-elect), Matt Betton (vice president), Jack Wheaton (secretary), and Clem DeRosa (treasurer). In addition, the organization drafted a constitution that included several broad, noble goals:

1. To foster and promote the understanding and appreciation of jazz and popular music and its artistic performance.
2. To lend assistance and guidance in the organization and development of jazz curricula in schools and colleges to include stage band ensembles of all types.
3. To apply jazz principles to music materials and methods at all levels.
4. To foster and encourage the development and adoption of curricula which will explore contemporary composition, arranging and improvisation.
5. To disseminate educational and professional news of interest to music educators (in a newsletter).
6. To assist in the organization of clinics, festivals and symposiums at local, state, regional and national levels.
7. To cooperate with all organizations dedicated to the development of musical culture in America.[12]

The birth of the NAJE and this list of purposes were long-overdue jazz-education milestones. Coupled with an equally important MENC symposium on Youth Music in the summer of 1968 at Tanglewood (which discussed how school music departments could become more up to date and in tune with student needs and just how to go about getting students involved in school music),[13] these developments augured well for the health and advancement of collegiate jazz and music education at large.

One discerning and experienced member of the jazz community, however, Fr. George Wiskirchen, placed the burden of NAJE's future success more on the individual teacher than on the organization itself. "The founders have high hopes," wrote Wiskirchen in his *down beat* Jazz on Campus column, "but unfortunately, by themselves, this handful of leaders is incapable of making NAJE a success. Many professional organizations are still-born. It is to be hoped that this one will live and thrive, but that is up to the teacher in the field . . . If the NAJE is to grow strong . . . the educator in the field, the one nobody but the local PTA has heard of, has to become actively involved."[14]

A new collegiate-jazz festival was also unveiled in April 1968 at previously inconspicuous but picturesque Quinnipiac College, located at the foot of the Sleeping Giant Mountains in Hamden, Connecticut. The result of energetic ideas and actions on the part of two Quinnipiac music-department instructor/brothers, Sam and Don (Sonny) Constanzo, the first Quinnipiac Intercollegiate Jazz Festival went off without a hitch. "An advantage of localized festivals of this kind," wrote Stanley Dance in a *down beat* review of the inaugural event, "is the fact that the not-so-talented are less reluctant to expose themselves. . . . As judge Bob Share remarked afterwards, they hear what other superior groups are doing and are not only inspired by them, but are prompted to return to their own college with requests (or demands) for increased support."[15]

Progress was also being made with the second Intercollegiate Jazz Festival held June 20–22, 1968, in St. Louis's Kiel Opera House. There, the winners of six participating regional festivals (Mobile, Villanova, Cerritos College, California; Utah, Little Rock, Arkansas; and the Midwest Festival—which would evolve into the Elmhurst Jazz Festival in Chicago, Illinois) battled it out, and although John Garvey's University of Illinois Big Band "gave a surprisingly lackadaisical, unimaginative performance" in the semi-finals, it roared back in the final set as a "completely different band,"[16] and took top honors over other big bands from Millikin University and the Philadelphia Music Academy.

By June 1968, *down beat* magazine had other encouraging news to report to the jazz world at large: the Music Panel of the National Foundation of the Arts had added a jazz committee. Much like the establishment of the NAJE, this move did much to "legitimize" further the long-maligned improvisatory art. Composed of three respected professional musicians, a former college-president, a vice president of a professional music organization, a prominent jazz journalist-critic, and an active adviser to the jazz community (all of whom voted in an early meeting to remain anonymous so as to "remain free from outside influences"),[17] the committee would submit recommendations for grants to the music panel, subject to approval by the National Council on the Arts. "For the first time," noted the anonymous but internationally known jazz figure and music-panel member chairing the jazz committee in a June 1968 issue of *down beat* magazine, "there is a very real possibility that the United States government will give active support to this American music not overseas, but in its own country."[18] (The reference here was, of course, to yearly early- and mid-sixties government sponsorship of jazz tours undertaken by collegiate and professional jazz groups in various parts of the world.)

For the University of Illinois (the first band to win the CJF and the IMF in the same year), however, the party was far from over, and the band was soon off to Rhode Island and the Newport Jazz Festival in early July. Crushed into a bus for the two-day ride to the East Coast (a manner of travel that leader John Garvey would note in a short piece for the '69 CJF program was helpful in familiarizing the band's younger members with "the national consistencies of the Howard Johnson menu"),[19] the Illinois band members were rewarded for their cross-country pains with a two-day stint at Newport in the select company of Duke Ellington, Woody Herman, Count Basie, Dizzy Gillespie, and many more.

Originally scheduled for the opening "throw away" spot of the Saturday-evening performance, Garvey and his Illinois crew were moved to the final afternoon slot after an assistant festival producer heard them in rehearsal. Performing at the designated time, the band dazzled the scattered numbers in attendance and earned rave reviews. "The University of Illinois Jazz Band," trumpeted the *New York Times*, " . . . gave a performance that made the future of big-band jazz seem much more hopeful than did the four professional bands—Count Basie's, Duke Ellington's, Woody Herman's and Dizzy Gillespie's—that were heard on Friday night."[20]

"The Illinois Band," continued the review, ". . . not only matched the professionals in its ensemble and solo work, but its arrangements, written by students, were far more varied than the generally cut and dried orchestrations of the professional bands."[21] "The band could have more than held its own against professional competition on any of the evening shows," added Dan Morgenstern in a *down beat*/Newport wrap-up, "and it's a pity that more people didn't get to hear it. . . . Those who remained to listen stood and cheered on more than one occasion."[22] (Apparently, just being in the general vicinity of jazz giants wasn't enough, for a number of Illinois Band members proceeded to

jam with jazz-greats Rahsaan Roland Kirk and Sonny Criss at a large
Saturday-night party thrown by RCA Victor for the festival officials
at the Viking Hotel.)[23]

In the fall of 1968, Garvey and Co. next took their irrepressible
Illinois jazz sounds to Europe and Scandinavia on the CJF-won U.S.
Department of State tour. Over an eight-week period, the big band
(supplemented by potent jazz combos and a Dixieland group made
up of several big-band members) performed in Ireland, Yugoslavia,
Romania, Austria, Finland, Sweden, Norway, and Czechoslovakia,
consistently featuring charts written by past and present band members
at each concert locale. Assisted in its travels by various U.S. embassies,
the University of Illinois band also received support from foreign cultural and student organizations, as well as European banks, local jazz
buffs, and jazz-festival sponsors. Invariably, the band members recip-
rocated such hospitality by taking part in jam sessions with local musicians that often lasted late into the night. Lastly, University of Illinois
concerts were televised in Bucharest, Ljubljana, Belgrade, Vienna,
Helsinki, Oslo, and Prague, and the band was able to cut its first com-
merical album in Romania for Electrecord Records.[24]

In a final burst of late-sixties jazz/academic-landmark progress,
Gunther Schuller's breakthrough book *Early Jazz* emerged in 1968.
Although historical and biographical jazz collections or critical works
by Charles Delaunay, Hugues Panassié, Leonard Feather, Rex Smith,
Martin Williams, Nat Hentoff, Ralph Ellison, Whitney Balliett, Ralph
Gleason, Rudi Blesh, and others had previously appeared, it took a
renowned French-horn player, scholar, classicist, and jazz man such
as Schuller to approach the earliest periods of jazz history and subject
them to what a *Time* magazine book review termed the "same kind
of penetrating musical analysis usually accorded classics like Beethoven's
quartets or the Wagner Ring Cycle."[25] With the advent of *Early Jazz*
the improvisatory art could no longer be breezily tossed aside as crude
or backward music unfit for serious "study." All that remained now,
it seemed, was to push the Schuller work under the most stubborn
of academic college noses and wait for the results.

On a somewhat less encouraging, much sadder note, the late
months of 1968 witnessed the passing of sixty-nine-year-old Maher
Publication's president, John J. Maher, the man who had, in a real
way, singlehandedly saved the CJF from extinction in '66–67. (A few
months before his untimely passing, however, Maher—who had once
had a partnership in a famous 1930s Chicago nightclub known as the
Three Deuces—brought an old CJF friend, Charles Suber, back as pub-

lisher of *down beat* magazine.)

Taking over the reins of the eleventh CJF was former Melodon/ Notre Dame student/'67 CJF High School Festival head, Greg Mullen. The third CJF chairman to have studied and performed music to some formal degree ('65 chairman Daniel Ekkebus—a former Melodon—was the first; Notre Dame High School concert band member/'67 chairman Paul Schlaver, the second), Mullen was fortunate enough to already have six CJF's under his belt. Definitely an experienced hand, he soon set about putting together the '69 jazz event, and eventually succeeded in lining up such judges as trumpeter Clark Terry, composer/arranger/ saxophonist Ernie Wilkins, *down beat* editor Dan Morgenstern, trumpeter Thad Jones, alto-saxophone-great Sonny Stitt, and brilliant young composer Gary McFarland (Morgenstern, Terry, and McFarland all returning to judge the CJF for the second time). As always, there were cash awards and CJF plaques from the usual donors, though in truth (due both to CJF desires to reduce competition and the increasing difficulty of procuring more valuable goods from manufacturers), there was a noticeable drop in the number of instrument awards in 1969. Taking up this CJF prize slack, however, the Joseph Schlitz Brewing Company stepped forward once again to sponsor a trip to the Newport Jazz Festival for the Best Overall Group, a prize for which eighteen bands and combos from Illinois, Iowa, Pennsylvania, Michigan, Missouri, Ohio, and Massachusetts were scheduled to vie.[26] (In mid-to-late '68, Mullen had also made efforts to secure regional sponsors, whose support would allow additional bands outside the Midwest to attend the CJF and even explored the possibility of bringing a European jazz group to the '69 festival in conjunction with the newly formed European Jazz Federation.)[27]

Taking his lead from the past two chairmen, Greg Mullen opened CJF '69 with not one, but two prefestival concert/lectures. The first of these concerts, a jazz lecture-demonstration (sponsored in conjunction with the Notre Dame Music Department) was held on the evening of March 8 in the Notre Dame Memorial Library auditorium and featured Wilberforce, Ohio Central State College instructor/former Prestige and United Artists recording musician, Ken McIntyre. Utilizing various woodwinds to demonstrate improvisational techniques, as well as jazz elements developed and achieved over the course of the music's evolution from slavery to the present day, multi-instrumentalist McIntyre (who recorded in the early sixties with renowned jazzman Eric Dolphy) captivated the Notre Dame/St. Mary's audience.

The following evening, March 9, senior honors engineering student Bill Hurd (the musician who had urged a Notre Dame combo into the '66 CJF finals) and his quintet (including trombonist Larry Dwyer, a CJF soloist award winner in '65 and '66) continued the jazz-week proceedings with a live performance in Washington Hall.

Thursday evening, March 13, found the third annual CJF symposium under way in the Kellogg Center for Continuing Education. Still working under its original "Current State of Jazz" title, the symposium panel made up of Clark Terry, Gary McFarland, Ernie Wilkens, Fr. George Wiskirchen, Fr. Carl Hager (chairman of the Notre Dame Music Department) and *down beat* editor/panel moderator Dan Morgenstern tackled the question, "Where is the Jazz Audience?" Focusing on the relationship of jazz to rock and jazz's current lack of popularity, the panel discussed such topics as the new jazz-rock sounds of "Blood, Sweat & Tears," the black audience (or lack of it) for the music, and various jazz programs that had been taking place at the Kinetic Playground in Chicago and Fillmore East in New York City. (Prior to the symposium, Ernie Wilkins took time to drop in on an Afro American Culture seminar on Notre Dame's campus in order to speak to students on similar topics of interest, as well as on the past and present role of the black musician in jazz.)[28]

As the next day's Friday-afternoon music session began to roll into high gear, it became apparent that one of the expected judges, trumpeter Thad Jones, would not be able to attend. Once again, Father Wiskirchen (already on hand with his Melodons) was approached, and he quickly consented to fill in the judging gap. During the first session, the finally intact judging panel (Sonny Stitt had arrived late Thursday night after the symposium's end) witnessed, among others, a Northwestern University Avant-Garde Dixieland Ensemble (featuring vocals and kazoo), and a University of Illinois Quintet (co-led by pianist Ron Elliston, bassist Jeff Foote, and trumpeter/flugelhornist Cecil Bridgewater) that blistered through group arrangements of numbers like Ornette Coleman's "Invisible."[29]

Friday evening was once again University of Illinois concert night as the Ron Dewar Quartet unleashed its collective, polished jazz act early on, only to be followed by a CJF-record third Illinois entrant in the festival, the John Garvey-led Illinois big band. Presenting yet another riveting display of largely unequaled collegiate-jazz drive, precision, showmanship, and humor, the Illinois band stormed through arrangements by local music-educator and former Illinois/Notre Dame band-member Larry Dwyer and others to close down the night's session. (Particularly outstanding during the set was an Illinois rendition of "The Old Beelzebub Blues" which "combined banjo picking with a swaying reed section led by an E-flat clarinet and brass with plungers.")[30]

Between these Illinois group "bookends," of course, were sandwiched a number of other fine groups such as the University of Missouri Studio Band (within which could be found trumpeter Mike Metheny, whose younger brother Pat was a budding guitarist) and the Tom Ferguson-led Memphis State Statesmen (appearing this year minus the blazing red suitcoats that had made them stand out like musical sore thumbs at the '68 festival) which featured a raucous, crowd-pleasing vocal number by trumpeter Reed McCoy entitled "Put on Your High Heel Sneakers."[31]

"Just to be invited to participate is something of an honor," explained Memphis State leader Ferguson of his band's second straight CJF invitation. Aptly summing up collective '69 band-leader fears, Ferguson added, "But when you think about going up against bands like the University of Illinois, it stops you cold."[32] (Just to make sure and give his band an extra "up-against-Illinois" competitive edge, Ferguson commandeered the mezzanine of Notre Dame's LaFortune Student Center before his group's preliminary performance and held a 45-minute rehearsal that ended in a flurry of wild applause provided by dozens of surprised and enthusiastic Notre Dame students.)[33]

In regard to the '69 CJF's own brand of surprises, Fr. George Wiskirchen would not be one of the Washington Hall-held CJF high-school jazz festival judges for the first time since the event's inception in 1967.[34] As it was, of course, Father Wiskirchen's '69 CJF activity load was already heavy enough with collegiate-judging-panel demands and onstage Melodon performance direction to occupy his time. In 1969, however, there existed an even more important reason for his absence on this Saturday morning in March, something entirely experimental, rare, and unique for a collegiate jazz festival: a jazz mass.[35]

Composed by Jim McNeely, a Chicago-born pianist and former Notre Dame high-school Melodon who was presently a sophomore at the University of Illinois, the jazz mass (entitled "Masse en Masse") began at noon, Saturday, March 15, 1969, in Stepan Center and combined the talents of a Melodon Jazz Lab Band and vocal ensemble with traditional Catholic texts and audience-responsorial sections. Set up in front of the wooden CJF stage, the altar (consisting of the long wooden judges' table draped with a long, white linen cloth) was bare except for "a crucifix, Bible, wafers and wine."[36] Onstage, Father Wiskirchen (attired in full, red mass cassock and shoulder cloak) conducted the instrumental and vocal groups while a second equally colorfully garbed priest performed the actual service and administered communion to the 100 or more "souls" up early enough to attend.[37]

Expressing his hopes and fears about the mass and the role of jazz and other kinds of alternative music in the liturgy in a CJF '69 program article, Father Wiskirchen wrote:

> We need a new music, but is jazz a suitable genre for church use? . . . Since I have been unsatisfied with the efforts to produce a jazz liturgy that I have encountered and since I had some serious questions about the validity of jazz as a form of worship music, I decided to attempt to put together a jazz liturgy to test the possibilities.
>
> Throughout we felt that jazz is a musical art form that can communicate deeply and immediately with people. It is one of the most personal of the musical forms of expression. We felt, sort of intuitively, that it might have a definite place in the updating of worship or better, in the helping to make religion relevant for modern man or at least a segment of society.
>
> I honestly don't know if we have been successful.
>
> After our performance at CJF we will have to evaluate and assess. We welcome your help in our task. Maybe then we can answer our question.[38]

Roaring back to life after this more contemplative moment, the afternoon CJF music session presented fine groups from MIT, Michigan State, the University of Northern Iowa, and the Interlochen (Michigan) Arts Academy (the latter of which contained drummer Peter Erskine and trombonist Christopher Brubeck within its Studio Orchestra fold). Chosen from the preliminaries band and combo ranks for the evening's finals session were six groups: the University of Illinois Jazz Band and Elliston-Foote-Bridgewater Quintet, trombonist Dave Pavolka's Ball State Quintet, Michigan State University's Andy Goodrich Quintet, the Case Western Reserve Concert Jazz Ensemble, and the University of Nothern Iowa Jazz Band, a surprising and entertaining group of young musicians led by James Coffin from Cedar Falls, Iowa, a Midwest music mecca second only to South Bend.

Aptly termed the "Lew Alcindor of Collegiate Jazz" by Memphis, Tennessee *Commercial Appeal* writer William Thomas (who had accompanied the Memphis State Jazz Band on the '69 trek to Notre Dame), the University of Illinois made a UCLA-esque basketball roll to its third-straight CJF Best Big Band and Best Overall Group titles, thereby reaping the sizable Benny Goodman/Selmer trophy and a second consecutive Newport Jazz Festival trip. Not to be outdone, the Illinois Quintet containing Cecil Bridgewater took the Best Combo award. Of the Illinois band's overwhelming 1969 presence, the *Commercial Appeal*'s Thomas wrote:

> And then came the University of Illinois.
>
> Strong, masterful, exciting, the band exploded on the festival with a sound that has earned it the reputation of one of the best jazz machines in the country. And when a tall, cool Negro named Cecil Bridgewater ambled down front and raised a flugelhorn to his lips, it was all over.
>
> For a long moment, Bridgewater—an ebony young man with a natural hairdo and a goatee that reminds you of a billy goat's whiskers— faced the audience with a nonchalance that seemed to announce, "Now you're going to hear one of the best horns in the country." And when the last note died, the crowd knew it had heard something very special.
>
> In a single mass, the crowd came roaring to its feet, shouting, whistling, stomping, throwing paper cups and beating its hands. At that moment, nobody in the entire hall needed the judges to tell them who had won the 11th annual Notre Dame Collegiate Jazz Festival.[39]

Settling back down to award-distributing business, the CJF announced individual winners for 1969. Cecil Bridgewater was named Outstanding Instrumentalist and Outstanding Trumpet Soloist, while Illinois teammates Jim Knapp (Best Composer), tenor-saxophonist Ron Dewar (Special Plaque for Performance), Ron Elliston (Best Piano), John Monaghan (Best Big Band Bassist), and Chuck Braugham (Best Big Band Drummer) managed their own share of CJF awards. Divvying up the remaining honors were Ball State Quintet members Dave Pavolka (Best Trombone), Warren Jones (Best Flute), and Wayne Darling (Best Bass), and Michigan State band/combo performers Andy Goodrich (Best Saxophonist), Louis Smith (Best Miscellaneous Instrument—Flugel-horn), and Billy Parker (Best Combo Drummer). To honor an outstanding performance by Case Western Reserve alto-saxophonist Charles Barone, the category of Most Promising Soloist was also resurrected.

"For the first time in its eleven year history," proclaimed a post-festival article in the *Observer*, the Notre Dame daily student newspaper founded in 1966, "the promotional efforts of the CJF committee have put the Festival in the black financially."[40] "Attendance was way up over previous years," remarked Chairman Greg Mullen in the same *Observer* report. "I was happy to see a greater response from the Notre Dame student body. Many students here don't realize the national significance of this event. Also, they are often turned off by the esoteric sound of the word jazz. Once they come, they realize that the groups are tremendously exciting and that the festival is really a lot of fun. In any case, the important thing is not the financial but the musical success of the weekend."

On that encouraging closing note, CJF '69 ended, as did a decade of turmoil, debate, and development. There was a new president in office. There would soon be a man on the moon. And, in the 1970s, there would be another decade of collegiate jazz at Notre Dame to come.

The Modern Men of Dartmouth College exhibit their crackling brand of college jazz on the way to a finalist berth. Left to right, the "Men" are Bob Yassin (bass), Donald Miller (baritone-sax), Paul Roewade (drums), and trumpeter/leader Allen Houser.

(Photo courtesy The University of Notre Dame Archives)

University of Minnesota UJW Quartette members strike a pre-festival performance jazz pose with popular band leader/1960 CJF judge Stan Kenton. (left to right) Kenton, Jim Trost (piano), Dave Karr (tenor-saxophone), Joel Beale (drums).

(Photo courtesy *South Bend Tribune*)

1960 judges' panel: (left to right) Frank Holzfiend, Stan Kenton, Robert Share, Willis Conover, Charles Suber. *(Photo courtesy South Bend Tribune)*

The North Texas State Lab Band, named Best Overall Group and Best Band at the 1960 CJF. At far right (arms raised) is director Leon Breeden.

(Photo courtesy *South Bend Tribune*)

The Paul Winter Sextet—minus key trumpeter Dick Whitsell—performs during the 1961 CJF preliminaries. Personnel: (left to right) Warren Bernhardt, piano; Les Rout, baritone-saxophone; Paul Winter, alto-saxophone; Scotty Holt, bass; unknown trumpeter; Harold Jones or Morris Jennings, drums.

(Photo courtesy *down beat* magazine)

North Texas State's Leon Breeden (left) accepts an invitation to the Indiana Jazz Festival from Evansville, Indiana businessman/festival organizer Hal Lobree as victorious Lab Band members balance their 1961 CJF trophy and look on.   (Photo courtesy *South Bend Tribune*)

Bob James Trio member Ron Brooks accepts his Kay "Maestro" string bass prize from Charles Suber as Best Bassist at CJF 1962.   (Photo courtesy *Musical Merchandise Review*)

Father Wiskirchen's swinging Notre Dame High School Melodons in 1963 included trombonist James Pankow, a future founding member of the influential jazz/rock group "Chicago." (Photo courtesy Dave Larsen)

Urged on by future Earth, Wind & Fire and Earth, Wind & Fire hornmen Louis Satterfield (trombone) and Don Myrick (alto-sax), the Crane Junior College Jazzmen powered their way into the '63 CJF finals. Other personnel in the first all-black unit to perform at the festival are: (left to right) Fred Humphrey, piano; Ernest McCarthy, bass; and (second from right) Charles Handy, trumpet. (Photo courtesy Dave Larsen)

The University of Denver Stage Band, CJF 1963's Best Band.

(Photo courtesy Dave Larsen)

Creating a unique, freely-conceived jazz sound, Indiana University's Jamey Aebersold Septet slashed its way to both Finest Jazz Group and Best Combo awards in 1964. Personnel: (left to right) Tom Hensley, piano; Dave Baker, cello; Jamey Aebersold, alto-sax; Don Baldwin, bass; Dickie Washburn, trumpet; Preston Phillips, drums; Everett Hoffman, Jr., baritone-saxophone. (Photo courtesy Dave Larsen)

Selected as both Finest Jazz Group and Best Combo at CJF '63, the University of Michigan's Bob Pozar Trio also managed individual musician awards for Bob Pozar (Best Drums), Ron Brooks (Best Bass), and Mike Lang (Best Piano). (Photo courtesy Dave Larsen)

CJF '64 judges' panel confers. (left to right) Cannonball Adderley, Robert Share, Oliver Nelson, Gary McFarland.   (Photo courtesy Dave Larsen)

CJF 1964 Outstanding Instrumentalist Bunky Green was tabbed by the
State Department for a tour of North
Africa with a sextet after the sixth
festival.

(Photo courtesy Dave Larsen)

North Texas State tenor-saxophonist
Billy Harper, named Most Promising
Instrumentalist at CJF '64.

(Photo courtesy Dave Larsen)

Horn section of Chicago's Crane Junior College Jazz Interpreters, CJF 1964's crowd-favorite group. (left to right) George Patterson, alto-sax; Cleo Griffen, trumpet; Charles Kinnard, tenor-sax.   (Photo courtesy Dave Larsen)

"Strong but sometimes verbose" Indiana University/Jerry Green Sextet trumpeter Randy Brecker (shown performing at CJF '64) took home the Best Trumpet award in 1965.

(Photo courtesy Dave Larsen)

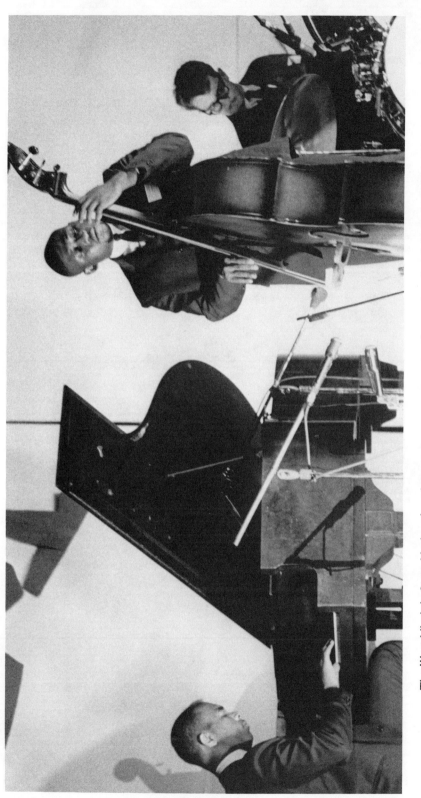

The West Virginia State Modern Jazz Interpreters concentrate on the music at hand during CJF '64. Selected for a State Department tour of North Africa that year, the group returned in 1965 decked out in colorful African tribal robes. Personnel: (left to right) Robert Thompson (Best Pianist, 1965), Reggie Minor (Best Bassist, 1965), and drummer Tom Roberts. (Photo courtesy Dave Larsen)

Walden String Quartet member John Garvey leads the 20-piece University of Illinois Jazz Band to a Best Big Band award at CJF '64. Trumpeter Cecil Bridgewater can be located in the back row, behind the tuba player. (Photo courtesy Dave Larsen)

The West Chester State College Criterions—one of CJF 1966's powerhouse finalist big bands.
(Photo courtesy *South Bend Tribune*)

The Notre Dame Jazz Sextet horn section in action at CJF '66. Personnel: (left to right) Bill Hurd, alto-saxophone; Mike Turre, tenor-sax; and Larry Dwyer, named Best Trombonist for the second consecutive year. (Photo courtesy *South Bend Tribune*)

Roosevelt University Jazz Quintette trumpeters Oscar Brashear (left) and Charles Handy (right) heat up the 1966 CJF/Fieldhouse stage. (Photo courtesy *South Bend Tribune*)

'67 CJF Chairman Paul Schlaver (left) poses for a moment with judges Donald Byrd (center) and Herbie Hancock (right) during a festival break. After the Friday evening preliminaries session, Byrd and Hancock would take part in a jam session with student musicians. (Photo courtesy *South Bend Tribune*)

Representing California's Santa Rosa Jr. College, 1/1 = One duet drummer Michael Brandenburg (left) and pianist Jack Tolson (right) presented experimental, offbeat works and managed a 1967 finals berth. In addition, Tolson emerged as a new breed of CJF Outstanding Instrumentalist. (Photo courtesy *South Bend Tribune*)

Judge Donald Byrd and Notre Dame Music Department Chairman
Father Carl Hager share a laugh during the 1967 CJF Symposium.
(Photo courtesy The University of Notre Dame Archives)

Making use of a two-channel, reel-to-reel tape machine during the preliminaries, the
University of Illinois Dominic James Quartet both surprised and delighted the CJF crowd
on the way to the 1968 finals. (Photo courtesy *South Bend Tribune*)

A tight, swinging, vibes-oriented group, the Leon Schipper Quintet dazzled the judges and the crowd with original compositions and exciting musician interplay on the way to a Best Combo Award in 1967. (Photo courtesy Bruce Harlan)

Perplexed by the theatricality of the University of Illinois band, 1967 CJF judging panel members (left to right) William Russo, Robert Share, Don DeMicheal, and Lalo Schifrin faced one of the more difficult Best Band decisions in CJF history. (Photo courtesy *South Bend Tribune*)

A last-minute addition not even listed in the 1968 CJF program, the Indiana University Randy Sandke Sound Band (spearheaded by tenor-saxophonist Michael Brecker and trumpeter Randy Sandke) seemed a shoo-in for the Best Combo award until a startling jazz/rock finals session burst of song.　　　　　(Photo courtesy *South Bend Tribune*)

'69 CJF judges' panel: (front row, left to right) Gary McFarland, Sonny Stitt, Ernie Wilkens; (back row, left to right) Father George Wiskirchen, Clark Terry, Dan Morgenstern.

(Photo courtesy *South Bend Tribune*)

John Garvey and the University of Illinois Big Band jazz juggernaut on its way to a third consecutive Big Band award. Also selected as Finest Overall Group, Illinois was soon off for the Newport Jazz Festival and, thereafter, a State Department European tour. *(Photo courtesy South Bend Tribune)*

Held Saturday morning in Stepan Center, the 1969 CJF Jazz Mass composed by Jim McNeely involved the Father George Wiskirchen-directed Notre Dame High School jazz lab band Melodons and vocal ensemble (on stage), traditional Catholic Mass texts and audience responsorial sections.

The University of Illinois Ron Elliston–Jeff Foote–Cecil Bridgewater Quintet: CJF 1969's Best Combo. Personnel: (left to right) Jeff Foote, bass; Rick Kvistad, drums; Larry Cangelosi, tenor-sax; Cecil Bridgewater, flugelhorn. (Not shown: pianist Ron Elliston.)
(Photo courtesy *The Commercial Appeal*)

Chapter 3

THE SEVENTIES

> It was a beautiful experience. Young cats were aspir-
> ing to play, and not necessarily trying to play rock. It
> inspired me to see that there still are young people in-
> terested in playing jazz. —Joe Farrell, speaking of his
> first Collegiate Jazz Festival judging experience, *down
> beat*, June 25, 1970.

1970 Although the third Intercollegiate Jazz Festival (held for the second straight year in St. Louis) offered jet another dynamic musical package in late May 1969, it was the final hurrah for the event
itself. Soon after the '69 IJF wound down, organizer Bob Yde
clashed with various festival jazz educators over the direction the
IJF should continue to take while making known his desire to emphasize folk and pop brands of music over jazz in order to cater more
definitely to current collegiate tastes. The jazz educators, of course,
found this a bit hard to swallow, and as a result, the IJF jazz event
dissolved amid the ensuing schism and chaos.

Intent on his idea, however, Yde convinced a number of regional
IJF feeder festivals (including the one at Villanova) to go along with
his pop-festival conception. Banding themselves together on the other
side of the music fence, the IJF jazz educators sought out a new jazz
locale for the spring of 1970 and eventually found one in the as-yet
unfinished John F. Kennedy Center for the Performing Arts in Washington, D.C. Enamored with the jazz-festival idea, opera-singer George
London (the projected center's artistic director and an enthusiastic jazz
fan as well) gave the event unanimous support. Unfortunately, Mr.
London could not yet offer the educators a festival stage, so the first
reconstituted event (held under Kennedy Center auspices) was eventually scheduled for the Krannert Center at the University of Illinois

in Urbana, Illinois, the undisputed hotbed of late-sixties collegiate jazz. Produced by Willis Conover, the event now proudly bore the title of "the American College Jazz Festival."

Meanwhile, at Notre Dame, the shrouded specter of CJF competition again arose from the shadows of the sixties. With the diversity of foreign music influences (much of it due to the Beatles and their incorporation of Far Eastern sounds into their revolutionary late-sixties albums), a new set of metrical alternatives (as opposed to straight 4/4 swing), thanks to Ornette Coleman and the jazz "avant-garde," and a different array of instruments now at hand, it had become increasingly obvious over the past few years that making judgments about music played at festivals or on records was a delicate, difficult matter.

Summing up much of the gnawing feeling about competition at the CJF and elsewhere, a letter printed in *down beat* in the summer of 1969 by one concerned 1969 CJF participant and observer, Michigan State University big-band drummer, Cameron Phillips, seemed to call the tune.

"The Notre Dame festival," began Phillips, ". . . showed itself this year [1969], in my opinion at least, to be in need of some rather careful consideration and fundamental revision if it is to continue as a forum for *creative* collegiate jazz players. . . . I would suggest as a solution," he advised, "simply eliminating all the awards, prizes, tours, winners, etc. Let the State Department get their publicity elsewhere and let the musicians and the audience explore their music unencumbered."[1]

Realizing that things were ripe for change, the CJF's first female chairperson, Ann Heinrichs, a St. Mary's College junior from Fort Smith, Arkansas, sent out a questionnaire in late 1969 to "judges, consultants, musicians and band directors" who had been connected with CJF in the past, in order to "determine whether the festival should eliminate the Best Overall Group, Best Big Band, and Best Combo Awards."[2] As Heinrichs soon discovered, "The response was overwhelmingly in favor of eliminating these awards and reducing the competitive nature of the festival in general."[3]

Since the majority of those schools and individuals replying to the questionnaire also felt it was "an unnecessary and nearly impossible task to choose one collegiate band as the 'best,' "[4] Heinrichs decided to do away with the Newport Jazz Festival trip as well as the self-limiting top-group (Combo and Big Band) awards. In their place, she substituted a process whereby three finalist groups in both the Big Band and Combo categories (a total of six groups) were to be singled out as "outstanding" and receive cash awards ($50 for combos, $150 for big bands). In addition, several individual awards were added, thereby ensuring the judges' ability to "alter and supplement the prize list" as they saw fit.[5]

"By reducing the competitiveness of the festival in this manner," noted an awards-change explanation in the CJF '70 program, "CJF hopes to encourage greater freedom of artistic expression and place the emphasis of the festival on musicianship. Performance in the finals of this year's CJF will be an opportunity for displaying musical virtuosity without the pressure of added competition."[6] No doubt this development was welcomed by all. As a result, the six groups singled out for the finals in 1970 would for once be playing for the music and themselves, not against the other finalist bands. After twelve years, the festival was, perhaps, becoming more of a festival after all.

By the end of the 1960s, the number of "stage bands" (more and more frequently referred to as "jazz bands" or "jazz ensembles") existing on the high-school level was approximately 10,000 – double the number that could have been found in the decade's first year. Similarly, by 1969, 135 colleges offered academic credit for jazz-related courses, whereas in 1960, barely 20 did. As far as stage-band events or college jazz festivals (more often than not taking their lead from Notre Dame) were concerned, the dozen or so existing in 1960 had increased to roughly 75 by 1969.[7]

In other related areas, college and high-school jazz-education programs had been vastly expanded; a collegiate-jazz competition had taken place on a national level; various college groups (initially chosen from the Notre Dame event) had toured distant parts of the world at the behest of the U.S. State Department; and clinics with professional jazz musicians (a rarity in the late fifties and early sixties) now abounded – many as adjunct events to the collegiate festivals themselves. Finally, numerous volumes on jazz-band organization and teaching methodology had emerged to improve the education of teachers and students. In short, though there was still a long way to go, essential and dramatic jazz progress had been made – even in such unlikely locales as South Bend, Indiana.

Along these lines an age-old complaint arose during the 1969 CJF symposium, something not unakin to: "Between one CJF and another we're starved for jazz, but what can you do in a place like South Bend?"[8] In response, most of those attending the symposium at the Kellogg Center for Continuing Education gave a nod or small smattering of vocal assent, figuring, as they did so, that, as usual, little would be done about their predicament. To the surprise of many, '69 judge Clark

Terry suddenly pierced the thickening fog of South Bend jazz despair and said, "Don't just sit there and complain. You've got to go out and do it yourself."⁹

Describing the progress made in Baltimore on a local level by the Left Bank Jazz Society, as well as the efforts of jazz organizations in other towns, Terry continued to challenge those in the audience to do something other than wring their collective South Bend hands. Finally, the exasperated-but-well-meaning trumpeter declared, "Look you get your group going and I'll come out and play your first gig. For free."¹⁰

Sparked by Clark Terry's perhaps too-generous offer, a few of those in attendance (including CJF adviser Richard Bizot) called a meeting a few weeks after the '69 CJF. Of those who had expressed a desire to attend, about a dozen or so showed up. Organizing themselves as a nonprofit group and taking on the name "The Michiana Friends of Jazz," Bizot and a number of Michigan and South Bend businessmen and women, including Bill O'Connell, Alice Rupert, Larry Powell, and others, put on their first concert within a month with the Bill Hurd Quintet.

In August of '69, an exhausted but amiable Clark Terry kept his word and flew in to South Bend from Denver late on a Saturday afternoon. Taking time to catch his breath with an hour's sleep, the talented musician proceeded to knock out an enthusiastic audience of 500 with his hot trumpet play at the South Bend campus of Indiana University (known locally as IUSB). "To be perfectly honest about it," revealed Richard Bizot in the 1970 CJF program, "Clark did not play for free. In order to avoid hassle with the union we had to pay him scale. It was a funny feeling writing a check to Clark Terry for $27.83."¹¹

Buoyed by the tidy bankroll brought in by Clark Terry's concert, the Michiana Friends of Jazz hosted two more concerts in late '69/early '70—the Elvin Jones Trio at Washington Hall and the Harold Land-Bobby Hutcherson Quintet at IUSB. Membership continued to pick up, and by the spring of 1970, the number of "friends" had expanded to 75. In addition to the concerts, members were apprised of jazz developments in the area by an informal network of communication, and many lent their full support to CJF promotional efforts and those of local high-school jazz programs as well. Though still far short of a jazz mecca, South Bend was apparently making admirable jazz progress in its own quiet way.

A week before the 1970 CJF, the annual prefestival concert/lecture was conducted by alto and soprano saxophonist/educator Jamey Aebersold in Notre Dame's Memorial Library Auditorium. A professor of music at Indiana University at New Albany and a faculty member of two summer jazz clinics, Aebersold (a former CJF award winner) had just released his innovative album entitled, "A New Approach to Jazz Improvisations," which offered listener/musicians an instructive "record course" in jazz improvisation complete with an instruction booklet. Performing on Sunday afternoon, March 15, Aebersold explained various jazz styles and idioms to the audience before joining other members of an onstage quintet to illustrate and improvise various points in the lecture. Cosponsored by Notre Dame's Black Studies Program and the '70 CJF, the event continued the music-educational tradition of the CJF and provided audience members yet another chance to hear top-notch jazz.

Also free and open to the public once more was the 1970 CJF symposium, held, as usual, on the Thursday night before the opening day of the festival. Devoted this year to the question of Jazz and Rock, the symposium featured a panel made up of North Texas State educator/composer/bandleader Leon Breeden, saxman/flautist/1959 CJF participant Joe Farrell, Chicago-based AACM (Artists for the Advancement of Creative Music) pianist Richard Abrams (making his first outing ever as a judge of a musical event), and returning '69 judges Ernie Wilkens and *down beat* editor/panel-moderator Dan Morgenstern. Rounding out the symposium panel was none other than Voice of America jazz broadcaster Willis Conover—back for the third consecutive year as CJF emcee. (In what was most certainly a Conover-related matter, tapes of the 1970 CJF were scheduled to be internationally broadcast by the Voice of America.)

After dealing with the given symposium topic and various audience questions for roughly two hours, the panel (as recorded by *Observer* reporter Steve Novak) reached a consensus, noting that "for some unfortunate reason, jazz has not enjoyed the success it should have in recent years, while predominantly white rock groups borrowing—and, as Willis Conover put it, 'sometimes stealing'—what black blues and jazz musicians have done, become popular successes."[12]

"A generation of American youth," continued the *Observer*'s Novak, "are growing up with the mistaken impression that the blues were discovered—or invented—by the Rolling Stones and John Mayall. There is a growing danger that they will live their lives under another misconception—that Blood, Sweat & Tears and Herb Alpert play jazz (after all, wasn't Alpert elected to the jazz hall of fame by the people who vote in the *Playboy* poll?)." Fortunately, concluded the writer, the 1970 CJF symposium offered a timely, if not entirely necessary way to "deal with this strange delusion."[13]

Opening strongly, the initial Friday-afternoon CJF '70 music session featured two eventual combo finalists, the Midwest Collective from Indiana University and Graffiti, a combo led by three-time CJF award-winning trombonist Dave Pavolka that was made up of students from five different universities (Ball State, the University of Illinois, Drake, Indiana University, and Eastern Illinois). Just as potent, the evening session showcased Notre Dame's own Larry Beachler Sextet (made up of alto-saxophonist Jack Leo, drummer Pete Szujewski, guitarist Norm Zeller, bassist Jack Prendergast, trombonist John Buchanan, and pianist Nick Talarico)—the first Notre Dame entry since the Bill Hurd/Larry Dwyer finalist combo in 1966. Also on the night's agenda was MIT's Richie Orr Quintet (with Notre Dame's alumnus/MIT graduate-student Bill Hurd on flute and saxophone), James Coffin's driving University of Northern Iowa aggregate, and the University of Illinois Jazz Band II, with tenor saxophonist Ron Bridgewater, pianist Jim McNeely, and vocalist Dee Dee Garrett (soon to marry trumpeter Cecil Bridgewater and become Dee Dee Bridgewater) whom Dan Morgenstern would later note in a *down beat* festival review, was the band's "undisputed star."[14]

Bringing up the rear for the eleventh straight year was the Notre Dame High School Melodon band. As usual, however, Father Wiskirchen had a few surprises in store. Combining original and adapted material (penned by John Redman and Melodon alumnus Jim McNeely) with diverse, imaginatively presented works drawn from Frank Zappa's Mothers of Invention, the jazz-rock group "Chicago," and experimentally inclined saxophonist Archie Shepp, the young Melodon band, as Dan Morgenstern pointed out in a post-CJF review, "almost stole the show and would have had a good chance to make the finals, had it been eligible."[15]

"The Melodons," continued Morgenstern, "have long stood for the best in high school jazz, but never before has the good Father had such a talented crew. For the first time in my hearing, there were good soloists in the band. These included two big-toned trombonists, a good clarinet and two excellent guitar players. . . . The band's material was, as usual, provocative and original—quite a step beyond many college bands." Noting that the group incorporated mellophones and psychedelic guitar effects into its presentation for "added color," the critic went on to pay additional tribute to the band's "hip little soul singer, Bob Green," before adding that at one point in the Melodon performance fellow-judge Richard Abrams turned to him to mention, "They must be midgets." "Indeed," continued Morgenstern, "it seemed improbable that a mere high school band should be capable of producing such thoroughly enjoyable music . . . not just school music, impressive for such-and-such technique and/or educational reasons, but *music*."

Featured at the Saturday-afternoon music session was another finalist combo, the HGJJK Quintet from Michigan State, and all the bands that were eventually finalists—Hank Levy's Towson State Jazz Ensemble, Tom Ferguson's Memphis State University Jazz Band "A," and Herb Pomeroy's MIT Festival Jazz Ensemble. "The most dramatic of the three," wrote Dan Morgenstern, "was the Towson State Jazz Ensemble from Towson State College, Baltimore, Maryland. Nearly 30 pieces strong (five assorted percussion players; two french horns; two basses; tuba and contrabass clarinet in addition to the conventional big band instrumentation), the ensemble performed compositions and arrangements by its leader, Hank Levy, with precision, verve and conviction."[16] (Two Levy compositions premiered at the festival—"Rock Odyssey" and "Antea"—would eventually turn up on trumpeter Don Ellis's "Fillmore" album within the year.) Morgenstern also went on to compliment Towson State trumpet soloist Tony Neenan and "miniskirted contrabass clarinetist Stephanie Tolan," who, he wryly remarked, was "a different kind of asset to the band—which is not to say she didn't play well."[17]

"Both for the sake of variety and in recognition of its musicianship,"[18] a fourth combo also received a noncompetitive Saturday-evening finalist slot by dint of a special honorary judges'-panel vote. Led by ex-Notre Dame-musician Larry Dwyer (currently a graduate student, pianist, trombonist, and composer in the University of Illinois #1 band), the seven-piece group known as the University of Illinois Dixie Band surprised everyone at the festival by spinning out updated versions of Louis Armstrong's classic twenties Hot Five/Hot Seven output and thereby becoming "the first traditional jazz band to appear at a college festival in years."[19]

Comprised of Fats Waller-admiring pianist Dwyer, trumpeter Ric Bendel, clarinetist Jim Cuomo, trombonist Rich Roush, tuba-man Dean Leff, banjo-plucker Terry Pettijohn, and drummer Chuck Braugham, the group (which had actually been formed in the fall of 1968 for the University of Illinois's CJF-won European trip and subsequently toured the Soviet Union with the big band in '69), tastefully swung through historic bits of early Armstrong hot jazz such as "Ory's Creole Trombone" as well as other memory-evoking numbers like Fats Waller's "Honeysuckle Rose" and George Gershwin's "I Got Rhythm."[20] "Judging from the enthusiastic audience reception, especially the packed finals house," wrote Dan Morgenstern, "the time may be ripe for yet another traditional revival."[21] (Of the Illinois Dixie Band itself, the critic remarked that since the members had come to traditional jazz relatively late, they lacked the "antiquarian attitude of most professional traditionalists," and brought to the music "a refreshingly independent spirit.")

In regard to the diverse play of other combos selected as "outstanding" finalists, the Midwest Collective from Indiana University was, to Dan Morgenstern's mind, "in a class almost by itself." Meanwhile, the Graffiti, led by Dave Pavolka ("a stunning technician") and bassist Wayne Darling ("a player with almost frightening chops and splendid musicality") earned Morgenstern's critical praise as a "polished unit" that emphasized "smooth ensemble work."[22]

Winners once more abounded. Wayne Darling of Graffiti took top honors as Best Bassist and Outstanding Instrumentalist; Shelby Janes, Paul DeMartinis, and Ken Sloane of the Midwest Collective won respective Best Piano, Saxophone, and Trumpet awards, and MIT trombonist Richie Orr finally broke Dave Pavolka's three-year stranglehold on the Best Trombone prize while managing a Best Composer award as well. Elsewhere, Towson State members Tony Heenan (Best Big Band Trumpeter) and Bill Reiber (Outstanding Drums and Percussion) carted off CJF plaques, while Warrick Carter of the finalist HGJJK Quartet shared drum honors with Pete Szujewski of Notre Dame's Larry Beachler Sextet. (Notre Dame was also well represented in 1970 by Best Guitarist Norm Zeller and the performances of other alumni such as MIT Best Saxophonist Bill Hurd and Illinois Dixie combo finalist member Larry Dwyer). Last but not least, singers Dee Dee Garrett of Illinois and Marilyn Walton of Elmhurst College took top vocal awards.

"The 12th annual CJF," summed up Dan Morgenstern, "maintained the high musical standards and superior production values one has come to expect from Notre Dame. This year the competitive aspects of the festival were toned down. . . . Thus, there was no need for the three finalist big bands and three finalist combos to perform competitively—a fact which resulted in more relaxed playing and few disappointed musicians." "The winning bands," he continued, "represented varying approaches. Each band was excellent in its own way, and it was good to have them judged equals."[23]

Turning to the judging panel, the critic noted that though it was "a diversified one," it also "operated without dissent." "It was a particular pleasure," he continued, "to serve with [Richard] Abrams, who, in his first outing as a judge, showed enthusiasm, understanding, and a truly open mind."[24] "Willis Conover," wrote Morgenstern in his festival wrap-up, "did his usual expert job of emceeing and added the prestige of his presence to the event, and the sound system, installed and supervised by expert technicians from Electro-Voice and featuring some exceptionally sensitive new microphones, was near perfect."[25]

"Perhaps most gratifying," concluded the *down beat* editor and CJF adviser, "was the record attendance, most of it coming from the Notre Dame student body—which has not been the case in the past. It was good to see adequate local support for what has consistently been one of the best (and best-run) festivals of its kind in the country. The chairman this year was a lady, Ann Heinrichs, and she and her staff did a fine job."[26]

1
9
7
1

With the shock of student killings at Kent State and the military invasion of Cambodia in 1970, the tenor of both campus and national protests against the Vietnam War rose to strident new heights. Spurred by these incidents, Notre Dame president Fr. Theodore M. Hesburgh (who had openly condemned the war effort as early as October 1969) eventually went so far as to join with other college presidents in signing an open letter that called for accelerated government withdrawal of military personnel in Vietnam.[1] With regard to more musically oriented matters, the unforgettable scene at Kent State had perhaps its most devastating jazz effect on the 1970 American College Jazz Festival (ACJF), held at the University of Illinois. There, instead of the usual hoopla and fanfare, arriving judges and student musicians were greeted by the stunning silence of a totally deserted campus, a development brought on by university officials who, fearing possible student reprisals and protests in the wake of Kent State, elected to close the school late in the week.[2]

Consisting of regional feeder festivals in the Southwest (University of Texas/Austin), Midwest (Elmhurst College/Elmhurst, Illinois), South (Springhill College/Mobile, Alabama), West Coast (San Fernando Valley College/California), New England (Quinnipiac College/Hamden, Connecticut), InterMountain (University of Utah/Salt Lake City, Utah), and Northwest (Olympic College/Bremerton, Washington), the 1970 ACJF had, to a great extent, absorbed and embellished Bob Yde's IMF framework. At each regional ACJF event, a festival manager auditioned tapes of bands and combos wishing to perform, selected entrants, decided on individual competitive guidelines, and organized clinics for participating musicians.

Out of this network, twenty big bands, combos, and vocalists were selected for the May 1970 ACJF held in the Krannert Center for Performing Arts on the University of Illinois campus. Boldly characterizing the controversy over competitiveness, the ACJF—despite competitive regional festivals—offered audiences a noncompetitive format at Illinois. Other special features of the 1970 ACJF included seminars and performances by outstanding guest bands from North Texas State, Millikin University (Decatur, Illinois), the University of Illinois, and Indiana University (all of whom had been invited to attend by ACJF executive-director Willis Conover). In addition, funds provided by the American Federation of Musicians made it possible for the ACJF to bring in professional jazzmen such as Cannonball Adderley, Benny Carter, Gerry Mulligan, Clark Terry, and popular vibist Gary Burton to perform with student groups.[3] (Two other jazz personalities, composer Lalo Schifrin and composer/arranger Quincy Jones also came to the ACJF just to listen but, caught up in the event's enthusiasm, eventually took their respective turns on stage, too.)[4]

By mid-to-late 1970, student groups—no longer strangers to foreign audiences as a result of numerous State Department tours—were also beginning to turn up with increasing frequency at major European jazz festivals, particularly the young-but-increasingly diverse and acclaimed one at Montreux, Switzerland. Appearing at the 1970 Montreux International Jazz Festival for the first time, collegiate jazz bands from MIT and North Texas State knocked out European audiences with their mature, savvy, swinging play. (Montreux audiences were so enraptured with North Texas's set, they demanded three encores and remained cheering on their feet as the band left the stage at 3:30 A.M.)[5] Making breakthroughs of its own in other jazz-oriented ways, the National Association of Jazz Educators noted proudly in late 1970 that membership had grown to 2,000 and now included educators in every one of the 50 states.[6]

Bolstered by record 1970 attendance figures and the second show of profit in its twelve-year history,[7] the 1971 University of Notre Dame Collegiate Jazz Festival embarked on additional radical changes in festival format. Taking note of the past year's elimination of overall band and combo winners in order to reduce competition and shift festival emphasis toward more thorough recognition of individual talent, the '71 CJF resolved to streamline things even further by eliminating the ill-attended Friday-afternoon preliminary session entirely. In its place in 1971, a revamped Saturday-evening session would—instead of showcasing non-competitive "finalist" bands—seek to present bands and combos still involved in overall festival performance. In this way, student musicians would be exposed to larger crowds, competition would be further reduced, and audience excitement would build more dramatically toward a CJF climax late Saturday night, at which point the judges would announce their selections for Outstanding bands and combos, as well as Outstanding individual soloists.

Another new feature of CJF 1971 would be the large-scale inclu-

sion of noncompetitive CJF guest bands. For the CJF (which had presented guest bands such as the Melodons, as well as CJF high-school
festival winners and vocal/instrumental guest groups for many years)
this move was designed both to ensure audience interest in each of
the three reorganized CJF music sessions and to provide listeners with
a wide-ranging look at groups performing outside the traditional festival structure. Scheduled to appear in 1971 as guest groups were the
Notre Dame High School Melodons (Friday evening), the University
of Illinois Dixie Band (Saturday afternoon), and the University of Illinois Jazz Band (Saturday evening).

Run once again this year by St. Mary's College senior Ann Heinrichs, the 13th annual CJF also expanded the number of bands participating in the adjunct five-year old CJF high-school festival from 14
to 20 and moved the high-school event's performance locale from somewhat cramped Washington Hall to the more comfortable confines of
the Little Theater at Moreau Hall on St. Mary's campus. (Participating
high-school bands would in 1971 continue to be judged by the same
criteria—taking into account, of course, the relative level of musician
maturity—as their collegiate counterparts, and festival winners would
once more grace the Saturday evening CJF/Stepan Center stage with
their potent high-school jazz-band sounds.)

Abandoning the ill-attended traditional Thursday-evening slot for
a more reasonable 4 P.M. Friday-afternoon time, the 1971 CJF symposium on the "Current State of Jazz" offered audiences a chance for
interaction with and up-close viewing of one of the most progressive,
diverse, and youthful judging panels in years. Made up of *down beat*-
editor Dan Morgenstern, vocalist Leon Thomas, bassist Charlie Haden
(recently acclaimed for his controversial 1970 album "Charlie Haden's
Liberation Music Orchestra"), renowned arranger Gerald Wilson, reed-
man/pianist Richard Abrams, and Willis Conover (who would also
double as emcee), the CJF judging panel was rounded out for the symposium talks by the welcome faces of Father Wiskirchen and Notre
Dame Music Department chairman, Fr. Carl Hager. (As it turned out,
honors for one of the more interesting—and odd—symposium conversation bits this year went to Leon Thomas, who grappled momentarily with a comparison between jazz and basketball, citing the curious
fact that Notre Dame basketball star Austin Carr was "actually playing a drum when he dribbles, only in this case, the drum moves up
and down rather than the hand. . . .")[8]

Once again, bands and combos from locales such as Michigan,
Tennessee, Pennsylvania, Massachusetts, Virginia, North Carolina,
Maryland, New Mexico, and Illinois appeared on the Stepan Center/

CJF stage—only to be out-shone for yet another year by a portly priest and his ever-hip young band from Notre Dame High School in Niles, Illinois. One of the first high-school groups to explore the big-band rock idiom as well as "free-form" group improvisation, the 1971 Melodon band under Father Wiskirchen stole the show from even John Garvey's slightly crazed University of Illinois group by staging choreographic numbers and borrowing heavily from rock to present original arrangements of contemporary songs such as Chicago's "Make Me Smile" and Al Kooper's "Easy Does It," both of which were crowd pleasingly rendered by vocalist Bob Green (all presented, of course, along with traditional jazz works).[9]

For the second straight year, Hank Levy's Towson State Jazz Ensemble rambled to one of the festival's outstanding big-band spots. A professional composer who had honed his 22-member student group (drawn from a school student body of just 5,000) into an "experimental laboratory playing charts that will be sent to the Stan Kenton Orchestra and the Don Ellis Orchestra for publication and their own use," Levy and the Towson band stood (according to the 1971 CJF program description) in the "unique position of playing next year's charts this year."[10] Leaning heavily on rock chord patterns and rhythms, unusual time charts, and intriguing melodic expressions, Towson State (performing music that Levy clearly interpreted as the "wave of the future") bowled over both judging panel and crowd and even moved one Notre Dame/*Observer* student reviewer to proclaim the Towson sound as some of "the most exciting music" he'd ever heard.[11]

Also selected as "outstanding" along with shoe-in Towson State were big bands from the Philadelphia Music Academy (including a young bassist named Stanley Clarke), Memphis State (led by Tom Ferguson), and Indiana State University (Terre Haute). All received cash awards of $150 as well as a CJF plaque. On the combo side of the festival, the University of Illinois's Organic Fusion (led by '71 Outstanding Instrumentalist/multireedman Ron Bridgewater and featuring electric-keyboardist Jim McNeely), vibist Tom Van Der Geld's University of New Mexico Neo-Classic Quintet, and an Indiana University Quintet, Whatever, were also selected as Outstanding and, for their efforts, took home plaques and cash awards of $50. Other individual winners of note included bassist Jon Burr of Illinois, flautist Tommy Lee of the University of Pittsburgh/Tommy Lee Quartet, Neo-Classic Quintet members Tom Van Der Geld (Outstanding Composer/Arranger) and reedman Roger Janotta (Best Miscellaneous Instrumentalist), and trombone/euphonium-man J.B. Buchanan (Best Miscellaneous Instrumentalist) of the Notre Dame combo entry, Coatis Mundi.

"If there was anything wrong with this year's Collegiate Jazz Festival," wrote *Observer* critic Mike Lenehan in reference to the event's heavy-duty, 23-band listening load, "it was that there was too much good music in too short a time." "Even a seasoned festival goer and avid listener like Dan Morgenstern found the schedule a bit heavy," he continued, "but given the usual [Student] Social Commission [concert] fare, that doesn't seem like anything to complain about."[12]

As the lid closed back down on the CJF 13 jazz box, it was left to judge Charlie Haden to sum up what the CJF was all about. "What I've seen here," said the impassioned bassist, who had struggled manfully the entire festival with a horrendous case of flu, "makes me think that there really is hope."[13]

1
9
7
2
With the rise in "blues consciousness" brought about by the Rolling Stones, Cream, the Animals, and a number of other rock groups, festivals showcasing many of the original black blues artists emerged in the late sixties and early seventies, most notably, in Ann Arbor, Michigan. Surprisingly enough, however, to complement the celebrated CJF, one such blues event also evolved at the University of Notre Dame—a sign, if ever there was one, that the blues were definitely back in business.

Notre Dame's "blues urge" began innocently enough in the spring of 1969 when J. B. Hutto and his Hawks came down from Chicago and played to a crowd of several hundred folks, only to be followed by Son House late that same year. In the spring of 1970, another small Notre Dame blues bash featuring electric-guitarist/vocalist Luther Allison took place,[1] and by September, a full-fledged two-day weekend blues festival in Stepan Center, featuring Fred McDowell, Otis Rush, J. B. Hutto and Jimmy "Fast-Fingers" Dawkins, Hound Dog Taylor, and Lightnin' Hopkins was underway. Despite a paucity of publicity, nearly 1,000 people turned out for the event, which had been arranged by Notre Dame Student Government Cultural-Arts Commissioner Bob Brinkman as a package deal with blues-manager Dick Wadderman. (Although Lightnin' Hopkins's performance was filmed for what would turn out to be a half-hour educational-television documentary, top audience-pleasing honors at the festival went to Otis Rush and his high-powered, horn-backed band.)

November of 1971 saw the emergence of a student-organized three-day blues event at Notre Dame termed the Midwest Blues Festival or MBF. Featuring artists such as Fred McDowell (in his last performance anywhere), Carey Bell, Howlin' Wolf, Little Brother Montgomery,

Otis Rush, Jimmy Rodgers, Buddy Guy and Junior Wells (in both acoustic and electric sets), and, last but not least, legendary bluesman Muddy Waters, the festival's twenty hours of top-notch blues were made available to the Notre Dame student populace and public-at-large for the surprisingly low festival-pass cost of $6 (by comparison, Ann Arbor had recently been charging as much as $30 for a three-day pass).

Run by student Perry Aberli (with the backing of Bob Brinkman's Cultural Commission), the 1971 MBF carved out a national name for itself and reaped enthusiastic reviews in *down beat* and other magazines. Unfortunately, due to losses in 1971 of several thousand dollars, the event was cut back to a series of Washington Hall-held miniconcerts in the fall of '72, featuring Shirley Griffith, Hound Dog Taylor, Big Walter Horton and Carey Bell, and Houston Stackhouse. Earlier that same year, of course, a certain Collegiate Jazz Festival on campus celebrated its fourteenth anniversary as the oldest and most prestigious event of its kind in the land.

By early 1972, faced with the emergence of yet another college-jazz event, the Wichita Jazz Festival (Wichita, Kansas), the 14th CJF—run by student Bob Syburg—was set to present seventeen collegiate bands and combos (from Arizona, Michigan, Indiana, South Carolina, Pennsylvania, Illinois, Ohio, Massachusetts, Wisconsin, and Maryland), and three guest bands, as well as the usual CJF high-school festival winners. In addition, an expanded, seven-member judging panel would include former CJF-award-winner Jamey Aebersold, Willis Conover, Mothers of Invention-drummer Aynsley Dunbar, Dan Morgenstern, '72 *down beat* magazine-selected Best Flautist Hubert Laws, composer George Russell and—in something of an early 1970s CJF coup—rapidly rising pop/jazz pianist/composer/vocalist Roberta Flack. Benefiting from a National Endowment for the Arts grant of $1,000,[2] (matched by CJF funds), CJF chairman Bob Syburg, a South Bend native and Notre Dame junior majoring in American Studies, Black Studies, and African Studies, also made plans to expand the already firmly established CJF educational framework to encompass not only the traditional symposium (returned this year to a Thursday-evening time slot), but also a Friday-afternoon jazz-history lecture by *down beat*-editor Dan Morgenstern as well as a series of Saturday-morning lectures, clinics, and informal talks in the Main Library lounge, the CCE, and the Audio Visual Auditorium led by attending judges Jamey Aebersold, Hubert Laws, Aynsley Dunbar, and Roberta Flack.[3]

Seemingly the result of Syburg's own concern with the history of black literature and related cultural developments, as well as the CJF's own history of black collegiate participation (stretching back to the first festival in 1959),[4] the '72 CJF would also feature more black musicians, bands, and combos than any other year in the past. Among these groups in 1972 was a large band from Chicago's Malcolm X College, a Chicago Art Quartet Plus One, and, as a guest band, the massive Alvin Batiste-led Southern University Jazz Band Jaguars from Baton Rouge, Louisiana. Other '72 guest bands would include the Melodons and '71 CJF combo/arranger winner Tom Van Der Geld's Children at Play quintet, the latter of which would also play at Nicola's Restaurant in South Bend (a new CJF after-hours jam spot) each of the three festival nights.[5]

In an effort to give the jazz symposium "greater definition" and offer audiences additional "insight into the workings of the judges' minds,"[6] the traditional discussion format was changed in 1972 to a *down beat*-magazine-like "blindfold test."[7] During this "test," recordings identified only to audience members were played for the judges. After each selection, the judges attempted to name artists and song titles, while offering spontaneous evaluations, criticisms, opinions, and asides. The brainchild of CJF-adviser Richard Bizot, the blindfold test idea was both entertaining and successful, and the panel made up of Conover (doubling again this year as judge and emcee), Dunbar, Russell, Aebersold, and Morgenstern (who simply could not be stumped) responded vividly to other related topics such as the ongoing jazz and rock dilemma, and the merits of "free-form" jazz versus traditional jazz. "Jazz uses rock ideas and rock borrows from jazz, so they are really one," concluded panelist George Russell, who went on to wonder aloud at one point in the symposium why it was that jazz, which "affects people all over the world," was so "totally misunderstood and unsupported in its native land."[8]

Reduced competitive elements in 1972 made for another, more relaxed performance year, and, out of the fourteen big bands that turned up at the festival, four were designated as Outstanding. These bands included the Towson State College Jazz Ensemble led by Hank Levy (this year featuring intriguingly named percussionist Obidiah Potsdam III), the swinging, bongo-energized Malcolm X College Afro American Ensemble directed by Charles Walton (which featured pianist Jodie Christian), Herb Pomeroy's MIT Festival Jazz Ensemble, and the Louis Smith-directed University of Michigan Jazz Band—all representative of a wide range of music styles and directions. (Hearteningly, in addition to the rise in black band/musician attendance, there was also a noticeable increase in female participation in 1972; unfortunately, there was also a marked absence of the avant-garde, with the exception of the noncompeting guest Van Der Geld quintet, which performed everything from "Charlie Parker tunes to free-form jazz.")[9]

The fifth and final Outstanding group selected at CJF '72, a combo led by trumpeter Benjamin Franklin Jones, was a story in itself. Not even listed in the '72 festival program, the Louisville, Kentucky-based Jones (whose group had been selected to perform at CJF '72 on the basis of its submitted tape but subsequently couldn't attend) pawned his only horn in order to get to South Bend and, as a result, arrived with neither instrument nor band in sight the day of the festival. Sensing a dedicated musician in the CJF crowd, chairman Bob Syburg scraped up a trumpet and mouthpiece for Jones and paired him up with a trio of University of Illinois band members in attendance that included pianist Jim McNeely, bassist Jon Burr, and drummer Phil Gratteau. Against all odds, Jones quickly accustomed himself to his borrowed instrument and unfamiliar surroundings, blew with a pro's aplomb on tunes like "Stella by Starlight" and " Now's the Time," and even plunked himself down at the piano at one point for an inspired original piece.

"I can't think of many other college festivals," wrote Dan Morgenstern in a postfestival *down beat* review, "where Jones would even have been given a chance to play, much less to compete. Most go by the rulebooks. But CJF has soul, and the fact that this unorthodox group walked off with honors proves its right to call itself a jazz festival."[10] (As might be expected, however, offering the trumpet-soloist award to Jones ruffled some feathers at CJF '72, particularly those belonging to one talented, self-assured Ohio State Jazz Ensemble trumpeter who made his displeasure known to several judges. "Personally," mentioned Morgenstern of the somewhat bitter young man, "I hope he gets sore enough to learn something and come back next year to prove it—the talent certainly is there.")[11]

Gifted soloists at CJF '72 abounded once more. Included among this "singled-out" crowd were Malcolm X College band members Bill Howell (Outstanding Instrumentalist) and soprano/tenor saxophonist Sonny Seals (Outstanding Reed Soloist), and University of Illinois pianist Jim McNeely (Best Piano) and bassist John Burr (Best Bass). Others singled out were three-time flute winner Tommy Lee of the University of Pittsburgh, and Towson State's Bret Hardesty (Best Electric Piano), drummer Dave Gimbel (Best Drums), and Best Composers Bunky Horak and Harvey Cooper. On a somewhat more offbeat note, MIT soprano-saxophonist Bill Hurd became the first CJF participant to win awards six years apart—1966 (Most Promising Instrumentalist) and 1972 (Outstanding Miscellaneous Instrumentalist).

Postfestival jam sessions held at Nicola's Restaurant with Tom

Van Der Geld's Children at Play were highlighted by various musician sitters-in, including judge Aynsley Dunbar, who stepped into the fray one night and "acquitted himself handsomely on a jazz turf."[12] As for the guest bands, the Melodons, as usual, did their incomparable high-school-band thing, the Illinois big band was no less than stunning, and the 35-man-plus Southern University Jazz Band under leader Alvin Batiste received the finest tribute of all — a standing ovation for its churning Saturday-evening set dedicated to Charlie Parker.[13] Without a doubt, it was another fine festival. Somewhat sadly, however, it would also be the last to benefit from the advice and counsel of faculty-adviser Richard Bizot, who was moving on elsewhere to teach.

"Thinking over the past five years has made me realize all the more how much I'll miss the CJF," wrote the departing Notre Dame English professor/jazz enthusiast in a fine '72 CJF program farewell note. "Or, to put it more positively, how much I'll remember about the CJF. The music I'll remember, of course, but most of all I'm going to remember the people: the musicians, the leaders, the other local jazz nuts whom the festival brings together once a year, the students on the staff, annual reunions with Willis and Shirley Conover and Dan Morgenstern. . . . Yes, that's the way to end: remembering such people and also trying to say thanks to them."[14]

(In Richard Bizot's honor, the name of the Outstanding Instrumentalist at CJF '72 and each year thereafter as well as those of Outstanding Instrumentalists dating back to 1968 — his first CJF adviser year — would be engraved on the Richard B. Bizot trophy, which would permanently reside in the Black Cultural Arts Center on the third floor of the LaFortune Student Center.)

1 9 7 3 Rebounding in '72–'73 from the loss of Richard Bizot with yet another faculty-adviser — University of Notre Dame Associate Director of Bands James Phillips — the CJF (run for a second consecutive year by chairman Bob Syburg) sought once more to expand educational opportunities for participating student musicians. Realizing, however, that the event's fairly well-established structure would no longer lend itself to excessive expansion or change, Syburg, Phillips, and crew decided instead that the best way to broaden festival horizons was to incorporate the traditional postfestival jam session (which ordinarily included students and attending judges) into the already existing festival performance fabric itself. In addition, the fifteenth CJF would present a second gala "jam" with the '73 judges, guest artists, dancers, and more on the Thursday night preceding the festival.

This reemphasis in 1973 of the most ancient of jazz-education tools—the "jam" session—was important to the CJF, for it not only further helped to bridge the educational distance between performing student musicians (onstage) and professional musician or critic judges (hidden behind adjudicating sheets and desks), but also continued to stress the noncompetitive "festival" side of the event. Additionally, these two "jam" innovations would do much to ensure attendance at the CJF. Now, more than ever before, the attending judges would become the CJF's main drawing card.

In terms of jazz education during this period, the University of Notre Dame was also making dramatic progress, for a jazz-appreciative fellow by the name of Fr. George Wiskirchen had moved on to his alma mater to teach in 1972. Leaving the Melodons and Notre Dame High School in Niles, Illinois, after sixteen nationally prominent years, Father Wiskirchen brought a wealth of jazz knowledge to the university, not to mention a crafty sixth sense regarding the many mysterious ways in which to instantly assemble a jazz program and band.

Formed in the fall of 1972 under the Good Father's direction, a twenty-one member Notre Dame Jazz Band (or NDJB)—though an extracurricular organization—could soon be heard on campus performing everything from big-band jazz to free-form improvisational pieces, thereby becoming the first group in the university's history to "link Notre Dame's name with jazz performance."[1] In addition to the NDJB, Father Wiskirchen was instrumental in the formation of an eight-member combo at Notre Dame that same fall and presented weekly educational LaFortune Student Center jazz lecture/concerts called Jazz at Nine which helped to expose jazz to "average college audiences" in 1972–73.[2]

While Notre Dame was eking out a jazz victory, however, there were still numerous academic obstacles and setbacks in the realm of collegiate jazz. First of all, the Washington, D.C./Kennedy Center-held 1972 American College Jazz Festival turned out to be an artistically sound but financially inept affair. Saved only by the last-minute intervention of American Airlines, the ACJF (produced by the Kennedy Center and the National Association of Jazz Educators) still owed $1,500 to each of the eight participating regional feeder festivals as late as January 1973, and was presently shopping for a new home.[3] On an even more serious note, the thriving, widely hailed University of Utah jazz-education program led by respected maverick teachers Dr. William

Fowler and Ladd McIntosh was suddenly terminated by the university in 1972, only to result in uproarious student protest, tense negotiations, and further jazz/academia losses.[4]

Bolstered by a $1,000 National Endowment for the Arts grant and $2,500 in matching funds put up by the University of Notre Dame, the 1973 Collegiate Jazz Festival run once more by Bob Syburg offered a bit more hope against this encroaching festival gloom.

Kicking off the event with a Wednesday-evening, April 11, cocktail party for Notre Dame faculty, CJF staff, and judging-panel members in the Morris Inn, the 1973 CJF officially opened on Thursday evening, April 12, with a Stepan Center benefit concert (sponsored by the CJF and the University of Notre Dame Black Studies Program) for the minorities scholarship fund of a national black sorority, Alpha Kappa Alpha. Included on the benefit bill was a riveting group of Southern University students under the direction of Alvin Batiste, a talented South Bend jazz/dance troupe, and an "all-star" jazz combo made up of CJF '73 judges such as saxophonist/flautist Joe Farrell, drummer Roy Haynes, flautist Hubert Laws, clarinetist Alvin Batiste, trumpeter Jimmy Owens, and tenor-saxophonist Jimmy Giuffre (a last-minute replacement for an ill and once-more-unable-to-attend Gil Evans), as well as non-CJF panelists Phil Upchurch and Richard Abrams on bass guitar and piano.

Running ably through numbers such as "Swiftly Fast," "On Green Dolphin Street," Duke Ellington's "Come Sunday," and Jimmy Giuffre's "Dervish," as well as some free-form improvisations and a song for three flutes and clarinet (featuring Laws, Farrell, Batiste, and Giuffre), the invigorating session finally closed down at 12:45 A.M. after a 45-minute Batiste blues original entitled "Moe Zartin." Thoroughly enthralled with each other's playing, the judges adjourned to a downtown restaurant-nightclub in order to "jam" some more. (Although also scheduled to perform or appear on the benefit-program bill, saxophonist Cannonball Adderley and Gary, Indiana, mayor Richard Hatcher were both unfortunately unable to attend.)[5]

Held for the second consecutive year in the Memorial Library Auditorium, the Friday-afternoon CJF symposium led by Fr. George Wiskirchen once more invoked a *down beat* magazine-like "Blindfold Test" format, as judges Farrell, Laws, Batiste, Haynes, Owens, Giuffre and perennial *down beat* editor/CJF judge Dan Morgenstern listened to selections that varied from Bach to rock.[6]

In addition to their respective judging and symposium chores in 1973, each attending judge was asked to name five favorite jazz recordings, which would then be donated by the CJF (with funds set aside from the festival budget) to the audio center of Notre Dame's Memorial Library for the educational/listening benefit of students and campus visitors. Conceived by CJF faculty adviser Jim Phillips, this "Collegiate Jazz Festival Collection of American Jazz Music" was designed to "advance familiarity with jazz among students and to further traditional educational aspects of the annual event."[7] As the 1973 CJF program also noted, "tapes of each year's outstanding [CJF] college bands will also be placed in the collection."[8] (In yet another of his many contributions to the CJF, Dan Morgenstern selected a starter set of records for the collection, including famed and at times difficult to obtain LP's by Louis Armstrong, Johnny Dodds, John Coltrane, Eric Dolphy, Miles Davis, Ornette Coleman, and many others.)

Presenting bands and combos from Michigan, Illinois, Massachusetts, Tennessee, Wisconsin, Ohio, Texas, and Indiana, the '73 CJF (which processed a record fifty-two applications and tapes), was once again a potent collegiate-jazz force. Highlights of the two-day proceedings included standing ovations for both the six-man Governor's State University Jazz Ensemble, and the high-school-festival winning Crown Point (Indiana) High School Jazz Band (which didn't even get on stage Saturday evening at the CJF until 2 A.M.), as well as a somewhat unique group from Bowdoin College (Brunswick, Maine) called Tamarack, which featured shoeless drummer Pete Goodwin, violinist Andy Munitz, and a riveting sound mixture consisting of jazz, rock and "Virginia reel type hill music."[9]

During the festival, there was also a crowd-captivating synthesizer original entitled "Bus" performed by the Tom Battenberg-led eighteen-piece Ohio State University Jazz Ensemble, an enthusiastic outing by the Notre Dame Jazz Band (returning to CJF action for the first time since Lettermen band days in 1966), and a stirring MIT Festival Jazz Ensemble version of "You Make Me So Very Happy," by jazz-rock group Blood, Sweat & Tears. In addition, the Melodons made a much-anticipated appearance, and a late-Saturday-evening judges'/award-winners' jam lasted until 3:30 A.M.[10]

Before the jam, of course, emcee Willis Conover moved to the onstage microphone for the fifth consecutive year and announced the Outstanding Bands and Combos. Included among this select number were such groups as the Ohio State University Jazz Ensemble, the Texas Southern University Jazz Ensemble (an often caftan- and dashiki-clad/politically hip black aggregate appearing at the CJF for the first time under the direction of none other than CJF '60 award-winner/

educator Lanny Steele), the University of Wisconsin Jazz Ensemble, the Modern Jazz Quintet from Indiana University, and the Governor's State University Jazz Ensemble (Chicago, Illinois).

Individual Outstanding Soloists included saxophonist Steele L. Seals (Malcolm X College), John Smarzewski (Triton College), and Eugene Vinyard (Governor's State), trumpeter Ben Franklin Jones of Tennessee State University's Jazz Ensemble, pianist Marsha Frazier and flautist Doug Harris of Texas Southern's fine group, violinist Andy Munitz of Tamarack, and CJF '73's Best Bassist/Outstanding Instrumentalist John Clayton, Jr., of the Indiana University Modern Jazz Quintet. (In fact, Clayton so amazed listeners with a stunning bass solo during a rendition of "Bye, Bye, Blackbird" that he received a standing ovation not only from audience members, but—in an unprecedented move—from several judges as well.)

Taking the stand to accept his various awards late that Saturday night, John Clayton, Jr., looked out into the audience, paused for a moment, and then leaned into the microphone to say: "You keep diggin' it, I'll keep makin' it."[11] At fifteen years of age, the CJF could scarcely have found a more apt spokesman or a phrase more energetically descriptive of the performer/listener jazz rapport it had tried so hard to achieve.

1 9 7 4 In June 1973, the American College Jazz Festival (still owing "a considerable amount of money to several [1972] festival creditors")[1] took place in Chicago's McCormick Place in conjunction with the National Association of Music Merchants' (NAMM) annual convention and exposition. Musically, the 1973 ACJF was once more a smash; financially (due to unforeseen hailstorms and Chicago-area tornadoes which helped to keep audiences at bay), it was a bust. Clearly, future festival prospects were not looking good; by early 1974, there would no longer be an ACJF.

In other developments, the University of Notre Dame Collegiate Jazz Festival lost one of its primary connections in mid-1973 when Dan Morgenstern stepped down as editor of *down beat* magazine to devote more time to writing and other jazz-oriented activities. Since 1968, Morgenstern had been a prime backer (and annual reporter) of the event, in the tradition of *down beat* editor Don DeMicheal and publisher Charles Suber years before.

With his departure, it seemed inevitable that the ample *down beat* coverage enjoyed over the years by the CJF would decline. Fortunately,

Ken Lee, a Notre Dame junior marketing major from Shreveport, Louisiana, and the first black Notre Dame student to run the CJF, had the courage and foresight to invite Morgenstern back to judge the 1974 festival—influential *down beat* editorship or not.

In the fall of 1973, while Ken Lee was gearing things up for the spring jazz blast, Notre Dame student Perry Aberli was once again putting on the Midwest Blues Festival. Returning this year as a two-night Stepan Center incarnation, the MBF featured Roosevelt Sykes, Houston Stackhouse, Joe Willie Wilkins and the King Biscuit Boys, and Hound Dog Taylor on Friday night, only to follow that stellar blues cast on Saturday night with Shirley Griffith, Yank Rachel and J. T. Brown, and riveting Chicago blues artists such as Son Seals, Mighty Joe Young, and Koko Taylor.

By 1974, in addition to the Midwest Blues Festival, the Notre Dame campus was also privy to three other student-run festivals during the academic year. These included a Sophomore Literary Festival (which brought in top-name writers, poets, and critics for a week of lectures, readings, and discussions each spring), the Collegiate Jazz Festival, and the Black Arts Festival, held for the first time in 1974.

Offering a "serious look at various black expressions in drama, art, and music" that would "examine the new directions and aims of Black people,"[2] the event entitled "Black Arts Festival, Black Perspectives in Transition," took place March 30–April 1 on the university's campus and included a "ritual" conducted by the Kuumba Workshop; an exhibition of Black Art by Donald Turner of Terre Haute, Indiana, in the LaFortune Student Center; a Sunday-afternoon Library Auditorium lecture by Congressman Charles W. Diggs; a Voices, Inc., "Journey Into Blackness" performance tracing black history from Africa through slavery to the present day; and, lastly, a Saturday-night jazz/ African folk-music performance by saxophonist Gary Bartz and his Ntu Troop.[3]

Following the pattern established by the diverse panels of previous early-seventies CJF events, the 1974 CJF judging panel featured such veteran judges as bassist Charlie Haden and drummer Roy Haynes (both making their second festival visits), young, versatile trombone wizard Bill Watrous (who would also hold a clinic at the CJF High School festival), CJF 1964's Most Promising Saxophonist Billy Harper, critic Dan Morgenstern, and pianist Lonnie Liston Smith (a late replacement for Ahmad Jamal, who was unable to attend). Representing the spectrum from avant-garde to bop, big band to jazz/rock, the judges (save Morgenstern and Haynes) were all in their thirties. As for the master of ceremonies, the 1974 choice was none other than Willis Conover.

Benefiting from yet another $1,000 National Endowment for the Arts grant, the '74 festival once again featured a Saturday-night "Judges' Jam" with judges and student award winners. In addition, the emphasis was placed squarely once more on the event's "festival" side. "We've tried," explained chairman Ken Lee just before the '74 CJF, "to eliminate as much as possible the competitive aspect in favor of just giving each group a chance to get up on stage and play."[4]

Kicking off what could best be termed "jazz consciousness week," Father Wiskirchen's Notre Dame Jazz Band and a smaller Notre Dame student combo known as Erg's Finger Circus gave an annual free concert in the Engineering auditorium on March 29. Featured during the concert were pieces by King Oliver, Archie Shepp, and Count Basie as well as a number of student compositions. In addition, former Louis Jordan bandmember and South Bend resident Curtis Johnson took the stand for several performance songs to showcase his talented tenor-sax play.[5]

Six days after the concert (and barely three days after the inaugural Black Arts Festival wrap-up), the main CJF event opened on Thursday evening, April 4, in the Main Library Auditorium with the traditional judges' symposium. Highlighted by further *down beat*-magazine-styled "Blindfold Tests" (undertaken by panel-members Conover, Morgenstern, Father Wiskirchen, Haden, Smith, Haynes, Watrous, and Harper), the symposium also hit on various music oriented topics, such as "improvisation" and the "controversial jazz of Miles Davis."[6]

For the fifth consecutive year, Electro-Voice donated a full sound system as well as top company technicians Bill Raventos and Bill Southerland without charge to the CJF,[7] thus ensuring that attending bands from West Virginia, New Jersey, Ohio, Wisconsin, Illinois, Louisiana, Maine, Massachusetts, Indiana, Michigan and Texas would be heard via the finest microphone and amplification systems available.

Playing to Friday night's sold-out, packed Stepan Center house were fine bands from Malcolm X College, Loyola University of New Orleans, and Notre Dame, and combos from Bowdoin College (Brunswick, Maine) and Waubonsee College (featuring "devilishly adept" guitarist Peter Hix),[8] as well as Notre Dame's own Erg's Finger Circus (comprised of trombonist Nick Talarico, tenor-saxist Charles Rohr, bassist Mike Nickerson, keyboardist Neil Gillespie, guitarist Bill Boris, drummer Ken Scarola, and conga-man Bob Smith). Undoubtedly, though, the evening belonged to the Loyola University Jazz Band, which reaped "response after response from the Stepan Center crowd" and went on to receive two standing ovations.[9]

"It might as well have been Stan Kenton fronting that fabulous unit," wrote *South Bend Tribune* entertainment-editor John D. Gardner of the Loyola band, "—brisk, precise, emphatic, clean, subtly versatile and with a strong flavor of Kenton-Ellis finesse; a simply dazzling organization with excellent soloists in all sections."[10]

Saturday afternoon unveiled five more bands and two combos including an unusual six-trombone-strong Jazz Trombone Ensemble from West Virginia University and the unrivaled big-band sounds of the Governor's State University Music Experience. As for the Saturday-evening session, it fairly exploded with talented combos such as the Governor's State University Jazz Sextet and the Indiana University Modern Jazz Quintet (once more containing CJF '73's Outstanding Instrumentalist/bassist, John Clayton, Jr.).

For the second consecutive year, the CJF also closed down with a dynamic Saturday-evening judges' jam. Making potent use of drummer Roy Haynes, electric/acoustic keyboardist Lonnie Liston Smith, trombonist Bill Watrous, bassist Charlie Haden, tenor-saxophonist Billy Harper, and (after a few numbers), CJF '74's Outstanding Trumpeter Walter Henderson of Governor's State, the invigorating jam session lasted until 3:00 A.M. Sunday morning.[11]

Outstanding bands and combos selected at CJF 16 included the Loyola University Jazz Band, the GSU Music Experience, the Waubonsee Jazz Quartet, the GSU Jazz Sextet, and the Indiana University Modern Jazz Quintet. In terms of individual awards, GSU bands snared seven awards in all, including Outstanding Band, Outstanding Combo, Best Reed Soloist (Vince Carter), Best Trumpet (Walter Henderson), Best Trombone (Billy Howell), Best Drummer (Curtis Prince), and Best Composer/Arranger (John Pate).[12]

Other winners of note at CJF '74 included Best Guitarist/Outstanding Instrumentalist Peter Hix (the first guitarist to win the overall instrumentalist category in CJF history) of the Waubonsee Jazz Quartet (Waubonsee College, Sugar Grove, Illinois), Ohio State drummer Jim Curlis, Waubonsee Jazz Quartet drummer James Keiser, flautist Jo Greene of Bowdoin College's Woodrose Combo, and the University of Wisconsin Jazz Ensemble's Kathy Otterson (Best Miscellaneous Instrumentalist/saxophone). Not to be left behind in GSU's band-award dust, Indiana University's riveting Modern Jazz Quintet managed to snare five awards for Outstanding Combo, Best Bass (John Clayton, Jr.), Best Drums (David Derge), Best Piano (Peter Bankoff), and Best Composer/Arranger (Charles Ellison, in a tie with John Pate of GSU).

1
9
7
5

After the 1974 festival, Ken Lee decided to step down and turn the CJF chairmanship over to Barbara Simonds, a Notre Dame junior art major from South Bend who had served as artist and photographer for the event during the previous year. Fortunately for the CJF, Lee would remain on the festival committee in 1974–75 and use his experience to help track down a new crop of judges.

By dint of the combined efforts of Simonds and Lee, the 1975 CJF panel soon tentatively materialized as one of the most impressive lineups of musicians, educators, and critics yet. Included among this judging "elite" were legendary tenor-saxophonist Sonny Rollins, '69 CJF Outstanding Instrumentalist Cecil Bridgewater (now a noted professional in his own right), Dee Dee Bridgewater (CJF 71's Best Vocalist and wife to Cecil), well-known studio/performing bassist Chuck Rainey, drummer Jack DeJohnette, flautist Hubert Laws, and critic Dan Morgenstern. As usual, Willis Conover was scheduled to emcee the CJF for the seventh consecutive year.

Late 1974, however, also witnessed progress in areas beyond the yearly CJF as both the fourth Midwest Blues Festival and a weekly student jazz program at the LaFortune Student Center rolled into view. Reduced once more to a one-day event, the Midwest Blues Festival (which featured Fenton Robinson, Big Walter Horton, and Muddy Waters) was another artistic success. A maverick student-government-funded event that operated (much like the Collegiate Jazz Festival) without the benefit of "official" office, desk, or phone, the MBF and its organizer, Perry Aberli, hoped to expand the event back to two-day proportions by the fall of 1975.

Meanwhile, the LaFortune Student Center rathskeller Nazz Coffeehouse[1] (previously an uneventful student recreational or study hangout) suddenly found itself privy in late 1974 and early 1975 to a bi-weekly, Wednesday-night series of performances by the University of Notre Dame Jazz Band and two smaller Notre Dame combos—all led or supervised by Fr. George Wiskirchen. Soon playing to wall-to-wall crowds, the bands helped to introduce rock-accustomed student ears to the intricate ways of the improvisatory art of jazz. (On the nights when it became apparent that neither combos nor band would appear due to conflicting class schedules or commitments, Father Wiskirchen played jazz recordings and offered commentaries on jazz trends and developments.)[2]

Continuing the application procedures established by the previous sixteen Collegiate Jazz Festivals, the 1975 festival committee presented the 45-plus college band and combo audition tapes submitted for review to a three-man judging panel made up of Fr. George Wiskirchen and two *down beat* magazine critics.[3] Whittled down to seventeen collegiate groups from Ohio, Illinois, Indiana, New York, and Texas, the '75 CJF opened on Friday, April 11, with a 3–5 P.M. question-and-answer symposium in the Nazz Coffeehouse that included attending judges Sonny Rollins, Cecil and Dee Dee Bridgewater, Hubert Laws, Chuck Rainey, Jack DeJohnette, and Dan Morgenstern.

For the third consecutive year, Father Wiskirchen's Notre Dame Jazz Band eased things up a bit for attending bands by taking the stage first. Breaking the Friday-evening ice, the band scored well with an arrangement of "Scarborough Fair" and a much livelier Jimmie Lunceford number entitled "Close Out."[4] Up next on the Friday-evening agenda was an eventual Outstanding Band Award winner, the Cliff Colnot-directed Northwestern University Jazz Ensemble, which featured one of the festival's two Outstanding Reed Soloists, Pete Grenier, and a young sophomore bassist named Steve Rodby. Brassy, urgent, and full of enthusiasm, the Northwestern musicians ripped through such works as "Groove Merchant" and "Blues Over Easy," before dramatically ending their CJF stay by walking offstage into the audience one by one during the final set song, only to complete this stunning bit of musical theatricality by offering a unified band/song closing blast from scattered Stepan Center locales.[5]

Other bands and combos appearing on the Friday-night jazz platform included Notre Dame's veteran combo, Erg's Finger Circus, Indiana University's Primal Scream, and a Bowling Green State University Lab Band. Also on the agenda was yet another eventual Outstanding 1975 CJF Band, the powerhouse Fredonia Big Band from New York State's Fredonia University, which brought the audience to its feet with originals such as "Kohoutek."[6] Officially over just past midnight, the Friday-night CJF jazz strains continued on into the early-morning hours at jam sessions (open to all musicians—including judges) held downtown at the South Bend Creative Musician's Club on 1911 S. Franklin Street.[7]

Saturday afternoon's music session began with a rarity—an opening band that would go on to snare an Outstanding Group Award. Directed by '64 CJF Outstanding Instrumentalist/educator/alto-saxophonist Bunky Green, the Chicago State University Jazz Band also went on to snare awards for members John Smarzewski (Best Reed Soloist), Al Keith (Best Bass), and Paulette Hradnansky (Best Trumpet Soloist). A University of Texas Big Band featuring Best Trombonist Mike Mordecai and Best Drummer John Treanor soon followed Chicago State's riveting lead, before a colorfully attired, conga-juiced Texas Southern University small Jazz Ensemble directed by energetic Lanny Steele proceeded to snatch up three more awards for group members Val Ewell (Best Guitarist), Mike Pritchard (Best Drummer), and Eugene Perry (Best Bass). Rounding out the afternoon action was a performance by the Governor's State University Jazz Ensemble (directed by former CJF Drum award winner Warrick L. Carter), which concealed within its saxophone section a graduate music student named Earl "Chico" Freeman.

Saturday evening opened with the CJF High School contest winners (Lincoln High School, Vincennes, Indiana, and Bloomington North High School, Bloomington, Indiana) taking the stage. Next, Lanny Steele and a much larger Texas Southern University Jazz Ensemble stormed aboard en route to an Outstanding Best Band Award and performed madcap, vibrant selections such as "Registration '74," a number as "full of energy and confusion" as the title seemed to suggest which "successfully implied the discord and noise [of registration] to create a pleasing effect."[8]

The Eastman School of Music's Inner Jazz Combo (which had recently changed its name to "Telestar"), featuring vibist Steve Rehbein, '75 Best Flautist Stephen Kujala, and Best Pianist/Best Composer-Arranger John Serry, Jr., emerged next. Performing several "delightful African and Indian compositions"[9] that were sparked by sterling Kujala flute solos, the group easily took the festival's fifth Outstanding Band Award. Finally, after stirring performances by Ohio State and Govenor's State bands, the Eastman Jazz Ensemble led by Rayburn Wright ambled out to grab firm hold of the sixth and final Outstanding Band Award.

Presenting a "nothing short of sensational" opening set, Eastman was ably sparked by CJF '75 Best Trumpeter Al Vizzuti and tenor-saxophonist George Ross, who "offered a championship solo" on an original Ross piece entitled "Reflections," which "brought the crowd to its feet in standing ovations shortly past midnight."[10] Bolstered by blistering Kujala, Ross, and Serry flute, saxophone, and piano solos, subsequent Eastman renditions of Chick Corea and Duke Ellington numbers proved equally "irresistible" and left the crowd cheering for more. (Fortunately for the crowd, the Eastman aggregate continued to perform a second guest-band set while the judges retired to the back of Stepan Center to deliberate.)

Returning with their verdicts shortly after 2 A.M., the judges left it up to Willis Conover to read off the winners' names. Terming the '75 CJF "one of the most enjoyable festivals" he'd ever attended, Conover went on to declare that it had also been "one of the toughest festivals ever judged."[11] "And believe me," the much-respected jazz broadcaster added, "I don't say that every year."

Because of the unusual excellence of the year's participating collegiate groups, the judges found themselves forced to select six winning bands and combos, four Drum winners, three Best Trumpeters, two Outstanding Reed Soloists, two Best Guitarists, two Best Bassists, and three Best Arranger/Composers, in addition to the other soloist awards. At the top of the heap, however, was Eastman's George Ross, who was selected as the festival's Outstanding Instrumentalist for 1975.

As for the much-awaited judges' jam with Sonny Rollins, Jack DeJohnette, Cecil and Dee Dee Bridgewater, Hubert Laws, Chuck Rainey (the first primarily electric bassist to judge the CJF), and pianist Muhal Richard Abrams (who had driven in from Chicago on Saturday night just for the jam session), it began well into the wee hours of Sunday morning on a somber note with an arrangement of "Amazing Grace" dedicated to the memory of Jim Ward (a CJF staff member who had passed away in January and to whom the festival had been dedicated). Joined by several award-winning student soloists, the professional jazzmen continued on with the jam at length, eventually sending the bleary-eyed crowd home much too close (as had been the case with the two previous Saturday-night judges' jams) to dawn.

1
9
7
6
By 1975–76, jazz education had reached a point of undeniable pervasiveness in school systems across the country. Though still hampered by the same old difficulties, there were "more than 500,000 student musicians participating in jazz-related ensembles and courses supervised by a 'jazz educator.' "[1]

Nearly 4,000 colleges offered at least one jazz course for credit or the opportunity to participate in a jazz ensemble by 1975–76, and—at the most favorable extreme—a few such as the Eastman School of Music, the University of Colorado, the University of Illinois, the University of Miami (Florida), Indiana University, Wesleyan University (Connecticut), and North Texas State University were even tendering post-graduate jazz programs of study.[2] In addition, the role of the professional musician/jazz clinician was clearly established, and, with the gradual improvement in student technical jazz-performance abilities over the years, the top collegiate bands were now, in truth, more often than not, the equals—or betters—of first-rate professional bands.

By 1976, college band arrangements were also, for the most part, top-notch, dynamic, and challenging—the majority written by student band members themselves. In addition, jazz educators were better organized on local and national levels—most conspicuously by the National Association of Jazz Educators (NAJE), which held its first national convention in Chicago in 1974. By the 1970s, honorary university degrees had also begun to trickle down to jazz musicians such as Duke Ellington, Eubie Blake, Herbie Hancock, and others. In addition, yearly elementary, high-school, and college jazz festivals numbered close to 170—many of them originating with the help of *down beat* magazine—and most incorporating the noncompetitive format instituted over the years by the CJF and other festivals.[3] This was obviously a time for jazz education to hold its head high. Or was it? How accepted were the jazz curricula in the college music-education ranks?

Writing about the situation in Leonard Feather and Ira Gitler's *Encyclopedia of Jazz in the 70's*, educator, critic, and *down beat* publisher Charles Suber ventured the position that the impressive jazz-education figures might be a bit deceiving. Citing the fact that few colleges required any sort of jazz course for a degree in music (or, for that matter, jazz teaching competence for a degree in music education), Suber also went on to point out that, despite the gains, "Most colleges—even those with a considerable jazz emphasis—did not consider a jazz ensemble to be a 'major ensemble' like the concert band or orchestra."[4]

In addition, Suber continued, due to "tight budget" constraints and "tenured traditionally oriented faculty," the brunt of jazz teaching at universities was usually borne by one overworked educator. Even more importantly—as Suber viewed it—"jazz education in the schools in the 70's faced a fundamental internal challenge . . . [from the] . . . majority of jazz educators who had relatively little professional experience." "The influence," he continued, "of the contemporary, professional jazz musician—so important to the history of jazz education—had been diluted in the expansion of all those stage bands and jazz programs."

Echoing Suber's insights, Fr. George Wiskirchen wrote in a lengthy November 1975 *Music Educator's Journal* article that "all is not well. We are still not devoting the time and energy required to develop improvisational skills. We are still too deeply enmeshed in pop music."[5]

At Notre Dame, however, while the Collegiate Jazz Festival chairmanship was juggled back and forth before finally finding itself secured in the hands of senior arts-and-letters student Damian Leader, the fifth Midwest Blues Festival kept the blues rambling healthily on. Held once more in Stepan Center in November 1975, the two-day festival poured a well-deserved spotlight on such artists as Blind John Davis, Fenton

Robinson (just released from Joliet prison a few weeks before the MBF), Big Walter Horton, Otis Rush, Martin, Bogan & the Armstrongs, Son Seals, and Albert King (the latter augmented by a four-piece horn section and ever-present triangular-shaped guitar, "Lucille").

Speaking candidly in a *Scholastic* interview the week before the fifth blues blast, MBF coordinator Perry Aberli (now a Notre Dame graduate student) revealed future hopes for "having the artists coming in on Thursday night . . . coming to classes on Friday, talking in Lit classes, Black culture classes, or even some seminars all Friday afternoon. On Saturday, it would be feasible to have meetings with the artists, maybe in LaFortune, similar to the CJF setup. That might start happening next year, or it might not, but ideally that is what we are trying to do."[6]

Continuing the recent Collegiate Jazz Festival tradition of delegating judge-procurement responsibilities to another CJF staff member, Damian Leader tabbed junior management major/South Bend native and '76 CJF cochairman Michael Dillon for the difficult job. Soon, Dillon had rounded up multireedman Joe Farrell, critic Dan Morgenstern (back for his tenth CJF judging year), Chicago band leader/trombonist Dave Remmington, '62 CJF multiple-award-winner/pianist/arranger Bob James, and (after a phone call to the Windy City and the AACM) avant-garde-oriented Art Ensemble of Chicago bassist Malachi Favors, drummer/percussionist Don Moye, and trumpeter Lester Bowie.[7]

A truly diverse group that spanned straightahead bebop, pop, and free-form jazz, the CJF judging panel gathered once more on Friday afternoon—this time in the recital room of the new music building just south of the LaFortune Student Center—for the traditional CJF symposium. Moderated by Father Wiskirchen and Dan Morgenstern, the symposium featured topics ranging from the festival itself to personal careers and the current state of jazz. Eventually, the session broke into "quite a heated debate . . . over whether or not the future of jazz was heading towards a synthesis with rock."[8] "Most of the judges," recalled senior Jim Schwartz in a *Scholastic* piece in early 1977, "resented the identification with rock because to their minds rock is simplistic both in conception and in execution."[9]

Working without the services of judge/emcee Willis Conover for the first time in eight years, the 1976 CJF broke out of the starting gates with Father Wiskirchen's best Notre Dame big band yet, featuring trombonist Nick Talarico on his own arrangement of "Dem Ole Bonehead Blues," and other eye-opening numbers such as Frank Zappa's "Waka Jawaka."[10] One of the festival's two Outstanding Pianists, Alan Gerber, turned up next in a combo from Indiana University called "Moses," only to be followed—in a CJF first—by an Oakland University (Rochester, Michigan) "A-Fram" band featuring tuba soloist Brad Felt, who was later singled out as the festival's Miscellaneous Instrument Award winner.

Appearing as the fourth group of the night was a Notre Dame jazz combo destined to go down in CJF history. Composed of guitarists Bill Boris and Kevin Chandler, pianist Neil Gillespie, and drummer Steve Calonje, the group—in an unheard-of move—started off its set with only Boris and Chandler onstage in a swinging acoustic-guitar jazz duet. Catching judging-panel members and crowd off-guard with mellow, swinging, extended jams on such songs as "Autumn Leaves" and the "Woody Woodpecker" cartoon-show theme, the two musicians eventually went on to win soloist awards for Acoustic Guitars—a category created especially for them by the judges.

One of the few combos to appear at the CJF without the benefit of woodwinds, the Notre Dame combo soon expanded after the duet to include drummer Calonje and pianist Gillespie. Blasting away at the ecstatic, partisan audience with numbers like Chick Corea's "500 Miles High," the four-man group went on to capture "the crowd's as well as the judges' hearts" with Calonje's own dynamic composition, "Asphyxiation."[11] For its brilliant jazz efforts, the Notre Dame combo received one of the festival's Outstanding Group performance awards, thereby becoming the first Notre Dame group to ever win such an award in the eighteen-year history of the university's Collegiate Jazz Festival.[12]

Complete with a truly "tight" saxophone section, the Northwestern University Big Band containing '76 Best Bassist Steve Rodby and '75 Best Reed Soloist Pete Grenier churned on stage next en route to an Outstanding Performance award.[13] Following Northwestern's fine outing was a jazz presentation by yet another Outstanding Performance group, the Fredonia State University Jazz Ensemble led by pianist Emil Palame. During the group's performance, Fredonia's drummer, John Alfieri (selected as one of the 1975 CJF's Best Drummers) added extra drama and professionalism to his school's act by easily covering up the loss of a high-hat cymbal early in the set "with a loose and friendly stage presence."[14]

After the first festival session had ended, the Notre Dame Jazz Band and other student musicians from various colleges headed out to jam at a new downtown South Bend music spot located at 129 North Michigan Street known as Vegetable Buddies. Set to specialize in blues, rock, and local jazz, the rough-wood-paneled restaurant/music emporium (whose owner's lifelong dream was to book rock genius Frank

Zappa) opened its doors to CJF participants on both festival nights and planned to celebrate its grand opening the following week on April 9 with the venerable blues string band of Martin, Bogan & the Armstrongs.

Saturday afternoon found Best Flautist Michael Neal leading a Washtenaw Community College (Ann Arbor, Michigan) Big Band, followed by the Western Michigan Jazz Orchestra, and an Ohio State Jazz Quintet. Finally, Kent State's Big Band (showcasing Best Electric Bassist Gary Aprile) appeared before an MIT Jazz Quintet enthusiastically closed things down.

Saturday evening (the traditional CJF drawing card) played to a full house once more and found the CJF High School Festival-winning aggregates and a Governor's State Big Band (featuring 1976 Outstanding Instrumentalist/Best Saxophonist Earl "Chico" Freeman, Best Vocalist Myran Parker, and Best Arranger Vandy Harris) leading the way. Leaving the stage after a smoking set, Governor's State left little doubt of its claim to one of the year's Outstanding Performance awards.

John Garvey's University of Illinois Big Band also checked in Saturday night with a fine set that included a number laced with entertaining Russian Volga River boatmen's chants. Fifth on the evening's agenda was a hot Chicago State Jazz Combo entitled "Changes" that was supervised by Bunky Green. Thrilling the audience with versions of such songs as Charlie Parker's "Donna Lee," the Chicago State combo walked off with an Outstanding Combo award as well as individual awards for Best Reed Soloist (John Smarzewski), Best Piano (Dean Gant), and Best Bass (Al Keith).[15] Although passed by for Outstanding Band consideration, the Indiana University Big Band directed by 1975 CJF Outstanding Instrumentalist Dr. George Ross also riveted audiences with Ross's own '75 festival hit "Reflections in Ebony," and managed Outstanding Drum and Trombone awards for band members Larry Banks and Flip Miller. Last up on the evening was a Northwestern University combo, led by bassist Steve Rodby and soprano-saxist Pete Grenier.

Invited back in 1976 as a noncompetitive guest band on the basis of its dynamic, award-sweeping CJF '75 performance, the Rayburn Wright-directed Eastman School of Music Jazz Ensemble brought the house down with a special rousing set featuring a number of spotlit guest solos by well-known former Blood, Sweat & Tears trumpeter (and Eastman alumnus) Lew Soloff. Late in the set, judge Joe Farrell ambled over to stage side, opened a small black case, assembled his flute, and strode ever-so-casually up the stage stairs. Waved on by Soloff, Farrell was soon at the microphone taking blistering solos and occasionally trading fours with the bemused trumpeter throughout the remaining band numbers. It was a fitting end to the 18th CJF, which—due to the extreme diversity of musical talents on the judging panel—became the first festival in recent years to run through its entertaining, educational paces without the benefit of a full-fledged judges' jam.

1
9   Although jazz was certainly reaching the much-larger rock masses
       by 1977 via jazz/rock "fusion" artists such as Herbie Hancock,
7   Miles Davis, George Benson, Lonnie Liston Smith, Freddie Hub-
7   bard, Gary Burton, John McLaughlin, Chick Corea, Billy Cobham,
       Joe Farrell, and groups like Blood, Sweat & Tears, Weather Report,
       the Crusaders, Chicago, Dreams, Return to Forever, and many
more, South Bend, Indiana—though harboring acclaimed yearly festivals at the University of Notre Dame dedicated to blues and jazz— still fell far short of "music-mecca" designation.

Attempting to spark renewed campus and community interest in the CJF, 1977 chairman Mike Dillon decided to institute a closing Friday-night judges-only jam. Traditionally, the Saturday-evening music session, with its bands, awards announcements, and judge/student jams had been the primary CJF draw. Bolstered in 1977 by a National Endowment for the Arts grant, however, Dillon determined that the key to increasing both educational benefits and Friday-night crowds lay with the judges themselves.

In recent years, the judges' jam had, without a doubt, become the CJF's top attraction. Unfortunately, it rarely took place at a reasonable hour on Saturday night, and, ordinarily, when it did, few were left awake in Stepan Center to appreciate it fully. By moving the jam to Friday evening and ensuring that it would include the judges alone— a real, professional jam involving seasoned professionals (with, of course, an award-winners' jam to take place in the usual closing Saturday-night spot)—the festival would once again streamline itself and seek to provide the finest educational opportunities for participants and patrons.

Before Mike Dillon could effect such '77 CJF changes, of course, there was a blues festival to soak in and enjoy. Offering what *Living Blues* magazine would term " . . . a moveable feast of Chicago-tinged stylings" that "kept alive the flickering flame of blues festivals in the Midwest,"[1] the Midwest Blues Festival once again took charge of the campus in the fall of 1976. Run by student Bob Kissell (with Notre Dame faculty member Perry Aberli's never-too-far-away advice and assistance), the sixth MBF presented a tantalizing two-night roster of Stepan Center acoustic and electric acts which included Johnny Shines, Magic Slim & The Teardrops, Robert Lockwood, Jr., Sunnyland Slim, Fenton Robinson, Lazy Bill Lucas (who continued to play piano downtown at Vegetable Buddies after the Saturday MBF session until 3 A.M.),[2] and Big Guitar Red, John Wrencher, and Floyd Jones.

(Unfortunately, the event was marred when MBF headliner Albert King was hit "squarely on the head" by a beer bottle tossed by a carried-away member of the crowd during a festival-closing set.[3] As might be expected, King wisely stopped performing and left the stage. Stunning both coordinator Kissell and the enthusiastic crowd—the majority of whom were extraordinarily well-behaved—the "bottle incident" seriously jeopardized the event's future for the following fall.)

For the 19th annual CJF, Mike Dillon tapped into the rich vein of versatile New York City studio-session men and recording artists during his year-long search for judges and eventually came up with a panel consisting of pianist Bob James, drummer Bob Moses, alto-saxophonist David Sanborn, trumpeter Randy Brecker, and bassist Will Lee. Not only was this the youngest panel of judges yet, but it also contained no less than three former CJF award winners in Sanborn (Best Reedman, 1966), Brecker (Best Trumpeter, 1965), and James (Best Pianist/Leader, 1962). In addition, all of the judges were well-versed in current jazz/rock "fusion" modes as well as straightahead bebop and big-band jazz forms. Filling in the gap left by critic Dan Morgenstern (who could not attend in 1977), *down beat* publisher Charles Suber returned to the CJF after a ten-year absence to emcee the jazz proceedings.

Once again presenting twenty-two hours of the best in collegiate jazz at rock-bottom prices,[4] the 1977 CJF opened for the fifth straight year with Fr. George Wiskirchen's Notre Dame Big Band, which cruised enjoyably through Ernie Wilkins' "Slats," as well as other songs such as "Mr. Smoke" (featuring eventual Outstanding Keyboardsman Neil Gillespie), a Nick Talarico-arranged "I'm Glad There Is You," and, last but not least, Jim McNeely's "Spring Song."[5]

After Ohio State's pianist John Emche-led combo had made its way through such intriguingly titled songs as "Porcelain Steakhouse," the predictably unpredictable 41-piece Lanny Steele/Howard Harris-led Texas Southern University Jazz Ensemble amassed itself onstage. Featuring no less than ten saxophones and two vocalists, the band ripped through a TSU multireedman Kirk Whalum number before moving on to Howard Harris's tribute to deceased black jazz artists entitled "A Jazz Memorabilia." "Tribute to Elizabeth" (an original by TSU's lone African student, Richard Asikpo) followed, as did "I Remember Oliver," by CJF '75 Best Composer Horace Young, III, and a Lanny Steele arrangement of "The Song is You." Leaving the stage to a standing ovation, the Texas Southern band easily walked away with an Outstanding Performance award, and reaped individual awards for group members Herbert Perry (Outstanding Trombone), Richard Asikpo (Outstanding Arranger/Composer), Wendell Moore (Outstanding Guitar), and Toni Neely (Outstanding Vocalist). In yet another unprecedented CJF move, the judges also voted unanimously to offer a Best Bass award to the *entire* three-man TSU bass section.

The second standing ovation of the night soon went to another Outstanding Performance award winner, this time a Fredonia State University combo led by pianist Emil Palame featuring the '77 festival's Outstanding Tenor-saxophonist, Gary Keller. Following the supercharged Fredonia group, a Northwestern University Big Band coolly ambled in and mopped up the third 1977 Outstanding Group award. If Texas Southern's entire bass-section award was unprecedented, the sweep Northwestern's bassist Steve Rodby made at CJF '77 was surely the most exciting of all. A senior classical-bass major at Northwestern who juggled Chicago studio bass work and house bass gigs at Joe Segal's Rush Street "Jazz Showcase" with regular classwork, Rodby snared both Electric and Acoustic Bass awards in 1977 en route to becoming the third bassist in CJF history to win the overall Outstanding Instrumentalist award.[6] Clearly, Rodby (who had befriended three young musicians named Pat Metheny, Dan Gottlieb, and Lyle Mays a few years back at Illinois high-school summer music clinics) was a musician on his way.[7]

Last on the Friday-night bill-of-fare, of course, was the muchheralded judges' jam. Beginning at 12:30 A.M., the jam opened with a "soulful, bluesy presentation" by alto-saxophonist David Sanborn, accompanied by Bob James on acoustic piano, Will Lee on electric bass, and Bob Moses on drums.[8] Joined on the second tune by trumpeter/judge Randy Brecker, the judges' surging talents finally coalesced into a juggernaut jazz whole on the jam's third number, an extended instrumental version of Leon Russell's "This Masquerade." Featuring Bob James on a Fender Rhodes electric piano the number was also highlighted by several bits of interwoven alto-saxophone/trumpet play by Sanborn and Brecker. Ending after only 45 minutes because of "technical problems" that included persistent Sanborn saxophone mouthpiece difficulties, the jam, according to *Observer* student-newspaper critic Sean Coughlin, "left the overflow crowd very satisfied, as did the rest of the evening's performance."[9]

Saturday afternoon was highlighted by two more standing ovations offered, respectively, to the Tom Ferguson-led Memphis State University Jazz Ensemble and the Allan Horney-directed Eastern Illinois University Big Band. On a more offbeat, experimental note, the session also included a performance by the University of Iowa "Citizen's Band," a group that emphasized the "percussive and rhythm sections" instead of horns, and which played an "avant-garde progressive" brand of jazz otherwise unbroached at CJF 19.[10]

Saturday evening found the 12th annual CJF High School jazz festival winners taking the stage first. Moved by the performance of the Forest View High School Band (Arlington Heights, Illinois), *Observer* reporter Coughlin noted that, had the group been entered in the CJF, "it would have . . . blown many of the more experienced college bands out of the competition."[11]

On the college side, the Fredonia University Jazz Ensemble moved into view first and soared through student leader Emil Palame's "Martian Shopping Spree," "Call On Me," and "Bigfoot" on the way to a standing ovation as well as eight group and soloist awards (in conjunction with the Fredonia combo). Included in the Fredonia hoard were awards for Outstanding Combo and Band performance, Outstanding Saxophone (Gary Keller), Drums (Bob Leatherbarrow), Trumpet (Mike Kaupa), Keyboards (Palame), Arranger/Composer (Palame), and Honorable Mention Saxophone (Barry McVinney).

Other groups performing at CJF 19 included a Notre Dame Combo (made up of drummer Steve Calonje, pianist Neil Gillespie, guitarist Bill Boris, and bassist Cedric Williams), Herb Pomeroy's MIT Festival Band (featuring one of the '77 CJF's Outstanding Composers in Toru "Tiger" Okoshi), and the University of Notre Dame Greg Shearer/Bill Boris guitar duet. Also showcased were an Outstanding Combo award winner from the Wisconsin Conservatory of Music and the festival's final Outstanding Band Award recipient, the Pat Hollenbeck-led New England Conservatory of Music Medium Rare Big Band. (As for enjoyable CJF oddities, Medium Rare reedman Roland Rizzo received a unanimous miscellaneous award for his vocal impersonation of Louis Armstrong during the band's third song selection.)[12]

While the judges wrangled over the awards decisions in the back room behind Stepan Center's wooden stage, a CJF guest combo from the Eastman School of Music known as Gazelle (comprised of trumpeter Howie Shear, drummer John Alfieri, tenor-saxophonist Bill Kennedy, alto-saxophonist Bob Sheppard, and pianist John Oddo) dazzled the CJF crowd.

Among the plaques handed out late that Saturday night, a special one was offered to Fr. George Wiskirchen for his nineteen years of service as CJF "patron saint and spiritual advisor."[13] Due to the already advanced 3 A.M. hour, the scheduled award-winners' jam was scrapped. It would not appear again; in its place, the traditional postsession Friday and Saturday downtown-club jams would have to suffice.

1
9
7
8
After Mike Dillon's young, progressive '77 judges' panel, it seemed a bit surprising to find CJF '78 chairman/senior accounting major Jim Thomas assembling a more conservative, though just as dynamic and impressive adjudicating group. Composed of the perennial winner in the *down beat* magazine jazz poll, flautist Hubert Laws (back at the CJF for the fourth time), returning critic Dan Morgenstern, premier big-band and combo-drummer Louie Bellson, and pianist/composer/founding Modern Jazz Quartet member John Lewis, the panel was also graced in 1978 by 1960 CJF student musician alumnus/bassist Larry Ridley (currently a professor of jazz at Rutgers University) and saxophonist/flautist Lew Tabackin, who, along with pianist/composer wife Toshiko Akiyoshi had been the cocreator and molten improvisational core of the seventies headline-grabbing Toshiko Akiyoshi/Lew Tabackin Big Band.

Before it was time for collegiate jazz, of course, it was time for the blues. Run for the second year by graduate-psychology-degree-seeking student Bob Kissell, the seventh annual Midwest Blues Festival went decisively national in scope: ads were placed in *Living Blues* magazine, local radio spots were doubled, and all of the scheduled blues performers were lined up by mid-July (a new MBF record). Realizing that big blues names were an essential part of the "national" festival plan, Kissell went out and snagged Little Brother Montgomery, Edith Wilson, Sonny Terry & Brownie McGhee, and Son Seals for Friday-night's performance bill and pianist Big Joe Duskin, Mighty Joe Young, and Muddy Waters for the closing Saturday-night show.

Due to Kissell's efforts, the late '77 MBF—despite a short Muddy Waters set, and a near no-show by a stuck-in-the-snow Mighty Joe Young, as well as assorted microphone troubles and an accidentally tipped-over lighting equipment tree (no harm done)—was both a financial and an artistic success, drawing well both nights and exceeding all gate-receipt hopes. With the extra money, Kissell hoped to put on a one-night mini blues concert in Washington Hall in the spring.[1]

Held once more on Friday afternoon, April 7, 1978, in the Music Building, the '78 CJF colloquium (symposium) presented both the best-dressed and perhaps the most reserved judging panel yet. Low-key and puffing on a pipe that often seemed to be lost in his full beard, Lew Tabackin handled questions about the Akiyoshi/Tabackin band's Far Eastern music influences, and Dan Morgenstern spoke of his origins as a critic. Louie Bellson made particularly emphatic mention of his days with Duke Ellington's band in the fifties, as well as the important definition the Duke once offered him of just what "music" was—namely, "*Mass Unity Sounding In Concert*" (a phrase reiterated for the benefit of the CJF audience that evening by ultra-mellow, deep-voiced

Notre Dame student jazz combo member and '78 CJF emcee Dexter Gourdin).[2]

Friday night's agenda included performances by a University of Iowa combo, the perennial MIT Festival Band, an Ohio State combo, and the Loyola University of New Orleans Big Band, the latter two groups of which received Outstanding Performance awards. (In addition to the combo award, Ohio State combo members John Emche, Randy Mather, and Jim Rupp went on to receive respective Best Piano/Composer, Tenor-Sax, and Drum awards.)

Striding to the stage near midnight for the second annual Friday-night Stepan Center CJF judges' (only) jam, Hubert Laws, John Lewis, Lew Tabackin, Louie Bellson, and Larry Ridley put on a one-hour-plus show, a tour de force that was quickly declared by Dan Morgenstern to be "the best CJF jam yet."[3] Clearly a unified, musical bunch, the judges brought the crowd to its feet numerous times, most notably after an extended, breathtaking Hubert Laws piccolo-flute solo, and a jaw-dropping ten-minute Louie Bellson solo extravaganza. Rarely seen grabbing the solo limelight, Bellson's thunderous, yet immaculate and logical show of improvisational skin-slinging skill was a true delight as he worked from his patented double-bass drums to a row of sound-alterable tom-toms, and then let the solo drumbeat die to a dull pulse, only to churn it back subsequently to dazzling volcanic life.

Larry Ridley eschewed pizzicato-style bass-string plucking technique at one point in the jam and turned to his bass bow to good, chamberlike jazz effect; John Lewis, in natty three-piece suit and with an unusually soft-spoken, gentle manner offered delicate but unerringly on-the-mark chording and light, lithe, meaningful solos; Lew Tabackin — clearly delighted to be in Lewis's company — took a full, rich, outstanding tenor-sax solo on a romantic, moody mid-jam ballad. All in all, it was a stunning, educational, and uplifting display — a one-in-a-million CJF jam.[4]

Appearing Saturday afternoon and night were Outstanding Bands such as Pat Hollenbeck's New England Conservatory of Music Medium Rare Big Band, a Dan Yoder-led University of Iowa Big Band, and the Wisconsin Conservatory's Combo and Band, the latter two of which reaped six '78 CJF awards for Best Band, Outstanding Instrumentalist (Marcus Robinson/piano), Best Acoustic Bassist (Dick Scarpola), Best Guitar (Charles Small), Best Tenor-Sax (Steve Hollivan), Best Drums (Sam Belton), and Best Trombone (Harry Kozlowski).

Another energetic band that managed a Saturday-night standing ovation was the University of Notre Dame combo (made up of pianist Neil Gillespie, tenor-saxman Mike Stalteri, altoist Gerald Lawson, guitarist Greg Shearer, drummer Stu Monsma, and '78 Best Electric Bassist Cedric Williams), which featured a song dedicated to '77 drummer Steve Calonje, who had died tragically in a car accident over Christmas. Although the Notre Dame combo was not selected as an award winner in 1978, the group did find itself on the receiving end of some thoroughly encouraging postperformance critique-sheet remarks by judge Louie Bellson, who termed the combo a "fantastic" group that he would "love to get . . . on record."[5]

"I started out last night keeping my scoring conservative," explained the world-class drummer during the Saturday-night session (which featured a scorching guest-band set by the Bunky Green Quintet during judging deliberations). "But by the end of the show, I was putting stars and plus signs after everybody's name. Tonight I'm up to four and five stars. It's too hard to pick a winner. Everyone's so good—they have to be to be performing at this festival. The talent in universities all over the country is simply astounding." Asked if the big bands might not be involved in yet another renaissance, Bellson quickly replied, "You know what? They never left. Jazz is not dead. You people in the universities, you're bringing it back. You're giving it new life."[6]

"One of the most significant observations I made at the twentieth Collegiate Jazz Festival," noted *Observer* reporter Frank Laurino on the Monday after the event, "was the incredible amount of talent on stage. This is a tribute to the many fine jazz programs at major universities around the country, of course. But, more, it's a tribute to the meaning behind the CJF—the promotion of America's sole claim to musical art. And the CJF does it with class: no hype, no commercialism, just a sincere dedication to providing that special moment when musician and idea and instrument and sound and audience are one. That special moment called jazz."[7]

"The thing about the CJF, however," Laurino continued, "is that there are really no losers. To be good enough to perform in the most prestigious collegiate jazz festival in the country—maybe the world—takes a winner. To meet and talk with some of the renowned jazz greats: that's a victory."

In closing his '78 concert review, Laurino insightfully added: "If there were no such thing as the Cotton Bowl or the NCAA's, if the Golden Dome, Fr. Sorin and St. Rockne were figments of everybody's imagination, let it be known that this university took a stand for art in America. When I speak of Notre Dame, I won't just talk about home football games and pep rallies. I'll talk about the CJF."

It's sort of like treading furiously in a pool of fast dry-
ing cement, pulling out just as it hardens and walking
around on top for two days. —Joe Carey, 1979 CJF
Chairman, Chairman's note, '79 festival program

1
9   How does an undergraduate of sane mind and body end up run-
7   ning the world's foremost collegiate jazz festival? Difficult to say,
9   at best, but as cochairman of the previous year's CJF—the one
          who carries out most of the nitty-gritty, thankless, nuts-and-bolts
          details—it was assumed that, in the natural order of things, I
          would assume the chairmanship of the 1979 event. That was the
usual pattern. Unfortunately, there was little in that '78 staff post that
could have prepared a gangly English major for what was in store.

Running the CJF, as it turned out, was hardly the spontaneous,
toe-tapping joy that the actual event itself had appeared to be. Rather,
it was a year-long obsession, an incessantly demanding mistress who
teased an eager, expectedly naïve, twenty-year-old senior's jazz-
appreciative mind with what each day could—and often did—go wrong.
But it was also an unforgettable experience, a unique opportunity un-
available anywhere else to, in a sense, tap the pulse and core of a music
and a way of life—to feel, for once, on the inside of something important to creativity, art, and jazz.

My own formal music background, like that of most of the CJF
chairmen, was sketchy. Piano lessons as a teenager; an ability to lock
myself away on down days and play a loping—but to me best ever—
blues in the key of C; one struggling early-to-mid-seventies music-
theory course with Roger Mills, then director of the New Trier West
(Northfield, Illinois) high-school jazz program and band, and a fellow
who kept doing amazing things with the students he taught, which
were recognized both locally and nationally. (What I was doing in that
class I'll never know; I was the only nonmusic major there, and the
mere sound of the words "circle of fifths" still sets my head spinning.)

Once at Notre Dame, my brother Bill (then a junior) mentioned
that I should get in touch with a friend of his named Mike Dillon, who
was working on something called the Collegiate Jazz Festival. I hemmed
and hawed awhile, but soon trotted over to Fisher Hall to see Dillon,
who lived in a narrow single room that included a top-notch stereo
with a tall conga to one side (as well as a flute that he was learning
to play) and a mattress on the floor (a habit Dillon had no doubt picked
up during a stay in Japan the previous year in one of the university's
sophomore-year-abroad programs). The thing that really caught my

eye in the room, however, was the collection of albums it contained. It was awesome, extending lengthwise at forehead height from one end of the room to the door – at least a thousand albums – or so I thought. An unbelievable hoard.

We talked about music and the festival, listened to an Oscar Peterson album and some others, and then began to move on to the blues. I knew I liked things with a driving blues beat, but didn't know much about the music. Dillon played a few more albums, let me in on the existence of the upcoming fall Midwest Blues Festival, and wrote down the names of some blues albums to buy. It was all very eye-opening.

In charge of procuring the judges for the jazz festival in 1976, Dillon was in the process of finalizing negotiations with Stan Getz, Bob James, Steve Gadd, and other musicians and mentioned his need for a gofer-type assistant to book airline reservations for the judges, place and pick up ads, etc. He asked me if I'd like to help out. Figuring this was the way to go, I said, "Sure." Then Dillon let something frightening slip, something like, "You know, you could even run the festival next year, if you really wanted to . . . ," as if all that needed to be done was to give my name to the guy in charge. I don't remember exactly what I replied to that, but I got out of there fast.

The blues festival was mind-boggling that year, blankets stretched out everywhere in Stepan Center and a fog of cigarette smoke hanging in the air so thick you felt you could tie a rope around it and haul it home. The festival had the feel, the communal, overwhelming sweat and emotion that no blues record could ever convey. Man, was I a lost blues cause for two consecutive nights! What an instant music education! Within a few weeks I was buying blues albums like mad and trying to mimic Meade Lux Lewis's infectious "Honky Tonk Train Blues" boogie-woogie on piano.

Meanwhile, of course, I was hustling on and off for Mike Dillon and the CJF, which rolled around pretty fast. I recall a cocktail party at the University Faculty Club (next to the Center for Continuing Education building and just across from the Morris Inn on the tree-lined, southern drive up to the Notre Dame campus) where Malachi Favors of the Art Ensemble of Chicago was walking around with a cap pulled down tight on his head, looking friendly but a little out of place. Dillon made sure I shook hands with Favors, Bob James, Dave Remmington, Dan Morgenstern, and, I think, Lester Bowie, too, but it was all such a mysterious blur that it was difficult to remember all that was going on.

Friday night, the judges' jam failed to take place – despite the fact that the judges seemed to be making motions to pull out their instruments to play. (From a close-at-hand view of the stage the Art

Ensemble members of the panel appeared to be a bit argumentative about their music, as well as about the fact that it wasn't compatible with the other judges' brands of jazz.) Saturday afternoon and night were both thoroughly uplifting and exciting, although there was admittedly still so much to learn about in listening to a band (how to key in on soloists and various rhythmic band parts) that, after a number of performances, things once again began to blur.

I recall two distinct moments, though. One: watching Joe Farrell piece together his flute with a bemused nonchalance before joining Lew Soloff and the Eastman School of Music to play on the closing Saturday night. It was so unplanned, so riveting that it blew me away. Two: standing close to the side of the stage as it was announced that the Notre Dame combo and Notre Dame guitarists Bill Boris and Kevin Chandler had won respective Outstanding Performance and Acoustic Guitar awards. As it happened, Boris was my brother's roommate in 1976, so I had dropped by the room not infrequently to hear him practice and had gotten to know him a bit. His smile and totally surprised, disbelieving look as I grabbed his hand and laughed with him when he passed by on his way up to the stage told me a lot about the CJF, and the impact it had on the student musicians. (In addition, Boris achieved his acoustic award feats playing my brother's Guild guitar.)

Returning to Notre Dame in '77–'78 for my junior year after a year of study in Innsbruck, Austria, I was surprised one fall day by a call from a fellow named Jim Thomas, who identified himself as chairman of the Collegiate Jazz Festival. Thomas casually mentioned that '77 chairman Mike Dillon had offered him my name as someone to get in touch with for festival help. Out of the blue Thomas asked me to be cochairman for the '78 festival. Would I?!! I was flabbergasted. Mike Dillon, who didn't owe me a thing, had made good on his promise to keep my name in the festival fold. (I should have known he had something up his sleeve when I received a copy of the '77 CJF program in the Innsbruck mail and found myself listed among CJF staff members as a "foreign correspondent.")

Working with Jim Thomas in '78 was a learning experience. Jim had only been prizes chairman the year before, and I hadn't even been on campus, so we were both feeling our way along. But, while doing all the "inside" work (organizing the staff, working on publicity, advertising, and the CJF program; making all sorts of nuts-and-bolts calls and arrangements), I began to envy his "outside" position—the glamor spot, I thought, the one who contacted all the judges, talked to both the big names in jazz and the collegiate band directors, and shaped the year's event according to his own inner plan. Jim Thomas held a mysterious, intriguing connection to the world of jazz. He held all the cards. He was the lifeline, the mastermind of the '78 CJF.

Jim and I usually communicated by phone about festival details, often well after midnight due to our equally eccentric schedules. At times, however, in the months just preceding the '78 festival, when the CJF pressure cooker was really beginning to turn on its round-the-clock heat (it actually extended year-round), the phone often became more of an enemy than a friend, and more than once I resorted to shoving it angrily into a desk drawer to muffle its incessant ring and get some sleep.

I honestly doubt that anyone who hadn't been involved with the event could understand the day-to-day intensity necessary to organize a sprawling festival like the CJF with a small volunteer student staff, no office, no secretary, incredibly limited funds, and a not-a-little-frightening past reputation to live up to. Perhaps even we didn't quite understand; if we had, most of us might have thrown up our hands and given our respective jobs a quick heave. The pressure was just that intense.

Thomas, as I recall, was initially interested in obtaining the services of bassist Charlie Mingus and singer/songwriter Stevie Wonder for the '78 judging panel. Mingus was open to the idea at first but his health had deteriorated a bit by that point; as for Wonder, after some negotiation, his agent eventually balked, citing the multitudinous safety precautions necessary for the sightless artist to attend the festival.

For one reason or another, then, both potential judges fell through. Otherwise, in what appeared to be short order, Jim lined up Dan Morgenstern, Hubert Laws, Lew Tabackin, John Lewis, Larry Ridley, and Louis Bellson for the '78 judging panel.

Fortunately, the '78 festival itself was worth all the work. All the judges were immaculate dressers and gentlemen to the core. Bellson, in particular, stands out in my memory as a truly humane, genuine artist—perhaps only because I had the chance to talk to him a bit more after the traditional Friday-afternoon symposium. Embarking on a quick tour of the campus, Louie and I eventually ended up at Stepan Center in order to set up his drums for the judges' jam. The setup itself lasted about an hour and, at times, it seemed that even he—drummer extraordinaire—was baffled by some of the extensive drum hardware Ludwig had shipped along for the judges' jam. During the hour or two we spent together we talked about Pearl Bailey (his wife of many years) and her return to school to study French and religion. Louie thought that was just great. He also spoke of the rigorous physical regimen he adhered to in order to keep himself in top shape for gigs; jogging

five miles a day, eating certain foods, meditating, etc. In a totally seasoned, well-traveled professional's way, Louie also had a knack in the
few hours we spent together of remembering my first name and using
it in a warm, personal way, as if he'd known me for years.

The '78 jam was unforgettable. I also remember driving Hubert
Laws, Lew Tabackin, and John Lewis around campus with Tabackin
trying to pin Lewis down to a return engagement in the future, or the
time Hubert Laws threatened forcefully to wrest away the wheel of
the car I was driving after the Friday-night jam (we had gone the wrong
way and been stymied by a locked gate). Due to my unfamiliarity with
a stick shift, the car kept dying as I tried to reverse our direction in
the tight, cement-embanked road space. Frustrated and tired, Laws
finally suggested that I simply head over the five-inch curb and drive
down the sidewalk back toward Stepan Center. I hadn't thought of
that, but subsequently followed his advice, and got the judging car
back to the Morris Inn in good shape.

Other memories include Dan Morgenstern's lovely, ever-patient
wife Ellie and their nuclear-powered young son Adam running around
the Morris Inn lobby; Hubert Laws inquiring about male/female relationships at Notre Dame on the way to the airport and offering kind,
fatherly advice after my somewhat unencouraging reply: "Just get your
profession down. Once you get that down, then the women will come
around . . . "; being told, "You're in charge now" by Jim Thomas as
he took the judges into the room behind the Stepan Center stage to
select festival winners. (In charge? Who wanted to be in charge out
in Stepan Center? How I would have given my right arm to be in the
room itself, listening to what went on behind closed doors instead of
out there "in charge"!); lastly, Hubert Laws and Lew Tabackin performing classical-flute exercise duets—Tabackin on a 14-carat-gold
model flute—in a room at the Morris Inn for well over an hour after
breakfast Saturday morning to a slack-jawed audience of three, including me.

Tabackin's flute, I recall, was much breathier, Laws's more slick
and smooth. Clearly, they both got a kick out of working through the
exercise books. I'd never had such a direct, powerful, and thrilling
musical experience. It seemed at the time as if it wasn't really happening. Memories like that floated you along, made you want to do anything for the festival, even go through the year-long hellhole of hassles
and start from scratch again the next year.

As it turned out, that's exactly what happened.

The job of chairman had fallen to me in '78-'79 (as it had, I'm
sure, to so many others) by way of chance, friends, and some previous

festival experience. There were undoubtedly others on campus with
a vaster knowledge of jazz, others with greater organizational skill,
business acumen, or musical ability, but somehow, the responsibility
had fallen my way. Jim Thomas handed over to me the cardboard box
containing folders with CJF odds and ends, a few old programs, a '78
budget, guidelines and forms for band applications, and a small, grey
tin box filled with 3 x 5 index cards containing the names and numbers
of numerous jazz musicians, educators, and critics. That tin box *was*
the CJF. That box was really all I had to go on. That, and longtime
festival advisers like Father Wiskirchen and Dan Morgenstern. I had
been closely involved with the festival for a full year, knew some of
its ins and outs, and, yet, in reality had no firm idea of how to run
the event at all. Perhaps no CJF chairman or woman had (excluding,
of course, the two rare individuals in the past who had run the event
a second year). How quickly, though, you find things out.

It was a crazy year all right, crazier, I'd like (and would hope)
to think than most other CJF years. Naturally, I began, (as did, I'm
sure, every other CJF head) by revamping the index-card file of judges'
names, which seemed to be full of outdated numbers and addresses.
Many of the address cards, though precious artifacts, were practically
obliterated with the comments of past CJF chairmen about contact results, whom to call, why so-and-so could or couldn't attend in '72, '74,
'76—and whom to stay away from. Trying to expand the lists, I began
to pester Musicians Union 802 in New York City for various numbers
over a week-long period. As only two numbers could be released at
a given time, I began calling four or five times a day until the union's
telephone operator finally got so exasperated she mailed me the entire book of musicians' phone numbers and addresses.

During the summer of 1978, I also began what would become a
year-long habit: making lists of potential CJF judges. Some of the early
ones included such grandiose pipe-dream panel members as:

Kenny Clarke		Oscar Peterson		Miles Davis
Dave Brubeck		George Benson		Red Garland
Jim Hall	-or-	Ray Brown	-or-	Philly Joe Jones
Percy Heath		Max Roach		Buddy DeFranco
Jean-Luc Ponty		Joe Venuti		Richard Davis

	Ron Carter		Ron Carter
	Dave Brubeck		Joe Sample
-or-	Philly Joe Jones	-or-	Stanley Turrentine
	Stanley Turrentine		Billy Cobham
	Noel Pointer		Joe Kennedy

The permutations were endless and all—seemingly—beyond reach. Feeling the need for a guide of some sort through the morass of names, I bought a horde of jazz history books, devoured them and began calling the biggest, most revered names I could find.

At first, however, I was really just too petrified to even think of ringing up any revered jazz personality with my trusty Student Union/ CJF billing number, but, eventually, I worked up the nerve to call my first potential judge, legendary drummer Max Roach, at his Connecticut home. To my complete surprise, Roach bought the whole stumbling festival story I offered and agreed to attend. On a roll, I tried to track down violinist Stephane Grappelli (initially through Dino De-Laurentis Films on the West Coast because Grappelli was then recording the soundtrack for the DeLaurentis movie, *King of the Gypsies*) and pursued pianist Oscar Peterson and guitar virtuoso Joe Pass with abandon. Eventually, I got ahold of bassist Ron Carter's number, talked up a storm, and he, too, agreed to come. It was incredible—midsummer, and I already had Max Roach and Ron Carter in the bag, with Grappelli, Pass, and Peterson, I was sure, next in line. A dream band that would surely blow the CJF audience away!

It was, however, not to be.

After six months of negotiations, Max Roach dropped out in January 1979 for various reasons, thereby following the lead of Ron Carter who had backed out just before Christmas. Stephane Grappelli was committed for awhile after four or five months of phone calls to his New York agent but then suddenly demurred, with elegantly lettered thanks for the invitation. As for Oscar Peterson and guitar-wizard Joe Pass, they remained unreachable enigmas most of the year. I even tried to track down octogenarian violinist Joe Venuti, but he was ill and soon to leave the world of jazz altogether. (Along these lines, alto-saxophonist Paul Desmond, the musician I would have done anything to snag for the CJF, had defeated my efforts before I'd even had a chance by sadly passing away the year before.) It was a learning experience.

En route to CJF '79, however, there were many, many delightful moments that fall to few collegiate folk. I spoke to Dizzy Gillespie while he watched his favorite soap opera, "As the World Turns"; Bill Evans and his unusually protective manager Helen Keane; Pablo Records head Norman Granz (who told me once after a morning call somehow got through to him at his California office, "Not to call so early again"); Benny Carter (just emerging from the shower); Orrin Keepnews, J. J. Johnson, George Avakian, Jack Whittemore, Carl Jefferson, Larry Ridley, Marian McPartland, Chicago "Jazz Showcase" owner Joe Segal, San Francisco/Keystone Korner owner Todd Barkan, and Father O'Brien—

manager to piano great Mary Lou Williams. (Unfortunately, though I thought the famed pianist's strong religious affiliations and the lure of Notre Dame would win her over, Father O'Brien was only interested in larger projects for his client. And what is more, Mary Lou was somewhat ill.)

During the year, I also made efforts to contact Gary Burton, Dave Brubeck, Herb Ellis, Keith Jarrett, Kenny Burrell, Elvin Jones, George Benson, Jaco Pastorius, Benny Goodman, Joe Zawinul, Wayne Shorter, Tony Williams, Jim Hall, Roy Eldridge, Herbie Hancock, Freddie Hubbard, and a hundred more. I even wrote to Danish bass-sensation Niels-Henning Orsted Pedersen, and expatriot tenor-sax greats Johnny Griffin and Dexter Gordon at European addresses, offering to fly them in to the CJF from any European locale.

Despite the initial judging-panel cancellations, however, things suddenly began to look up. Dan Morgenstern had, as usual, agreed to come and continued to offer essential advice and information whenever it was needed from his East Coast Rutgers University Institute of Jazz Studies office. Clarinetist Buddy DeFranco, listed in one jazz text as "a largely forgotten man," was tracked down at an obscure Florida club and also agreed to attend. Wakened one Sunday morning to pick up the phone and do an instant, though drowsy, CJF song and dance, I also convinced bassist Richard Davis to attend. (Davis had received a letter describing the festival and its educational efforts the week before.)

Finally, in early 1979 the ice broke, and negotiations with tenor-saxophonist Stanley Turrentine's agent Richard Carpenter succeeded. The following day, a phone call to legendary drummer Philly Joe Jones at his Philadelphia (where else?) address resulted in yet another affirmative answer. Soon a letter from pianist/composer Toshiko Akiyoshi's agent bearing additional good news arrived from Los Angeles.

Philly Joe Jones, Buddy DeFranco, Richard Davis, Toshiko Akiyoshi, Stanley Turrentine, Dan Morgenstern. Perhaps there was hope after all. Still, the whole judging panel assembly process gnawed at me incessantly. Too many prospects had canceled out already, and they were so important to the festival. Perhaps too important.

The judges' jam was the big event these days and, in a real sense, it was the ultimate reflection of the chairman's efforts that year. Not only did the judges have to fit into the bass/piano/percussion/brass/critic categories necessary to ensure appropriate, balanced student band and combo critiques, but their respective jazz-playing styles had to be compatible in order to play as a unit during the judges' jam as well. In choosing the judges for the '79 CJF, I had hoped to highlight neglected instruments such as violin and clarinet. For educational reasons, I also tried to select musicians whose collective experience encompassed the entire spectrum of jazz: big band, bebop, fusion, swing, etc. Lastly, I hoped to turn the spotlight a bit on women in jazz and with the recent addition of Toshiko Akiyoshi to the judging panel, this final goal seemed to be well within reach. Each chairman, I guess, wants to do things in his or her own way and leave an imprint while benefiting the bands and the audience in the most extensive way possible.

Working along the lines of expanding festival horizons, I also began to dig into CJF history for a historical '79 program piece, carting weighty, bound year-by-year volumes of the Notre Dame *Scholastic* from the publication's second-floor LaFortune Student Center offices to my room in the Old Fieldhouse (where I resided in '78–79 as live-in custodian) in order to leaf through each volume slowly and xerox old CJF articles and reviews. (At one point, the *Scholastic* volumes had grown so high that people entering the room didn't realize I was there, hidden behind the stacks piled in front of a beat-up couch.) In addition I also sought to land a name emcee who could add both education and entertainment to the festival. An offbeat list of potential emcee names early in the year included Robert Klein, Bill Cosby, Dick Cavett, Martin Mull, and, of course, jazz-enthusiast Woody Allen. Calls were placed to Michael's Pub in New York (where Allen played clarinet each week), but the comedian/filmmaker remained elusive. Dick Cavett's New York office responded to my letters in December, expressing Cavett's thanks for the CJF invitation, but mentioning that his schedule was full for the spring. Finally, a California lead was established in January 1979 with Tim Hauser, founder/member of the internationally popular/vocalese-oriented group known as the Manhattan Transfer.

A perpetual nostalgia buff, I had been an admirer of the Transfer since their debut album and CBS-television miniseries in 1976. In addition, I'd caught the group live twice—once in Chicago in 1976 and again in London in 1978 while traveling between semesters during my sophomore year abroad. The dazzling, brilliantly choreographed London show had evidenced a quantum leap in the Transfer's maturity and direction. Needless to say, snagging Tim Hauser and his Transfer talent and aura was something I'd had in mind for a long time. Better still, it also added a vocal/educational dimension to the CJF.

In other areas, contact was also made with Tim Owens, producer of the critically acclaimed National Public Radio series "Jazz Alive!" in the hopes of securing a future festival broadcast on NPR. An extensive proposal was also sent to WTTW (Chicago's highly regarded public-television station) for possible television broadcast of the festival.

(WTTW eventually considered the proposal but turned it down in January because of the distance to South Bend.)

(In 1978–79, another television lead also arose and vanished mysteriously via a series of intriguing conversations with Notre Dame alumnus/trustee John Schneider, then a high-ranking CBS vice president. During the year, Schneider heard my CJF story and mentioned that he had been hoping to broadcast the Collegiate Jazz Festival on CBS for several years. After a number of phone calls, Schneider promised he would continue to "work on the idea" and get back to me. I never heard from him again.)

During the summer of '78, I'd also seen a number of historical jazz films shown at the Chicago Public Library by Delmark Records founder and Chicago Jazz Record Mart-owner Bob Koester. Figuring that the educational aspect of the event could be greatly enhanced by such a visual jazz presentation, I made initial contact with Koester, but later stumbled across the world's foremost collector and presenter of jazz films, Dave Chertok. Borrowing some money from another wing of the Notre Dame Student Government Cultural Arts Commission, I booked Chertok into Washington Hall the week of the CJF. (To reserve a hall—or Stepan Center, for that matter—on campus, you had to wend your way through the curling subterranean passageways below the Center for Continuing Education in order to find the calendar office and fight with the folks there for a locale and date that wasn't booked up through 1995.)

Figuring that CJF audiences should be exposed to as many types of jazz as possible, I also tried (at Father Wiskirchen's suggestion) to reunite the Memphis Nighthawks, a popular Midwest dixieland/traditional band made up of ex-Illinois tenor-man and CJF award-winner Ron Dewar, local Chicago trumpeter Steve Jensen and several other talented musicians—to no avail. After some additional brainstorming I then got in touch with world-class country-swing/jazz mandolinist Jethro Burns in Chicago, a musician over whom I had gone wild on recent albums put out by legendary Chicago folksinger Steve Goodman in the mid-to-late seventies.

During my freshman year at Notre Dame, Goodman and Burns had turned up for an unforgettable Stepan Center concert that ended with the two musicians jamming around on yuletide carols such as "White Christmas" on electric guitars. As it turned out, Burns—one-half of the famed country-music/humor duo known as Homer and Jethro until partner Henry (Homer) Haynes's untimely death in 1970—was scheduled to put out a straightahead, swinging jazz album in 1979. Produced by well-known mandolinist David Grisman, the album, "Back to Back," would feature electric mandolinist Tiny Moore, bassist Ray Brown, and drummer Shelly Manne. Tickled to death to be able to gather up some Chicago musicians and jam away at the CJF as the Saturday-night closing guest-band act, Jethro responded to my invitation with an immediate affirmative reply.

Do most festival organizers try to bring in performers they'd like most to meet? I know I did. I wanted to meet Jethro Burns, Tim Hauser, Stanley Turrentine, Philly Joe Jones, and the rest. I also wanted to talk to men who had played with Charlie Parker, John Coltrane, Miles Davis, and the greats and present them to CJF audiences.

(Strangely, it was also an offbeat dream of mine to corral folk-singer James Taylor—a crafty, jazz, gospel and rhythm and blues-conscious musician—for the judging panel. Though such a development never came to pass, I felt an affinity of sorts with Taylor when I discovered that '79 judge Richard Davis had once played on a Carly Simon album. Simon, of course, was married to Taylor at the time.)

Somewhat sadly, Toshiko Akiyoshi wrote in February 1979 to say that an unexpected commitment had come up and she couldn't attend. With that lettter both the panel and my idealistic hopes to focus on women in jazz were back to square one. Trying to replace Toshiko, I went after Dave Brubeck, but found his agent fearing for his aging client's ailing back (Brubeck was recuperating in the Caribbean at the time). In addition I made attempts to get ahold of pianist Red Garland through Todd Barkan (owner of San Francisco's Keystone Korner jazz club).

Finally, because I had long been a fan of the funk/jazz/fusion giants known as the Crusaders (and, it seemed, couldn't play enough of their infectious music on a weekly, Friday-night, midnight-to-3 A.M. WSND-FM student jazz radio show of mine that I was sure no one ever listened to), I took a shot at snagging electric/acoustic keyboard wizard and Crusaders cofounder Joe Sample. Oddly enough, I never talked to Sample once during the four-month negotiation period. Instead, I dealt exclusively with his agents at the Greif-Garris Agency in Los Angeles. Why I pursued this far-fetched Crusaders lead, I'll never know. But I called four or five times a week (sometimes even a day) and wrote numerous letters for months. Finally, a glimmering of light appeared at the end of the tunnel. Sample could attend in 1979 because of a break in a Crusaders tour. When word of Sample's acceptance arrived, it was mid-March, with the festival barely two or three weeks away. For once, things seemed fairly firmed up—or so I naïvely thought.

Two weeks before the '79 festival, deep trouble in the judging panel began to brew with Stanley Turrentine and his agent. Without a doubt, Turrentine was the musician I wanted most, the judge who would knock the audience out during the jam and give the collegiate students and bands a thrill. Turrentine had that hard-booting, full-bodied tenor-horn sound that couldn't miss. He had also committed to attending the festival four months previously, and until this point negotiations had proceeded in an amicable, trouble-free manner. But now his agent would make me pay dearly for believing in such commitments. Now, of all times, with the festival only a few days away.

Wondering why there had been such a sudden shift in Turrentine's commitment, I placed several calls and determined that one of the worst possible situations had evolved: there was some sort of record-company contract trouble with Turrentine and a possible lawsuit somewhere in the works. Suddenly, the musician's agent refused to take my calls (occasionally the agent would answer—it was hard to miss his gruff, brusque voice—and ask who was calling; upon determining it was I, he would then explain that the fellow I was seeking "was not in"). To complicate matters further, Turrentine changed telephone numbers and went into seclusion.

Sensing the CJF dream band was going down the tubes, I knew I had to act fast. Unfortunately, it was now too late to contact many other artists. I felt hung out to dry, devastated, and at a loss. I had been foolish to believe that someone's word was his honest bond.[1]

Suddenly, there still seemed to be a ray of hope. Somehow, I wrangled Turrentine's new number, talked to the artist again, and found him to be Mr. Peacefulness-and-Light, supercool, amiable, and, most importantly, still sure he was coming to the CJF. We talked awhile, and I even told him we would stock his favorite liqueur, Courvoisier, and reminded him to bring his horn for the judges' jam. Talking to Stanley Turrentine, however, was one thing, and talking to his agent quite another.

Turrentine's agent brushed off my final phone calls, telegrams, and mailgrams full of flight confirmations, and finally crushed the last of my young, idealistic hopes on the phone one night about ten o'clock—the first time I had been able to reach him in days and barely a week before the festival. Angrily chewing me out for catching him just about to go to bed—the agent emphatically explained that, no, Stanley couldn't attend the CJF because, of all disturbing things, the festival "was on his [Turrentine's] birthday." His birthday? He couldn't come because it was his birthday? What kind of excuse was that?

I felt set up and knocked down flat. Worse yet, Dan Morgenstern—my CJF ace-in-the-hole and the man who had missed only one CJF

in ten years—had notified me a few weeks earlier that due to a conflicting music conference he also would have to bypass the 1979 festival.
In one fell swoop two major festival cogs had been suddenly removed.

    (On an even more saddening note, fusion-drum giant Billy Cob-
ham called me early on a late-March Sunday morning to say he'd just
received my letter—sent months ago—and wanted to come to the '79
CJF because he was deeply interested in what we were doing and in
the educational side of jazz. In what was the most difficult, agonizing
decision of the year, I told Billy Cobham—whose representatives at a
large New York booking agency had practically laughed me out of town
a few months back during my initial contact attempt, saying the money
I offered wasn't nearly enough and that there wasn't a chance Cobham
would ever attend—that I had already received a commitment from
Philly Joe Jones and couldn't afford to invite a second drummer. Boy,
was he one sad musician. Here I was, losing judges left and right,
forced—because I had given my word to Jones—to turn down a high-
powered star like Billy Cobham.)

    Dan Morgenstern, however, knew of my Turrentine bind and of-
fered to help while I worked out last ditch, "man-going-down-for-the-
last-time" calls to anybody, anywhere: J. J. Johnson, Blue Mitchell,
Leonard Feather. Help! After leaving some frantic messages with Morgenstern's answering service, Dan stepped into the void and offered
the name of Fantasy Records-producer Orrin Keepnews, whom he
thought might be able to help. Within minutes, I was on the phone
to Keepnews and in the midst of a good, long, recuperative talk. Listening in disbelief as he filled me in on Turrentine's agent and the situation at hand, Keepnews then had a few things to say. Sensing the
precariousness of my problem, Keepnews generously offered me the
Florida telephone number of legendary cornetist Nat Adderley, whom
he knew to be on vacation at that time.

    Whether someone got to Nat first to explain the story or not, I'll
never know, but he was so receptive to the judging idea on incredibly
short notice that I nearly dropped the phone. Within a matter of
minutes, Nat Adderley was coming to the '79 CJF. Flush with this last-
minute windfall, I called Father Wiskirchen late that night and told
him I'd gotten Nat, whom Father himself had suggested offhand as
the judging panel's perfect complement just the other day. In his laconic,
gruff-but-well-meaning way, Father George gave his approval of the
impressive juggling feat I had just accomplished. Then he chuckled
diabolically, and said, "Well, that's great. Now all you have to worry
about is the airline strike."

    Airline strike? I had read of it approaching, but no, it would never take place this week, the week of the CJF. With all the judges' tickets already booked and forwarded to California, Pennsylvania, Florida, and Wisconsin how could anything that brutal happen now? I looked over the judges' reservations and noted that most were scheduled to fly into South Bend on United Airlines. Picking up that day's newspaper, I slowly read the numbing news: it was none other than United Airlines that was going on strike.

That was it. I knew it was over. A CJF without judges. Why was this happening? It didn't make any sense. I was just a kid trying to organize something way beyond my control and nothing—Nothing— was going right. Trying to hang onto the last thread I had, I spent the next three or four hours rearranging the judges' flights—all barely a week before they were scheduled to arrive. Mailgrams with new flight times went out that night to all of the judges—even Stanley Turrentine (for whom, I noted in the mailgram, I would keep a ticket waiting in his name at New York's LaGuardia airport until the festival began on April 6).

As might be expected, the 1979 CJF jazz week itself did not begin as planned. By now, however, that was par for the course. Scheduled to kick things off Tuesday, April 3 in venerable Washington Hall, jazz film collector Dave Chertok (whose fight had also been rearranged at the last minute) got as far as Chicago on the afternoon of the appointed presentation day. Unfortunately, a horrendous rainstorm had swept over Chicago the day before and continued to rage. As a result, the world's busiest airport, O'Hare International, had been forced to shut down, leaving Dave Chertok without a connecting flight to South Bend.

Somehow, my parents, who lived in Chicago, got wind of Chertok's predicament and, with saintlike speed, picked him up at the airport and sped off through the rain-slashed night for South Bend. The driving was abominable and slow, and I sat facing a scattered evening crowd at Washington Hall, giving progress reports as the scheduled film-showing time rolled by. How my folks did it is hard to say, but Dave Chertok, clutching his films and clearly the worse for wear, finally made it to the podium forty-five minutes late. I scrambled my way through the introduction and then hustled Chertok's film canisters up to the projection booth, taking quick looks at the understandably dwindled audience as I did so. However many there were in attendance, though, they were all in for a rare treat as Chertok rolled priceless hours of film of Thelonious Monk, Billie Holiday, Charlie Parker, Louis Armstrong, Dizzy Gillespie, Count Basie, and more. In short, it was an expertly narrated visual feast of jazz history.

Buddy DeFranco (an old pro hoping to rest a day before the CJF) was the first judge to arrive, coming in on Wednesday, April 4. His early arrival gave me a chance to have a few meals with him alone and talk about the festival and jazz in general. In his leisure suits and straight, oddly un-hip manner, DeFranco surprised me a bit, but his memories were certainly worth their musical salt. In particular, DeFranco made mention of several gigs with Charlie Parker and of walking through the streets of New York somewhere with Bird before one night's performance.

"We passed by a Salvation Army Band, you know, beat up trumpets, horns, and drums, just playing away," he explained, "and I didn't give it a second thought, but Charlie suddenly had to go back; he had to hear that band. So we stood there for about a half an hour, just listening. And you know, that night on the stand, while listening to Bird solo, I suddenly realized he was playing a fragment that the Salvation Army Band had played!"

DeFranco spoke too (raising his thick bushy eyebrows from time to time) of his Norman Granz-organized head-to-head meeting with keyboard phenom Art Tatum in the fifties,[2] a recording I had come across that year and thought out-of-this-world. "If only I could do it with Tatum again," mused the brilliant but too often neglected clarinetist over a Morris Inn meal. "I didn't have any idea what Art was up to then harmonically. Now I think I do. I wish I could have that chance."

After most meals I left DeFranco to practice alone in his room. By my clock, he put in at least two hours a day on his instrument—amazing for a jazzman in his mid-fifties—each time assembling his clarinet from a custom-designed businessman's type briefcase. So seemingly straight and yet so dedicated to jazz. While many might have written DeFranco off as a "forgotten man," I knew in those moments I was somehow glad he had come because deep down beneath the odd attire and dedicated air, DeFranco—leisure suits and all—had heart.

Philly Joe Jones and Nat Adderley arrived in Chicago on Thursday, April 5, but, due to the weather and O'Hare airport's continued shutdown, they had to be picked up and driven to South Bend. The storm, however, seemed to be abating. Somehow, Joe Sample and the Manhattan Transfer's Tim Hauser managed to get into Chicago from Los Angeles and catch a scheduled connecting flight to South Bend without trouble. But when I picked them both up at the Michiana airport, neither musician's luggage had arrived.

Back at the Morris Inn, I met up with Nat Adderley, who was dressed in his own inimitable way in a lambswool Marlboro Man jacket and Texas-size ten-gallon hat. Nat quickly directed me to Philly Joe

Jones, who was presently over in the Morris Inn bar. I almost didn't recognize the legendary drummer at first (personalities often look so different up close), but there he was, resplendent in dark sunglasses, wrist and neck jewelry, and a sharp, perfectly tailored double-breasted suit. The drummer casually sipped a cool-looking drink at a small table by the wall and glanced across the table momentarily at his companion, Father Wiskirchen, who was puffing happily away on a cigarette and ogling Philly Joe. A gentleman through and through with an unmistakable aura of the ultra-cool, Philly Joe Jones had a surprisingly light, gentle handshake for such a powerful, slashing drummer.

Heading out for a small off-campus CJF staff party held on Notre Dame Avenue, the now-ravenous judges were soon on their way to a dinner at Captain Alexander's, a large, comfortable restaurant located on the St. Joe River in downtown South Bend. Tucked into a far corner of one room, the after-dinner stories that emerged were as delectable as the food and ranged from DeFranco's tales of his year in Count Basie's '51 septet to hilarious tales exchanged by Nat, Philly Joe, Tim Hauser, and Joe Sample about being held at one time or another at gunpoint after performances by various shady characters. Philly Joe also told some risqué stories of his days in the famed mid-fifties Miles Davis quintet. Later that evening, Tim Hauser vigorously plied Philly Joe with questions about which singer he had enjoyed playing behind the most, finally getting the famed skin-slinger to shake his head reluctantly and say, "Sarah, it had to be Sarah [Vaughan]."

Late in the meal, CJF '79 production chairman Stan Huddleston appeared. Stan had kindly consented to pick up bassist Richard Davis at the Michiana airport and bring him back to the restaurant so that Davis and he could eat, but after introductions to all the judges, it quickly became apparent that Stan was alone. "Davis didn't come in," he explained slowly. "Because of the weather, all flights from Chicago were canceled." Once more, things had been rolling forward enjoyably only to grind to a halt.

What could we do now? We had no idea where Davis (who taught at the University of Wisconsin, and was flying in through Chicago from Madison) presently was. I knew the bassist had wanted badly to come and see Philly Joe and the rest of the judges but, faced with such obstacles, he was sure to head back home. The '79 CJF—and the jam— would have to go on without a bassist. (A talented equestrian, Davis had also requested that we track down a stable where he could ride in off-festival hours; with his sudden absence, however that assignment was shot, too.)

We took the judges back to the Morris Inn and then, at a late, tired hour, parted company. I headed for my Fieldhouse room and made as many calls as I could, trying to track Davis down in Chicago. It was hopeless. I gave up at 2 A.M.and went to bed. At 3:45 A.M. the phone rang. A familiar voice spoke out. "Joe? This is Richard Davis. I took a bus from Chicago to South Bend and managed to get over to a hotel lobby here downtown. Could you pick me up?" Could I pick him up? I threw on some clothes and a coat and, in complete disarray, ran out to one of the CJF cars (loaned to us in return for a program ad once more by the kind folks at downtown South Bend's Gates Chevrolet) parked (by virtue of special campus car pass) just outside the Fieldhouse and spun out of the campus, rubbing the tiredness out of my eyes. Totally out of sorts and somewhat unsure of where the hotel was, I mistakenly drove toward Michigan for awhile, but finally turned back and arrived at the hotel a little after 4 A.M. Richard Davis wasn't hard to recognize. Wearing a wide-brimmed, flat-topped Mexican hat and a woven gray poncho, he stood—unmistakably—inside the glass doors of the hotel lobby holding a cloth-covered upright bass. El Hombre himself. Without the beard I'd seen on so many album covers, Davis seemed older, smaller, less intense. We shook hands, loaded his bass into the rear of the station wagon, and drove back to the Morris Inn. I carried the bass to Davis's room and left him, all smiles, Mexican hat still in place, watching television at 5 A.M.

During the week leading up to the festival, other strange things had begun to happen. Suddenly, I was deluged by musicians who wanted to come to the festival. Trumpeter Freddie Hubbard's agent called and mentioned that the musician had read my letter of many months previously and now wanted to attend. Though tempted, I quickly realized there was no way the CJF could afford another artist and airfare. Besides, with the ongoing airline strike, reservations were nearly impossible to make. So I turned down Freddie Hubbard, explaining that we already had a commitment from Nat Adderley. Next Tony Williams's agent called expressing the well-known drummer's interest in coming. Again, I had to say no, Philly Joe Jones is attending, but please keep us in mind for the next year. Why, why, I kept muttering to myself, couldn't these guys have called a while back?

Sometime during that same week—I don't recall exactly when—a call also came through from someone I'd never heard of, someone who identified himself as Dan Henkin, former owner of the Gemeinhardt Flute Co. and a resident of Elkhart, Indiana (roughly twenty-five minutes east of South Bend). Henkin had a bubbling way of talking—although making perfect sense—and I wondered to myself at first what the hell he wanted. "Come out to my house for lunch Friday," he said to me, "Buddy DeFranco's an old friend. Bring the other judges, too, and whoever else you want." Why did I agree? I had no time for this luncheon. But I told Henkin fine, we'll come. Calling the judges on Friday morning from the Morris Inn front desk, I determined which ones would like to go. For the others, I drew small maps giving campus directions to the Music Hall for the afternoon symposium and put a staff member in charge of making sure the judges got to the hall on time.

Tim Hauser, Buddy DeFranco, '79 cochairman Barb Aste, and I headed out for Elkhart around 10 A.M. on Friday, got lost a few times, and finally pulled up at a palatial, French manor-esque brick home on the bank of the St. Joe River roughly an hour later. A Jaguar or some equally expensive sports car was parked in the driveway, flanked by an impressive boat resting regally on a trailer. Henkin, a round, friendly, Santa Claus-shaped figure in a business suit that seemed much too large even for his impressive frame, met us at the door with his much shorter, petite Japanese wife, Mary. Barb Aste and I exchanged glances, wondering what we had gotten ourselves into and how we would ever get Hauser and DeFranco back in time for the symposium.

We followed Henkin into a large, magnificent living room studded with priceless Japanese ceramic objects, vases, bowls, dishes, ivory carvings, custom-made Persian rugs, authentic pieces of wooden furniture from the Louis XIV–XV periods in France, and other works of art. Henkin's business associate joined us and nodded at everything Henkin had to say. DeFranco and Henkin talked about music like old pals and, on a less positive note, about popular modern-day performers like Billy Joel. Unfortunately, Joel had been a friend of Tim Hauser's in scuffling, pre-Manhattan Transfer/New York days, and Tim stepped in to defend him, receiving stern glances all around for his remarks. I kept my eyes on my drink and watch. Luckily, it was soon time for lunch.

We filed into an equally magnificent dining room and sat down to a startling five-course meal, prepared by the live-in chef. As I recall, there was even a little group playing classical music in the room. After dinner, Henkin brought the chef and his attendants out, explained that it was the chef's birthday, and had the chef take a bow. Already out of sorts from the activities of the last few days, I felt strapped onto a massive kaleidoscope of some kind that kept swirling mad colors around my eyes and head. During the meal, however, I finally got a chance to talk with Tim Hauser (who was seated to my right) about his vast fifties and sixties R & B record collection and vintage-car purchases as well as about the origins and successes of the Manhattan

Transfer, feeling somehow throughout our talk that he was being neglected amid all the CJF shuffle.

We arrived at the symposium only a few minutes late. Father Wiskirchen introduced DeFranco and Hauser and the others, and things got into high gear. The class was filled to capacity with students from Father Wiskirchen's riveting jazz-history course (of whom, as a second-semester senior, I was one)[3] and interested townsfolk. The conversation turned to the figures most important to jazz history. Philly Joe, Richard Davis, and Nat quickly mentioned the Miles Davis Septet and Quintet of the mid-to-late fifties, while DeFranco opted for Charlie Parker and Art Tatum. Nat then gave a hilarious lecture on fusion and a more serious one on how the judges would play that night, and offered other ever-articulate views on music in general. Philly Joe got laughs with an offhand remark terming himself the "Fuller Brush Man" and then noted that he always wanted to see the pianist's hands when he played drums for various timekeeping reasons. Tim Hauser and Joe Sample chipped in occasionally, but more often listen attentively to the others.

After the symposium (which Father Wiskirchen quickly termed as "the best one we've ever had"), Tim Owens and an assistant from National Public Radio's "Jazz Alive!" series introduced themselves. (Tim had finally agreed to fly out and cover the festival for the series after I had negotiated with him for several months.) As we walked back to the Morris Inn, I scrambled to give Tim a hurried festival history and update/interview, trying to compose my thoughts on the go and assure them that the festival taping would take place as planned.[4]

While talking to Owens and his note-taking companion, it suddenly dawned on me that I'd set up too much and that there was too much going on. I understood then why there hadn't been much radical change or innovation in the CJF for years. It was just so hard to get the event together and done that any extra dimensions, expansions, or new ideas couldn't—and really shouldn't—even come into play. But, in 1979, they had, and it was now up to me to deal with the structure I had set up as best I could.

Realizing that Turrentine was a no-show and that my hands were full, Father Wiskirchen stepped into the fray and contacted legendary Chicago alto-saxophonist/educator/former CJF award-winner and long-time friend Bunky Green the night before the CJF was scheduled to begin and somehow got him to agree to attend as the sixth and final judge. Despite this last puzzle piece falling into place, I couldn't eat anything at the dinner with the judges before the opening session at the Morris Inn. It was the most tense moment of my twenty-one-year-old life.

After some last-minute lighting trouble the festival opened with the judges in place on time. (To my relief, Electro-Voice had—after some hesitation—once more agreed to provide a top-notch sound system for the festival.) I coached the judges a bit as best I could about the CJF critiquing system and adjudicating sheets and explained a new Outstanding Group and Soloist sheet I had designed to simplify the process of keeping track of their ideas and views on things as they happened. Although the judges still appeared to be a little puzzled as they sat down in their chairs behind the judging table (set up about twenty feet from the front of the stage), it was apparent that they instinctively knew what was expected of them after a band or two had played.[5]

Father Wiskirchen's Notre Dame big band led off the Friday-evening music session for the seventh straight year. Dedicating the entire set to Charlie Mingus, the band cooked through Toshiko Akiyoshi's "Studio J," Jack Teagarden's "Muddy Water," a swinging version of "The Lunceford Touch" (arranged by Larry Dwyer), and Charlie Mingus's "Better Git It In Your Soul," the latter including refreshing group vocal touches. (After "Muddy Water," Tim Hauser ran backstage to compliment Notre Dame's powerful vocalist Karen Jadlos; he would continue to offer advice and praise to vocalists throughout the festival.)

If the Notre Dame Band's presentation didn't offer enough evidence of both a collegiate return to bop basics and an escalating interest in earlier types of jazz, the subsequent performances of the Washtenaw (Michigan) Community College Combo (which presented "Cherokee," John Coltrane's "Giant Steps," and trumpeter Clifford Brown's "If I Love You") and the University of Akron Ensemble (which played student originals and Jelly Roll Morton's "Black Bottom Stomp") took additional, strong, emphatic note of these trends.

As for the Ohio State University Sextet (led by Outstanding '79 Arranger/pianist John Emche and featuring Outstanding festival soloists such as trombonist John Fedchock, saxophonist Randy Mather, and drummer Jim Rupp), it turned the place upside down with a set-closing Fedchock bebop arrangement of the popular "Flintstones" cartoon-show theme (humorously entitled "Flintstoned"). Philly Joe Jones was so taken with the song, he ran backstage after the set to ask Emche and Fedchock to write the "Flintstoned" song out for him. He returned holding a sheet of notated paper and possessing a smile a mile wide.

Last but not least, Lanny Steele's 29-piece Texas Southern University Jazz Ensemble massed itself on stage. Because Steele-led groups had paid somewhat casual notice to required festival set-time restrictions in the past, I cautioned him before the performance to keep his set length within reasonable bounds. In response, Steele simply shrugged his colorful caftan-draped shoulders and nodded in quick agreement like a man who knows he's going to do what he wants anyway. Roaring through Kirk Whalums's "Blues at 5" (featuring the entire sax section), "When I Found You," and "Ohp Bop Bedop," as well as Lanny Steele's own "Homage to Monk and Miles (or a Rather Mysterious Blues)" and Eddie Harris's "Freedom Jazz Dance," the exotically outfitted band from Texas Southern University (also Joe Sample's alma mater) knocked the crowd out on the way to an Outstanding Group performance award (matching, of course, the group's other awards taken back to Texas in '73, '75, and '77).

The judges' jam was up next. It was what everyone, including the '79 chairman, was waiting for. Stepan Center was packed, people extending beyond the chair section on blankets all the way to the back and side walls. (For the first time in CJF history we had created a series of television spots to publicize the festival locally; obviously, the television, newsprint and radio package we had scrambled to create had paid off.) I watched the judges confer to select tunes for the jam and kept an eye on the stage crew as it arranged the grand piano for Joe Sample, set up an amp for Richard Davis's bass, and assembled Philly Joe's brand-new set of Selmer-shipped drums at center stage. After awhile, I moved over to the judges' now-vacated high-backed leather chairs and sat down along with other CJF staff members, each of us allowing ourselves for one moment the well-deserved comfort and luxury of the best seats in the house.

The jam: Buddy DeFranco (clarinet), Nat Adderley (cornet), Bunky Green (alto-sax), Richard Davis (bass), Joe Sample (acoustic piano), Philly Joe Jones (drums). Philly Joe moved downstage, introduced the musicians, and then sat down behind his drum set as the judges readied themselves to play. An incredible electricity spun through the Stepan Center air, riveting each member of the crowd in place. Finally, the front horn line moved to the microphones, adjusted various mouthpieces, nodded, and the musicians began the jam somewhat meditatively as the lights dimmed with Miles Davis's "All Blues" (which tied in well to the symposium mention of the Miles Davis Quintet and Septet as two of the most historically influential jazz groups).

Philly Joe's whiplash stick and cymbal work urged the beat on, and the sextet soon settled down into a more comfortable jam-rhythm groove. DeFranco, Adderley, and Bunky Green took long, blistering solos during the song, while Sample (who had once played in a Philly Joe Jones combo) displayed his thickly textured piano-chord prowess. The second selection, "Bye, Bye Blackbird," showcased Nat's patented deep backbend cornet play—the kind he unveils only when it's get-down-to-business blowing time. Meanwhile, Bunky Green (who hadn't arrived until early in the Friday music session and found himself forced to down a potato-and-steak dinner at the judges' table in between band critiques) cranked out another energy-filled alto-sax solo. Sample, Jones, and Davis also contributed stellar improvisational turns of their own. Things then quieted down during the set with "Easy Living," a ballad on which DeFranco, the elder statesman of the judges' crew (who hadn't played with Philly Joe since 1961, when the drummer unexpectedly appeared onstage with a DeFranco-led group) let his sultry, beautifully crafted clarinet play take charge. (Several more selections followed, the names of which escape recall.)

To me, the ballad was an unforgettable moment (as was, of course, the entire jam). As far as I was concerned, in light of the past crazed festival week, the fact that the judges' jam had taken place at all was a minor miracle in itself. And nothing, nothing in the world could beat watching the swarm of young preteen black and white kids surrounding Philly Joe after the jam to get his autograph.

Late Saturday morning (before the scheduled afternoon collegiate band/combo schedule), another '79 CJF experiment was set in motion: an informal coffee-and-rolls "rap" session at Stepan Center designed to give both judges and student musicians a chance to get to know each other on a first-name basis. The afternoon, however, belonged to the University of Iowa's big band and combo, both of which had been added on short notice to the festival agenda only after other bands had canceled out.

Led by tall, thick-shouldered Dan Yoder, the Iowa groups romped to Outstanding Performance awards, and managed individual soloist awards for Best Bass (John Shifflett), Best Piano (Tom Lyons), Best Alto (Bob Thompson), Best Trumpet (Ed Sarath), and Best Arranger/Composer (Sarath) as well. Featuring a number of student originals by Sarath, the University of Iowa Johnson County Landmark Big Band also acknowledged the late-seventies influence of the Toshiko Akiyoshi/Lew Tabackin big band (as did many others in 1979) with a rendition of Akiyoshi's "Road Time Shuffle."

Also on the afternoon schedule was a rather unique performance by trumpeter Jesse "Bob" McGuire of the Washtenaw Community College Big Band. Thoroughly proficient on one trumpet, McGuire leisurely walked downstage to the microphone at one point in the group's set, lifted one trumpet in his right hand and one in his left, and suddenly began to play both at the same time, eventually indulging in intriguing call-and-response bursts of left-right horn energy. Clearly an audacious, almost pretentious display, McGuire's talents gave the judges and the scattered members of the audience an added afternoon kick.

Saturday evening showcased the CJF high-school festival winners as well as eventual outstanding performances by the Tom Battenberg-led Ohio State University Jazz Ensemble and the Manty Ellis-led, eight-man-strong Wisconsin Conservatory of Music Ensemble IX combo. In addition, a potent, near-miss Outstanding award outing was offered by the Northern Illinois University Jazz Ensemble, which featured drummer Greg Rockingham extensively. During the set, a lengthy, soaring Rockingham stick-and-mallet drum solo rightly received a standing ovation and helped to earn him yet another Outstanding Drum award.

Closing down the '79 CJF was the Northwestern University Jazz Ensemble, which wowed judges and crowd once more with its patented all-band-members-walk-offstage-and-into-the-audience-for-the-last-notes-of-the-final-number act. What effect Northwestern's theatrics had on anyone else is hard to say. I do know that it left me both stunned, invigorated, and shaking my CJF chairman head in weary wonder. Moving the judges to the back room behind the stage to decide the outstanding bands and soloists, I watched as mandolinist Jethro Burns and his handpicked, youthful Chicago combo headed for the stage.

(Behind the stage a bit earlier in the evening, I had been enthralled by Jethro and his band as they casually sipped beers and picked around on bluegrass and swing tunes in a small circle in the back room. Listening to the group rehearse was a welcome escape from the rigors of festival-chairman duty and left me feeling as if I had stepped into another world entirely each time I entered the room. To say the least, it was a thrill. Father Wiskirchen's meeting with Jethro in that room was classic too.

Eyes wide as he entered the room, Father George laughed and then walked up and shook Jethro's hand. "Jethro Burns," he said warmly, pumping the acclaimed mandolinist's mitt, "I've been waiting a long time to meet you!" Father next moved to put his arm around Jethro's shoulder, saying as he did so, "What can I do to help you, what do you need? Just name it, it's yours." Never one to miss a comic opportunity in the making, Jethro quickly replied, "Father, I don't know if you can do anything for me, but my friend here has a problem." Father George looked suddenly serious for a moment and turned his attention to the young man. "But, what can I do for you, my son?" he asked. "Well, Father," explained Jethro, his timing perfect, as usual, "you see, Don here is a Cub fan." Sensing the joke, Father Wiskirchen put his arms around the young musician and advised: "My son, give it up. You've clearly lost your way.")[6]

Back behind closed doors, the judges, Barb Aste, Father Wiskirchen, and I sat around a long makeshift table (made out of two wooden boards resting on old sawhorses) and looked over the special judging sheets I had designed. Outside I could hear Jethro and crew rambling through "C Jam Blues." God, how I wanted to be out there to listen! But I was finally in the back room, wondering, as I had the whole year, exactly what it was that I was now supposed to do. Usually, judging sessions last for hours, but, because the judges got along so well and— I'd like to think—because of the new sheet, it all went smoothly, with few disagreements along the way.

DeFranco, as I recall, had a few things to say, mentioning that although the talent level was high these days, the students were often throwing "everything but the kitchen sink" into their solos, many not having yet realized that what was left unplayed was often as important as that which was. Philly Joe spoke up about the festival talent at one point, noting that he had gone through four or five separate outstanding personnel sheets because fantastic new soloists seemed to come along with the appearance of each new combo or band. Glancing at Philly Joe's comments, I noticed most were signed (in a round, flowing script), "Peace & Love, Philly Joe Jones."

The biggest argument of the session eventually arose over whether to give Jesse McGuire of the Washtenaw big band and combo an award for his prodigious two-trumpet (and straightahead) horn play. Nat Adderley, trying to figure out for a moment whom the others were presently discussing, suddenly leaned in, recognized the musician, and with a patented Adderley laugh, said, "Oh, Showboat, huh?" thereby breaking up everyone in the room. After Nat, Buddy, and Bunky had said their piece about the trumpeter, an impassioned Joe Sample finally turned the tide. "But the kid has the chops!" Joe exclaimed, cutting the air emphatically with his hands. "He's going to be a good studio musician some day! Why not give him a break? Whether he gets this thing or not may determine if he goes on! The kid has the chops!" Grumbling a bit, the judges conferred again and, somewhat begrudgingly, announced that a special Nat Adderley Award would be given to Jesse McGuire as Most Promising Trumpeter for 1979.

The judges' session over in record time, we all went back to the stage area and listened as Jethro Burns and his four-man band closed down a swinging set that had a considerable number of the CJF audience folk dancing in the aisles to the country-swing, Django Reinhardt-influenced, two-mandolin, one bass, one acoustic guitar beat.

During the awards presentations (announced by Tim Hauser) Philly Joe got up to shake hands with the drum award winners and Nat even moved to the stage to announce and present the Most Promising Trumpeter award to Jesse McGuire. It was a communal sort of thing. (Cochairman Barb Aste was also singled out by the judges for her enthusiastic personality, helpfulness, and overall "jazz joie de vivre" and managed a makeshift curtsy onstage to the crowd's delight.) And then, it was over. The judges huddled together to sign each other's programs; student musicians headed out for Vegetable Buddies to jam the night away. (Interestingly, Ed Locke—Roy Eldridges's New York-based drummer of recent years—had flown in for the CJF as a guest of one of the university deans. Eventually, Locke identified himself to the judges—many of whom were old acquaintances—and subsequently sat with the panel throughout much of the festival. In addition, Locke managed a number of drum solos at the Vegetable Buddies jam on Saturday night.)

Things were beginning to blur once more. I dropped the judges off at the Morris Inn around two A.M. and then headed back to Stepan Center to help junior chemical-engineering student/CJF production-chief Stan Huddleston—a tireless worker, and an entirely dependable, one-in-a-million CJF staff member—clean up the festival debris. We piled up chairs, moved this and that, swept the floors with huge push brooms, and finally turned off the lights and locked up the place around 3 or 4 A.M. Before leaving, I took a last look at the large, rich, colorful spray-painted canvas mural of jazz musicians (draped behind the sound and light technicians' platform) which had greeted CJF audiences as they came in.[7]

As Stan and I walked out to the car and loaded some miscellaneous electrical odds and ends into the backseat, I turned around, realizing this was my last chance to find a CJF successor (Barb Aste, a senior, wouldn't be around in '80), and said, "Stan, what would you think about running this thing next year?" Much to my surprise and tired relief, Stan said, "Sure, I'd like to very much."

Sunday afternoon, Buddy DeFranco held a clinic in the Music Hall with some local musicians. Earlier in the day, I breakfasted with Joe Sample and Tom Hooper (who had accompanied Joe to the festival representing the Crusaders' management) and then drove Sample, Hooper, Richard Davis, and Philly Joe to the airport with some staff member help. At the uncrowded Michiana Regional airport, Hooper took me cautiously aside (as if to prevent a mob fan attack of some sort on Joe Sample) and kindly offered me several copies of Sample's latest, predominantly acoustic piano albums, "Rainbow Seeker" and

"Carmel," for Father Wiskirchen, other staff members, and me—each signed by Sample himself.[8]

It was hard to see them all go, there was a strange parting sadness. Tim Hauser (who had gotten Philly Joe to agree during the festival to back the Manhattan Transfer at the upcoming summer Montreux Jazz Festival in Switzerland) was driven to Chicago early Sunday morning by ever-helpful CJF staff member/program-editor Tom Krueger (also a diehard Transfer fan) in order to try and catch a flight to Los Angeles in time to make a special party thrown by Hugh Hefner. Bunky Green left for Chicago on his own with his kind wife sometime before early afternoon. Finally, only Buddy DeFranco remained. After the afternoon clinic, he appeared visibly tired, and so we took off for the airport as soon as possible, arriving about 4 P.M. Shaking his hand, I thanked him again for coming. Turning back once before heading to the plane with his peculiar brown clarinet-briefcase in hand, DeFranco nodded approvingly and said: "That's quite a jazz festival you've got there. Invite me back anytime."

Late that afternoon I drove back over to Stepan Center to take one last look at the now-empty auditorium. The red, white, and blue bunting was still up around the judges' table and stage. It all felt empty, hollow inside. I walked up to the stage, recalling how I had scrambled to rent the black grand piano (and even helped to unload and push it on stage). I recalled the idiocies of the year, how so little had gone right (I hadn't even been able to book the judges' rooms in the Morris Inn—a simple, entirely minor thing—until March because of a huge Athletic and Convocation Center-held karate tournament that had been scheduled for the same weekend as the CJF) and then recalled how much I had learned about people, jazz, student musicians, agents, critics, and, most of all, myself.

It was disheartening to realize as I stood there that there would be no record, no historical glimmer or trace of the 1979 festival, for, as it turned out none of the university's student publications—the *Scholastic*, the *Dome*, or the *Observer*—had bothered to send any reporters at all. (In fact, since no one else would, it had fallen to me to write prefestival articles for the *Scholastic* and the *Observer*. In addition, I also wrote, laid out, and collated the artwork for the prefestival publicity brochure we ran off several thousand copies of that year.) A number of things had been attempted, many of them successful. New connections had been made, files had been expanded, and CJF history, however tentatively, had been explored.[9] It had all been a big, struggling attempt to add something to jazz.

I walked up the steps of the stage, over to the solitary grand piano, and sat down to play a half hour's worth of key-of-C blues, play-ing to myself, thinking no one was around to hear me, and comfort-ing myself with that thought. Leaving the stage, I turned, and saw someone smiling at me; the large, ever-friendly, black part-time care-taker of the center. He walked to the stage, sat down at the piano, and began playing a nice little blues of his own—just as I had. The caretaker turned to me once during his playing to smile and nod, and I smiled back. It was a small moment, but one that seemed to capture the essence of something I had tried to do. And I left him playing his own song, the echoes remaining in my mind long after the final Stepan Center door had shut tight on 21 years of festival memories left behind.

1964 CJF Most Promising Instrumentalist Billy Harper takes a towering solo during the Judges' Jam in 1974.   (Photo courtesy Ed Brower)

Judges (left to right) Dan Morgenstern, Jamey Aebersold, Willis Conover, Hubert Laws, George Russell, and Aynsley Dunbar attempt to identify recordings and performing musicians during the '72 CJF Symposium's *down beat* magazine-style "blindfold test."

(Photo courtesy *South Bend Tribune*)

CJF '72 judges Roberta Flack (left) and George Russell (right) relax for a moment with festival advisor Richard Bizot (center). A rising star, Flack had recently been named the number one Female Singer in the *down beat* magazine Readers' Poll.

(Photo courtesy *South Bend Tribune*)

Judges' Jam '74: Bill Watrous, the premier trombonist in jazz.   (Photo courtesy Ed Brower)

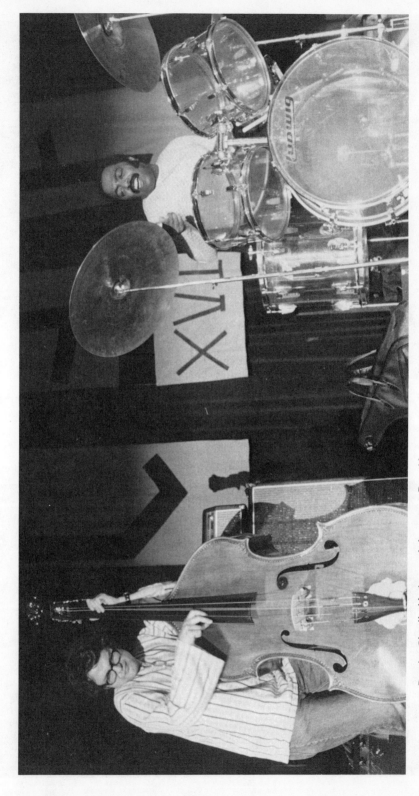

Bassist Charlie Haden and drummer Roy Haynes step into high gear during the '74 Judges' Jam.
(Photo courtesy Ed Brower)

Sparked by Best Trumpeter Al Vizzutti, the Eastman School of Music Jazz Ensemble stormed to an Outstanding Band award in 1975.   (Photo courtesy Ed Brower)

Flautist Hubert Laws (left), tenor-saxophonist Sonny Rollins (center), and trumpeter Cecil Bridgewater (right) hit a comfortable groove during the 1975 Judges' Jam.
                                                                (Photo courtesy Ed Brower)

Former Blood, Sweat & Tears trumpeter Lew Soloff performs with the Eastman School of Music Jazz Ensemble during a special festival-closing guest set at CJF '76.
(Photo courtesy Tom Paulius)

Chicago State's Changes Jazz Combo en route to an Outstanding Combo award in 1976. Pictured are: (left to right) Paulette Hradnansky (1975 CJF's Best Trumpeter), Best Reed Soloist John Smarzewski, and Best Bassist Al Keith.　　　(Photo courtesy Tom Paulius)

Judge Joe Farrell (right) jams with Lew Soloff (left) during the Eastman School of Music's closing guest set in 1976. (Photo courtesy Tom Paulius)

Fredonia State's Gary Keller digs into a solo and wraps up a CJF '77 Outstanding Tenor-Saxophone award. (Photo courtesy Leo Hansen)

Judge David Sanborn takes the 1977 Judges' Jam spotlight. In 1966, Sanborn performed as a student musician at the CJF and took home a Best Reed Soloist award.

(Photo courtesy Leo Hansen)

Tim Hauser, founder of the internationally popular vocal group, The Manhattan Transfer, emcees the jazz proceedings at CJF '79.

(Photo courtesy Kevin Pritchett)

Father Wiskirchen and the Notre Dame Big Band. Dedicating its entire set to ailing bassist Charlie Mingus, the group opened up the CJF for the seventh straight year.
(Photo courtesy Kevin Pritchett)

'79 Outstanding Arranger/Composer John Emche at the piano.
(Photo courtesy Kevin Pritchett)

The University of Akron's Mark Lopeman: CJF 1979's Outstanding Instrumentalist.
(Photo courtesy Kevin Pritchett)

Outstanding vocalist Toni Neely belts out a tune during Texas Southern's rousing CJF set. (Photo courtesy Kevin Pritchett)

Crusaders co-founder Joe Sample takes a rare acoustic piano turn during the CJF '79 Judges' Jam. (Photo courtesy Kevin Pritchett)

Neglected bebop clarinetist Buddy DeFranco unleashes his potent technique on the 1979 CJF crowd.
(Photo courtesy Kevin Pritchett)

CJF '79 judge Richard Davis: educator, performer, nonpareil bassist, and accomplished equestrian.
(Photo courtesy Kevin Pritchett)

Washtenaw Community College Big Band and Combo trumpeter Jesse McGuire. His unexpected two-trumpet-at-once display helped earn him a special Most Promising Trumpet award in 1979.

(Photo courtesy Kevin Pritchett)

Affable Nat Adderley mulls over a CJF student musician performance.
(Photo courtesy Kevin Pritchett)

Chapter 4

THE EIGHTIES

1
9
8
0
Following on the heels of a surging '78 Midwest Blues Festival that featured Albert Collins, Martin, Bogan & the Armstrongs, and John Lee Hooker, among others, the November 1979 MBF closed out the decade strongly with such artists and groups as Roosevelt Sykes, Lonnie Brooks, Professor Longhair and the Blues Scholars, Suzanne Prince, Eddy Clearwater, Big Joe Williams, and the Carey Bell Blues Band featuring Lurrie Bell. Although hampered by student Cultural Arts Commission budget cuts, the event's attraction was such that people even braved a severe snowstorm to dance enmasse in the aisles at Stepan Center once more. (Unfortunately, the weather also managed to keep away the capacity crowds needed to help the MBF break even and survive; financially unsuccessful in 1979, the event was clearly headed for a serious case of the soon-to-be-cancelled blues.)

Budget cuts also radically affected chairman Stan Huddleston's plans for the nonprofit Collegiate Jazz Festival in '79–'80. As a result of the cuts, the traditional Saturday-night guest band was scrapped; in its place, the final performing collegiate band of the night would play a second noncompetitive set while the judges deliberated. In an even more drastic move, the CJF high-school jazz festival—a staple since 1967—was also cancelled. Taking the place of the high-school band winners that had so rivetingly opened or closed Saturday-evening CJF music sessions for the past thirteen years, a noncompetitive guest college group, the Washtenaw Community College Big Band (selected from submitted taped auditions) would perform. For a festival entering into the 1980s, this was hardly an auspicious start.

With the advent of a new decade and the close of another, of course, music-critic minds often start to spin, and the seventies and eighties proved no exception. Tops on the list of jazz-in-general assessments were the reemergence of bebop and the refreshing, riveting em-

155

brace by many professional and student jazz musicians of not only current musical developments but historically sound and revered ones as well. The once all-pervasive force of jazz/rock fusion had, it seemed, finally given way to a "simultaneous diversity" within the music itself.[1] Losses during the past decade had, of course, been high (Duke Ellington, Louis Armstrong, Charlie Mingus, Cannonball Adderley, Joe Venuti, Johnny Hodges, to name a few), but, somehow, jazz—despite its expansions, detractors, critics, and scars—had once again survived.

By 1980, jazz had made important inroads into radio play, critical print coverage, video, and general audience exposure, as well as the area of government funding, particularly from the National Endowment for the Arts, which had increased its jazz allotment tenfold over the decade's first year.[2] On the college and high-school jazz-education side of the situation, there were more programs, bands, top-notch professional-caliber charts (for performance), student compositions, collegiate festivals, qualified teachers, and, perhaps most interesting of all, more student band recordings.

In the past, only the foremost jazz programs at North Texas State, Berklee, Indiana University, the University of Illinois, and others had the pull, access to facilities, and engineering know-how to record affiliated bands and combos. By the end of the 1970s, however, student bands and combos in all parts of the United States were either checking into the studio to record an album on a yearly (or biyearly) basis, or were at least considering recording options in their future plans. Though often printed in small quantities by labels such as Mark Records and Crest Records, and as a result more difficult to obtain than standard commercial releases, such albums were both the bedrock of an expanding and increasingly important body of collegiate-jazz prowess and a way of exchanging musical ideas among schools. In a sense, the rise of student recordings in the seventies offered one of the most tangible gauges of jazz-education progress in the academic arena.[3]

In late March 1980, sixteen bands and combos from Ohio, Iowa, Indiana, Alabama, Illinois, Wisconsin, Michigan, and Massachusetts gathered for the twenty-second running of the Notre Dame Collegiate Jazz Festival in South Bend. Reflecting the "diversity" of the eighties, the festival promised to feature bands "playing every form of jazz from Dixieland to Swing, Bebop to Fusion."[4] As had been the case throughout the mid- and late-seventies, plaques and cash awards would be awarded to individuals and schools singled out as "Outstanding" by the CJF judging panel, which was made up this year of pianist/educator/ National Public Radio "Jazz Alive!" series narrator Dr. Billy Taylor, tenor-sax giant Zoot Sims, bassist Milt Hinton, guitarist Herb Ellis, drummer Tony Williams, and critic Dan Morgenstern. Once again, as had so often been the case since 1959, the Selmer Company had offered to pick up most of the plaque costs.

Friday evening found Father Wiskirchen and the Notre Dame Jazz Band in the traditional leadoff spot.[5] Also appearing was an Ohio State University Jazz Nonet (featuring a "fiery, anti-tonal tradeoff between electric and acoustic bass" during a Chet Baker arrangement of Cole Porter's "Love for Sale"),[6] as well as the University of Iowa's Johnson County Landmark Big Band (featuring Best Composer Ed Sarath, Best Electric Bassist John Shifflett, and Honorable Mention Drummer Mike Tomaglia). In addition, Indiana University's Energy Liberation Unit, a "standout among combos"[7] led by '76 CJF Drum award-winner Larry Banks and '80 Best Pianist Jim Beard performed. All three groups received Outstanding Performance awards. (On an equally stirring collegiate-jazz note, a band from the state of Alabama—one of the few remaining states never to have been represented at the event—also took part in the CJF, closing down the Friday session.)

As for the 1980 judges' jam with Zoot Sims, Billy Taylor, Herb Ellis, Milt Hinton, and Tony Williams, it was nothing short of a swinging, boppish smash "worth double the price of admission."[8] Beginning with a rousing Sims tenor-sax outing and a "brilliant and thundering" Tony Williams drum solo on "The Girl from Ipanema" that brought the crowd to its feet at song's end, the set continued with "The More I See You," featuring smooth, lightning-quick guitarist Herb Ellis.[9] Pianist Billy Taylor then took over the solo spotlight on "All The Things You Are," while "the judge of judges," Milt Hinton, turned in a stunning bass solo during his own "extraordinary arrangement of the traditional spiritual 'Joshua Fit the Battle of Jericho.' "[10] "Those who went to see this group jam," concluded *Observer* critic Chalon Mullins, "went away psyched."[11]

Saturday afternoon featured bands from Purdue, Michigan State University, and the University of Wisconsin-Milwaukee, as well as a Notre Dame Jazz Combo made up of saxophonist Pat McKrell, trumpeter Keith Winking, pianist Mike Franken, bassist Michael O'Connor, guitarist Paul Bertolini, and drummer Don Ginocchio. Also appearing during the afternoon session was a fourth Outstanding Performance group, the Aaron Horne-led Northeastern Illinois University Jazz Ensemble. As for the evening session, Morris Laurence's Washtenaw Community College Big Band kicked things off only to be followed by the Pat Hollenbeck-led New England Conservatory of Music Medium Rare Big Band, a group that offered audiences what was clearly the performance highlight of the 1980 CJF.

"From the first notes of the first tune, Horace Silver's 'Room 608,' "
remarked the *Observer's* Chalon Mullins, "you could feel the audience
hold its breath to catch every phrase. . . . Then there was the music.
It was varied from Wayne Shorter . . . and Chick Corea to Duke Ellington and Jelly Roll Morton. It was superbly arranged by leader Pat
Hollenbeck right down to the band's punctuation of and counterpoint
to the always excellent solos. And it swang. Oh, brother, it swang!"[12]
For its efforts onstage, the Medium Rare Big Band received a wildly
cheering crowd demand for something no other band in the history
of the CJF had been privy to: an unheard-of encore! Surprised and
obviously moved, the group gladly returned to the stage to play Duke
Ellington's "Things Ain't What They Used to Be."[13]

Although a University of Iowa jazz combo (also selected as an
Outstanding Performance Group) and swinging combo or band aggregates from Ohio State, the University of Wisconsin-Madison, and
the University of Akron all made stellar showings thereafter, none
could dim the luster of the Medium Rare Big Band's "rare" encore
outing. Soon, individual soloist awards were offered to the University of Akron's Jack Schantz (Trumpet) and reedman John Orsini (Outstanding Instrumentalist), and Medium Rare Band members Ed Jackson
(Alto-Sax), Ed Felson (Acoustic Bass), Stephen Johns (Drums), Andy
Strasnich (Flute), and John Shapiro (Vibes). Other winners included
Purdue University trombonist Don Hill, powerful Northeastern Illinois
drummer Greg Rockingham, University of Wisconsin-Milwaukee guitarist Bill Martin, and Ohio State tenor-sax man Randy Mather.

"As evidenced by the vast majority of both big bands and combos
at this year's event," wrote *South Bend Tribune* critic Stephen Mamula
the week after the festival, "there seems to be a definite renaissance
of straight-forward swing as well as a variety of the earlier genre (bop,
boogie woogie), as opposed to the jazz rock fusion bag that was so influential five years ago and the atonal 'awareness' of ten years ago. . . .
Concerning the soloists, the bulk of the students seem to be yearning
toward a predominantly lyric quality in their playing, as opposed to
the rapid-fire 'impress your peers' pyrotechnics that prevailed and carried so much weight in years past."[14]

> The festival definitely possesses a special appeal [explained chair-
> man Stan Huddleston—the second black Notre Dame student to run the
> event—in his CJF program prologue]. Perhaps it's the feeling of excite-
> ment which so many tend to associate with the big band sound. Maybe
> it's the uniquely convivial atmosphere which goes hand in hand with
> the festival-style format. It could be the fact that the CJF gives us a pre-

view of tomorrow's professional jazz talent by featuring today's finest college jazz bands.

Whatever the case, the CJF's appeal seems almost timeless—like jazz itself—which Max Roach describes as "America's Classical Music." The union of jazz and education is a significant step in the development of cultural arts in the United States, and CJF has been an integral part of the union through thick and thin, providing, in the opinion of many, the best in college jazz.[15]

1 9 8 1 On April 10, 1980, after a special meeting of Notre Dame Cultural Arts Commission and Student Union personnel, the Midwest Blues Festival was cancelled due to a lack of student interest. Citing a variety of factors such as poor attendance (despite the fact that snowstorms on both festival nights in 1979 had kept crowds away), loss of money (despite the fact that the event had lost money in the past and had still been renewed; on several occasions—as recently as 1978—the MBF had actually even made money), and student apathy (the real root of the problem), the incoming and outgoing student-government heads expressed hurried regret over the cancellation and then quickly rushed to expedite plans for a Stepan Center country-rock festival designed on the basis of a student-interest survey.[1] With the heart-felt loss of the MBF, the heyday of the seventies blues bash was over.

"I expected it," remarked MBF founder and six-year past-chairman Perry Aberli after the decision, ". . . within the Cultural Arts Commission in particular and the Student Union in general, the University has consistently identified art as an upper class kind of thing, and the Blues Festival as something non-cultural. The Festival was never really understood as something cultural like, say, the Collegiate Jazz Festival or the Sophomore Literary Festival, but I think the Blues Festival presented more culture than the others."[2]

Spanning twenty-three years and four decades of jazz (the fifties, sixties, seventies, and eighties) the 1981 CJF headed up by Notre Dame student/'80 CJF cochairman Tim Griffin (an event more fortunate than its much younger and now-fallen fall blues festival brother) returned in the spring of 1981 with high-school festival once more intact. Featuring sixteen bands and combos from Indiana, Illinois, Ohio, Iowa, Michigan, Massachusetts, Oklahoma, and Texas, the CJF once again also found itself host to a top-notch panel of judges including bassist Richard Davis, drummer Mel Lewis, reedman/flautist Joe Farrell (back as a judge for the fourth time), former CJF award-winner/current Stan Getz combo-pianist Jim McNeely, clinician/onetime Stan Kenton trumpeter Mike Vax, and the director of the Institute of Jazz Studies at Rutgers University, Dan Morgenstern.

Gathering for the traditional CJF symposium on Friday afternoon in the large, low-ceilinged, first-floor Music Building classroom, the judges treated yet another packed-to-the-walls student and townfolk crowd to a lively question-and-answer session dealing with their respective, varied careers and the current state of jazz. Asked what he looked for in a student musician at a festival such as the CJF, bassist Richard Davis replied, "People who are into jazz are into creating music . . . I try to relate to the musicians personally; you get a better feedback then."[3]

Opening up the 1981 Friday-evening session was, as usual, the University of Notre Dame Jazz Ensemble. The first of two large ensembles in existence at Notre Dame in 1981 in addition to four combos and "an improvisational workshop with varying instrumentation,"[4] the Father Wiskirchen-led group had made its first tour earlier in 1981, playing at various Chicago locales over a three-day period before finishing up with a concert at Quincy College, in Quincy, Illinois.

Following Notre Dame's jazz effort, a Northeastern Illinois combo featuring perennial Best Drummer Greg Rockingham took the stand and soon played its way into an Outstanding Performance award, as did the evening's third group, the Ohio State University Jazz Ensemble led by Tom Battenberg. Also acquitting itself well was a University of Iowa combo with Best Arranger/Composer Bret Zvacek in tow. Finally, the Aaron Horne-directed Northeastern Illinois Jazz Ensemble arrived onstage to knock the crowd for yet another CJF loop with "explosive musical arrangements and . . . exceptional musicianship" en route to a standing ovation and a second consecutive CJF Outstanding Performance plaque.[5] Last in the evening, of course, was the traditional judges' jam—this year featuring Jim McNeely, Richard Davis, Joe Farrell, Mike Vax, and Mel Lewis—which continued on at length "until the crowd had its fill of music."[6]

Saturday afternoon and evening showcased bands from Michigan State, the University of Akron, MIT, Oklahoma's Central State University, and Texas Southern University, and combos from Notre Dame, Indiana University, Ohio State, and the University of Illinois. Rounding out the triumvirate of Outstanding Band award winners was the Dan Yoder-led Johnson County Landmark big band from the University of Iowa, which dazzled the judges midway through the evening session. Closing down with the usual early-Sunday-morning student-jam-session festivities at downtown locales, the twenty-third CJF continued the tradition of presenting the finest in collegiate jazz.

Sizing up the event that had been—as usual—a full year in the making, '81 chairman Tim Griffin termed the CJF ". . . a major stepping stone for a student performer." "The people who stand out here," continued Griffin, who was undoubtedly looking back over the long history of CJF contributions to professional jazz, "will be in the music business in the future."[7]

Offering additional insights in a 1981 CJF program interview, Fr. George Wiskirchen made particular note of the "good community spirit . . . where bands aren't pressured like at some of the other festivals, which have become very competitive." "Any rivalries here," Wiskirchen continued, "are friendly ones. An important part of that and of the festival overall is that it is not run by a college, faculty or music department. Instead, the festival is organized, promoted and run by students, most of whom are not even particularly jazz musicians. . . . This festival and the others help . . . I think, because they [the student musicians] get a chance to hear what other groups are doing, see their limits and expand their possibilities."[8]

1982 Run by student Kevin Bauer in 1981, the twenty-fourth Collegiate Jazz Festival sought once more to bring together the top student bands from across the United States. By March, groups from Indiana, Virginia, Illinois, Ohio, New York, Wisconsin, Michigan, Massachusetts, and Iowa had been selected to attend and play before a judging panel slated to include pianist Billy Taylor (back for the third time), longtime Count Basie band reedman/arranger Frank Foster, drummer Shelly Manne, bassist Charlie Haden (also returning for the third time), cornet giant Nat Adderley, and critic Dan Morgenstern.

Attempting to expand the educational aspect of the CJF and bring home an appreciation of jazz history to the Notre Dame/St. Mary's community on a more personal basis, the 1982 CJF arranged for acclaimed scholar/musician/educator Dr. Billy Taylor to spend the entire week leading up to the early-April event as an "artist in residence" at Notre Dame. Lecturing and performing to "packed houses," Taylor (who termed the CJF "the finest collegiate jazz festival in the country")[1] also generously took time to work closely with Father Wiskirchen and the Notre Dame Big Band, which would once again open up the Friday-evening CJF musical festivities.

Before the CJF began, however, one last-minute judging-panel change was made. Hampered by theatrical obligations made to the Boston/Stamford, Connecticut musical *Mahalia!* which dealt with the life of singer Mahalia Jackson, cornetist Nat Adderley was forced to cancel out a few weeks before the festival. (In his concerned, kindly way, Nat sought unsuccessfully to arrange for young trumpet-sensation Wynton Marsalis to attend as a replacement; in his place, former CJF judge/trumpeter Jimmy Owens eventually took a judging seat alongside his distinguished peers.)[2]

Friday night featured performances by a big band from Notre Dame as well as Outstanding award-winning bands from Virginia Commonwealth University and Northeastern Illinois. Also selected as Outstanding from among the evening's groups was the Northeastern Illinois combo. As usual, the session was highlighted by the perennial judges' jam—this year including Messrs. Haden, Manne, Owens, Foster, and Taylor.

Saturday afternoon and evening music sessions showcased bands from Ohio State, Fredonia University (New York), the University of Iowa (selected as an Outstanding Band for the fourth time in the last five years), Michigan State, and MIT. In addition, hot, diverse combos from Ohio State, the University of Wisconsin (the Black Music Experience Combo), Michigan State, Notre Dame (the Pauls Duo), and the University of Illinois (the Shambana Stompers) were interspersed throughout both Saturday programs with potent results.

As it turned out, 1982 was another University of Iowa year as the Johnson County Landmark Band snared awards for Outstanding Trombone (Bret Zvacek), Composer (Zvacek), Bass (John Shifflett), Guitar (Steve Grismore), and Special Lead Trumpet (David Scott). These awards, of course, were only in addition to the band's overall Outstanding designation and the rare CJF tribute the group received when the judges themselves rose to give the band a standing ovation.

Writing about the band on his judges' sheet (distributed after performances to the respective bands), ever-passionate humanitarian bassist/judge Charlie Haden noted: "Best Big Band I've heard in a long time!" before adding to this line a thoughtful commentary that seemed to say much about jazz education and the roles of student performers and judges in any festival.

"I don't think," the bassist continued, "that I have the right to set myself up as a judge for anyone's creative gifts. I'm just happy to see all of you wanting to play creative music. This means that even if you don't go on to a career in music, there will be that many more sensitive and good human beings in the world."

"Internalizing the experience of improvisation brings a person closer to the human and creative qualities inside themselves. This will hopefully enable them to become people who have reverence and concern for life."[3]

(Speaking for the students, 1982 Best Trombonist and Composer Bret Zvacek—who helped to stretch the University of Iowa's skein of consecutive Best Composer awards to five—summed up the feeling of many by stating he felt "quite fortunate that the atmosphere is such that student compositions and arrangements can be played at events like the CJF.")[4]

1
9
8
3
For the Collegiate Jazz Festival, 1983 was a particularly meaningful year. Not only was the event set to celebrate its twenty-fifth anniversary as the oldest, largest, and most prominent festival of its kind in the world, but it would include among its judging ranks a head-turning twenty-one-year-old trumpet whiz-kid by the name of Wynton Marsalis.

A scholarship graduate of the Julliard School of Music and an alumnus of legendary drummer Art Blakey's Jazz Messengers group as well as the possessor of an impressive 1982 *down beat* magazine Jazz Album of the Year award, Wynton Marsalis, in the words of renowned jazz-critic Leonard Feather, had quickly become ". . . a symbol for the fledgling decade." With his sharp double-breasted suits and outspoken, ever-knowledgeable classical/jazz manner, Marsalis would most definitely bring the CJF's jazz-education message home to those his own age—or older—onstage and in attendance. Due to the efforts of Notre Dame junior/CJF chairman Bob O'Donnell and his staff, Wynton Marsalis would also be joined on the judging panel in 1983 by his tenor-saxophonist brother Branford Marsalis, veteran numero-uno bassist Ron Carter, drummer Tony Williams, pianist Jim McNeely, and critic Dan Morgenstern.

Assembling for the Friday-afternoon symposium in the Music Building, the judges (excluding Tony Williams, who would not arrive until early that evening) fielded a wide range of questions posed by members of Father Wiskirchen's jazz-history class, as well as the hordes of other Notre Dame/St. Mary's students and townfolk crammed into the room on chairs, along window ledges, and against walls—many even stretched out or seated cross-legged on the carpeted music room floor. Father Wiskirchen, as usual, sat quietly to one side of the judges, who were seated in the center of the room on plastic chairs arranged in a makeshift line. One large arm draped over the edge of a grand piano, Father George carefully eyed the proceedings from his perch

to make sure (as festival adviser) that things went according to symposium plan. As might be expected, articulate and outspoken Wynton Marsalis did much of the responding to queries that drifted back
and forth from the current direction of jazz to the status of the electric
bass and guitar to the state of college bands in general and the role
and progress of women in jazz.

> I'm just trying to learn how to play [the young trumpeter began],
> I'm just thinking about what I'm playing. It's just like talking. You hear
> something and pick it up. I have a different idea of the words. People
> ask, "Where did you study?" and offer it as a compliment. I don't see
> it that way. I learned by my record player, through jam sessions, and
> performing on bandstands and hanging out listening to people. And peo-
> ple don't want that answer. . . .
> A lot of people confuse articulation with intelligence. If you know
> European music, that's important, but what distinguishes the music [jazz]
> is that it's *the* American music—and I don't mean Gershwin. . . . If you
> have a college band, I think it's imperative to be familiar with the music
> of Duke Ellington—the period 1930-31. Or Count Basie, Fletcher Hender-
> son, Thelonius Monk—these are key figures in this music whose work
> is important to know and understand so that you know how to incor-
> porate their ideas into your music. . . . [in regards to women in jazz]
> We don't discriminate, it's just a matter of being lucky. When I went
> to New York, I was fortunate enough to sit in with Art Blakey. . . .
> You have to listen to all things. You imitate everything around you.
> The main thing in playing jazz is listening. By looking at the situation
> and studying it, solutions come to mind. You have to intuitively know. I
> listen to the bass. That's my key. But the thing is to wind up playing you.[1]

For the silver-anniversary celebration, the CJF also took steps to
reduce competitiveness further and insure a "festive" festival time for
attending bands. "We sharply deemphasized the competitive aspect
of the festival this year," noted chairman Bob O'Donnell in the 1983
CJF program, "because although we do believe in defined standards
of excellence, we also appreciate any serious attempt at making high
quality music."[2]

"This year," explained a separate program note, "judges will
award 'Outstanding Instrumentalist' certificates to each individual that
they feel merits such an award. Consequently, these awards will be
based on the personal judgment of each individual judge, rather than
the quality of the participants as related only to each other. This year's
committee feels that this change will enhance the festival aspect of CJF
as well as introduce a new standard of excellence to the judging."[3] In

addition to these developments, the festival was also scheduled to be professionally videotaped and digitally recorded for local Public Television broadcast, as well as national and international broadcast by the Voice of America and National Public Radio's well-known Jazz Alive! radio series.

Swinging things to life for the eleventh consecutive year, the Father Wiskirchen-led Notre Dame jazz band (which had ventured on concert tours of Indiana, Illinois, and Michigan during the 1982–83 academic year) contributed yet another admirable opening CJF musical statement. Up next was one of the festival's two eventual Outstanding Combos, the Northeastern Illinois combo. Offering hot, occasionally funky bebop works that brought the crowd to its feet, the group would eventually go on to reap Distinguished Performance Citations for trumpeter Rod McGaha, alto-saxman Arthur Porter, drummer Greg Rockingham, guitarist Charles Smith, and bassist Kenny Davis. Following Northeastern's fine outing were potent, swinging big bands from Michigan State and Virginia Commonwealth University (Richmond, Virginia) — both of which also managed to snare Outstanding Performance plaques.

As if responding directly to Wynton Marsalis's symposium comments about Duke Ellington, the set by the black-tuxedo/formal-dress-attired Virginia Commonwealth band featured no less than two of the Duke's songs, "Rockin' Rhythm" and "I Got It Bad And That Ain't Good" (the latter showcasing Vocal Citation recipient Delores King). In addition, the group seemed to reflect 1980s eclectic student interests in past jazz roots, ballads, and bebop with presentations of Hoagy Carmichael's "Skylark," Al Cohn's "Some of My Best Friends," and Dizzy Gillespie's "Things to Come." The evening's final big band from Ohio State, on the other hand, featured original compositions by Arranger/Composer Citation recipient Vince Mendoza such as "Secret Love," "Make Someone Happy," and "Scherzo for High Hat and Jazz Ensemble."

Taking the Stepan Center stage for the silver-anniversary Collegiate Jazz Festival judges' jam, Jim McNeely, Ron Carter, Tony Williams, and Wynton and Branford Marsalis conferred for a moment and then unleashed their potent brand of jazz.

The unnamed opening number was fast and furious, with brilliant solos by Wynton and pianist McNeely, only to be followed by a second (also unidentified) boppish tune on which Branford and Wynton again took the solo limelight. Both brothers appeared suave and utterly cool but thoroughly dedicated to the task at hand. Both could have also easily won any CJF best-dressed-musician contest hands down. In fact, Branford's dapper navy-blue suit and purple cravat-and-pocketchief ensemble and brother Wynton's fisherman's-knit sweater and elegant-looking slacks seemed somehow to lend a new dignity and pizzazz to the onstage jazz craft—a dignity that was certainly not lost on the attending student players, any number of whom (perhaps following the Marsalis's sartorial lead of the past year) turned up at the 25th CJF wearing ties, double-breasted suits, and jackets.

During the set, Wynton, in particular, was allowed to solo at length, squeaking here, flinging off technically astounding flurries of 16th notes there, mocking a phrase impolitely, and then bending back deep to bring it to full-throttle completion. It was undoubtedly his show. For the third number (a fast bop version of "Surrey with the Fringe on Top"), Branford switched to soprano saxophone, Wynton soloed majestically again, and Jim McNeely did his subtle, crystal-clear keyboard logic routine once more. Fairly short in comparison to past extended judges' jams, the set ended after only thirty-five minutes. Linking arms in a line, all five judges returned to take several bows while the crowd gave tumultuous approval of their individual and collective efforts.

Saturday afternoon featured a Notre Dame combo (including Distinguished Performance Citation recipient/trombonist Kevin Quinn) and ensembles from MIT, Texas Southern, Purdue University, and Fredonia College, the latter of which was selected as the festival's third Outstanding Big Band. Saturday evening not only showcased the CJF high-school festival winners, but the Northeastern Illinois University Ensemble, the Loyola University Ensemble (New Orleans), a swinging Cincinnati College Conservatory Quartet, and the overpowering Eastman School of Music Ensemble and "Saxology" combo, both of which were awarded Outstanding Performance plaques, as well. (As in previous years, three such plaques were awarded in both band and combo group categories.)

In addition to the two Outstanding Group awards, Eastman band and combo members managed to receive nine Distinguished Performance Citations in 1983. These citation recipients included Jeff Beal (trumpet), Phil Tulga (trombone), Charles Pillow (alto sax), Joel McNeely (flute), Jeff Heimer (piano), Bill Grimes (bass), Bernie Dresel (drums), and Jeff Beal and Brian Scanlon (arranger/composers).

Departing for the traditional jam sessions (held this year in the ballroom of the LaFortune Student Center—drum set and other miscellaneous instruments provided by the CJF), the student musicians and remaining crowd members slowly began to disperse, carrying with them—as had so many musicians, students, listeners, critics, and crowds in festivals past—a bevy of memorable collegiate-jazz moments that could only have been heard at the unforgettable silver-anniversary CJF bash.

Summing up the sentiments of all those who had helped over the two-score-and-five years (some struggling, some plentiful, some fraught with cancellation peril) to make the Collegiate Jazz Festival a success, longtime CJF adviser, scholar, backer, and friend, Dan Morgenstern closed his sage opening notes for the '83 festival program with the stirring cry: "Here's to the next 25!"[4]

1
9   In early April 1984, the 26th Collegiate Jazz Festival once more
         played host to fifteen of the nation's top combos and bands from
8   Massachusetts, Indiana, Michigan, Ohio, New Jersey, Virginia,
         and New York. Turning again to a younger breed of professional
4   jazz musician, seasoned CJF chairman Bob O'Donnell and his stu-
         dent staff presented attending audiences and bands with a stellar
judging panel made up of twenty-year-old Jazz Messengers trumpet-sensation Terence Blanchard; swinging, popular Cuban saxophonist Paquito D'Rivera; pianist Joanne Brackeen; onetime Pat Metheny Group drummer Danny Gottlieb; internationally respected bassist Dave Holland; and the Director of the Institute of Jazz Studies at Rutgers University, Dan Morgenstern.

Featuring a female panel member for only the second time in CJF history (the first, Roberta Flack, appeared as a judge at the 1972 festival), the event also benefited tremendously from the addition of world-renowned jazz broadcaster, concert producer, writer, and educator Willis Conover as emcee. Returning to the festival fold after an absence of nine years, Conover once more added his vast knowledge of jazz history and musicianship to the collegiate proceedings.

Braving their way to Stepan Center in a driving rainstorm (which would continue throughout the duration of the festival),[1] CJF audiences were treated on the opening evening to performances by the University of Notre Dame Ensemble,[2] a Fredonia State College (N.Y.) Jazz Quintet and Ensemble, Eastern Illinois University's Kevin Gainer Quartet, and an eventual Outstanding Performance plaque recipient, the Herb Pomeroy-led Massachusetts Institute of Technology Ensemble. Closing down the first night's jazz feast was, of course, the judges' jam.

Taking the stage enthusiastically, judges Blanchard, D'Rivera, Brackeen, Gottlieb, and Holland launched into a dynamic, uplifting set of spontaneous jazz creativity that lasted an hour-and-a-half and brought jam-packed Stepan Center crowds to their feet on a number of occasions. Clearly, there was a potent current of performance electricity among the judges onstage. Few in attendance, however, could have predicted just where that spark might indeed lead the following night.

Saturday morning, April 14, saw the seventeenth incarnation of the Collegiate Jazz Festival High School Festival get underway at nearby Clay High School. Playing host this year to nine high-school bands from Ohio, Indiana, Illinois, Michigan, and New York, the festival also featured respected judges such as Kenneth Bartosz (Director of Jazz Bands at Loyola Academy, Winnetka, Illinois), Doug Beach (Director of Jazz Bands at Elmhurst College, Elmhurst, Illinois), and Tom Hilliard (teacher, composer, arranger, and leader of the Chicago-based Chamber Jazz Octet). Although noncompetitive, the high-school festival once again designated one or two bands as "Outstanding" and invited them to show off their respective jazz wares during the opening segment of the Saturday-evening CJF session. In addition, the festival distributed $6,000 worth of scholarships to the Berklee College of Music to "Outstanding" individual soloists and band members.[3]

Featured during the Saturday-afternoon collegiate-jazz session were bands from Roosevelt University (Chicago) and Western Michigan University, a John Stubblefield-led Rutgers Jazz Ensemble, and a Governor's State University combo, entitled Sanctuary. Also on the agenda was the University of Illinois Jazz Ensemble II, directed by Tom Birkner, who in 1981 conducted one of the CJF High School Festival's "outstanding" bands.[4]

Friday evening's musical offerings included two Outstanding Performance bands—the Michigan State University Jazz Ensemble and the New England Conservatory's Medium Rare band—as well as the William Paterson Jazz Sextet (William Paterson College, Wayne, New Jersey), a University of Notre Dame Jazz Quartet (featuring trombonist Kevin Quinn, pianist Peter Weiss, bassist Brian Burke, and drummer Chris Alford), and the Virginia Commonwealth University Ensemble, which performed an extended set dedicated primarily to compositions by Duke Ellington.[5] Finally, the much-anticipated University of Illinois Festival Band (a guest group directed by well-known educator/college bandleader John Garvey), emerged.

Climbing onstage one last time after the judges had returned from secluded backstage conferences, Willis Conover (who had agreed to broadcast tapes of the festival periodically over the next year on his internationally known Voice of America program, *Music U.S.A.*) announced the Outstanding bands and combos, as well as the noncompetitive Distinguished Performance certificate recipients (which were offered in even more plentiful degree than the previous year).[6]

And then it was over—or was it? Moving to the stage at this

already advanced hour—to the disbelief of several hundred stragglers remaining in the crowd—were the judges! In an unheard of act of Collegiate Jazz Festival enthusiasm and commitment, the judges (who had discussed the possibility of another joint performance among themselves that afternoon) had decided to jam a second time! Once again, Joanne Brackeen (sporting a white, Al Capone-style straw hat and a dark, baseball-pitcher-esque warm-up jacket), Paquito D'Rivera (white coat, flat-topped white straw Panama hat), Dave Holland (beard and loose-fitting Himalayan guru shirt), Danny Gottlieb (the longest-haired drummer/judge to attend the festival since Aynsley Dunbar in 1972), and Terence Blanchard (attired in natty suit, tie, slacks, and scholarly, wide-lens glasses) improvised energetically until the early hours of Sunday morning. (Due to the unceasing rain, and several Stepan Center ceiling leaks, a bucket had to be placed between Dave Holland and Joanne Brackeen to catch errant drops during the second jam.)[7]

Startling, provocative, and thoroughly dedicated to jazz, the twenty-sixth annual Collegiate Jazz Festival (which was videotaped for the second consecutive year and boasted an updated logo as well as streamlined, professional food-concession operations—the latter to ensure crowd comfort) had once more etched its way into the musical consciousness of attending young musicians, bandleaders, and jazz buffs.

"We are not able to reward the judges with the compensation they deserve, according to current professional standards," wrote chairman Bob O'Donnell in his 1984 CJF program note, "but the festival's excellent reputation throughout the jazz industry helps to override monetary considerations. We are concerned with jazz education, for both performers and listeners, and we believe CJF provides a very conducive learning environment. Of course, we also realize that CJF is a jazz celebration, and we hope to keep celebrating for another twenty-five years."[8]

1985 America's longest running collegiate jazz festival returned in the spring of 1985 to celebrate its twenty-seventh year of existence with a special judging-panel member in tow: guitarist Gene Bertoncini.

A late addition to the year's CJF judging crew (which also included tenor-saxophonist Jimmy Heath, pianist/1960 CJF student-performer Stanley Cowell, talented drummer Butch Miles, bassist/1984 CJF judge Dave Holland, and critic/jazz historian Dan Morgenstern), Bertoncini—a 1959 Notre Dame graduate and a performer at the first

Old Fieldhouse festival—was finally coming home. It had been a twenty-six-year trip, but worth the wait for the university's lone contribution to modern jazz.

One of the most versatile guitarists in the jazz world (a musician's musician equally adept in classical music as well as jazz), Bertoncini had performed over the years with Buddy Rich, Benny Goodman, the Paul Winter Consort, the NBC Tonight Show Orchestra, Tony Bennett, Clark Terry, Zoot Sims, Luciano Pavarotti, and the Metropolitan Opera Orchestra. Termed the "Segovia of the jazz guitar" by one impassioned critic, he had been quietly going about his jazz business for several decades while honing dual reputations as both a sought-after studio-session man and a teacher at Boston's New England Conservatory of Music and the Eastman School of Music in Rochester, New York.[1]

Linking up with gifted young bassist, Michael Moore, in 1977 to form a popular jazz duet, Bertoncini had gone on to release two albums (with Moore)—Bridges (1977) and Close Ties (1984)—each featuring varied, unique blends of classical and jazz works.[2] That the Collegiate Jazz Festival had taken the opportunity in 1985 to acknowledge his all-too-unsung talents and contributions to jazz was both a necessary step (with regard to celebrating Notre Dame's own history of student-jazz efforts) and indicative of why the CJF had earned the right to call itself a "festival" once more.

Opening for the nineteenth consecutive year with the traditional symposium, held Friday afternoon, April 12, in the Music Hall on Notre Dame's campus, the CJF was soon up and swinging again. During the symposium, several audience members took Miles Davis's recent recording and performance efforts to task, only to be successfully rebuffed by judge Dave Holland[3] (who had played with the famed trumpeter during the late sixties and early seventies). In addition, although working on but two hours' sleep after a late-night New York City performance and an early-morning series of flights to South Bend, judges Jimmy Heath and Stanley Cowell added their perceptive comments to festival-symposium lore and showed few signs of weariness.[4]

As for the festival itself, the first music session got warmly underway that evening with a performance by Father Wiskirchen's University of Notre Dame Jazz Ensemble, which presented several "tight" numbers before vocalist Ora Jones roused the crowd with a stirring rendition of "Got My Mojo Working."[5] Up next, an American Conservatory of Music (Chicago) combo attracted audience attention with "spirited" solos by pianist Bethany Pickens during songs such as "You Never Forget" and "Brazilian Breeze," before a Massachusetts Institute of Technology Ensemble emerged excitingly with "unique and different" selections, including "Amphibious Race," and "Tinsel Town Trap."[6] A synthesizer-juiced, electrified trio from Capital University (Columbus, Ohio) then added a different (and somewhat loud) twist to the night and, finally, one of 1985's Outstanding Performance bands, the University of Amherst Jazz Ensemble, wowed the packed Stepan Center crowd with "lively" renditions of numbers like "Scrambler" and "After You're Gone."[7]

Last, of course, but surely not least, was the judges' jam—featuring Stanley Cowell, Gene Bertoncini, Jimmy Heath, Butch Miles, and Dave Holland. Yet another roof-raising improvisational success, the jam brought magical smiles to each judge's face and, as usual, the crowd to its feet. After the last number, the judges linked arms and formed a line behind Miles's drum kit onstage and took several bows as the audience applause continued for several long minutes.

The Saturday-morning (and afternoon) CJF High School Festival entertained Clay High School crowds once more with performances by bands from Colorado, Indiana, and Ohio. Meanwhile, the Collegiate Jazz Festival's afternoon session featured ensembles from Ohio State, Northern Iowa, Michigan State, and Fredonia State University College, as well as a University of Notre Dame combo containing trumpeter Reg Bain, trombonist Kevin Quinn, guitarist Andy Boisvert, bassist Brian Burke, and drummer Mark Shepard.

Saturday evening was nothing short of a powerhouse musical affair. Launched with performances by fired-up Outstanding High School Festival bands, the session played toe-tapping host to Outstanding Performance groups such as the Virginia Commonwealth University Jazz Ensemble and the New England Conservatory of Music's Medium Rare band—a perennial CJF participant and crowd favorite. Also present and accounted for on the jazz agenda were Outstanding Performance combos from Fredonia State (the Fredonia Alternative Jazz Sextet) and William Paterson College (the William Paterson College Jazz Sextet). Closing down the jazz extravaganza were dynamic performances by the Eastman School of Music Jazz Ensemble and the United States Air Force Airmen of Note. Continuing the tradition of deemphasizing competition, nearly 75 Distinguished Performance citations were distributed to individual soloists at the discretion of the judges.[8]

"This 1985 CJF probably has the best collection of college bands and combos ever assembled here," read festival-chairman John Cerabino's closing 1985 program note. "They not only represent a wide range of geographic locations, but also perform in diverse and unique styles. Last month I read an extremely disturbing article in the *Chicago Tribune* on the 'death' of jazz. Well, my response to that ridiculous statement is embodied in the performances of the groups assembled here this weekend. If these bands are any indication of the future of jazz, as they truly must be, I can undoubtedly say that jazz is indeed alive and well."[9]

"There are some excellent musicians and bands here, and I'm glad to be a part of it," echoed judge Jimmy Heath. "How can they say jazz is dead when young people here are learning to play it?"[10]

Outspoken, talented trumpeter Wynton Marsalis dazzled CJF crowds in 1983 with his potent improvisations.
(Photo courtesy Karen Klocke)

Sartorially splendid young tenor-saxophonist Branford Marsalis solos majestically during the 1983 Judges' Jam. (Photo courtesy Karen Klocke)

Twenty-one-year-old trumpet whiz-kid Wynton Marsalis takes to the CJF Judges' Jam limelight with the urgent rhythmic backing of bassist Ron Carter (left) and drummer Tony Williams (right).

(Photo by Joe Carey)

Twenty-year-old Jazz Messengers trumpet sensation Terence Blanchard—youngest judge ever to attend the festival—commands crowd attention during the 1984 Judges' Jam.

(Photo courtesy Karen Klocke)

Swinging, popular Cuban saxophonist Paquito D'Rivera digs in during a Friday
night Judges' Jam solo turn in 1984.   (Photo courtesy Karen Klocke)

Tenor-saxophone great Jimmy Heath in action during the 1985 CJF Judges' Jam.
(Bassist Dave Holland visible at rear.)

(Photo courtesy Karen Klocke)

Guitarist Gene Bertoncini—Notre Dame's best-known contribution to modern jazz—
returned as a festival judge in 1985. (Photo courtesy Karen Klocke)

EPILOGUE

> I think the main function of the festival is that it is ed-
> ucational on many different levels. It's educational for
> the audience—one of the big things it does is build an
> audience for jazz among the people and the students
> that come to hear it. It's educational from the point of
> view of providing a motivating goal for the musicians,
> because they get pretty excited about it. And it's an
> educational factor for the students in my band, for ex-
> ample, to hear what other bands and musicians are
> playing. It's a learning experience, and also it's just
> plain good entertainment.—Fr. George Wiskirchen,
> CJF program interview, 1983

For nearly three decades, the University of Notre Dame Collegiate Jazz
Festival has been a potent force in the jazz-education world. Originated
in 1959 as a regional gathering of the collegiate-jazz clans, the festival
was expanded the following year to an event of national scope and
size that quickly caught—and has since kept— the attention of collegiate
and high-school musicians, educators, critics, and professional jazz
men and women across the United States.

An uncanny spawning ground for countless student musicians
who have gone on to successful professional-jazz careers—Joe Farrell,
Dave Baker, Gene Bertoncini, Marvin Stamm, Don Menza, Paul Winter,
Bob James, Oscar Brashear, David Sanborn, Randy and Michael
Brecker, Cecil, Ron and Dee Dee Bridgewater, Billy Harper, Bunky
Green, Chico Freeman, Jim McNeely, John Clayton, Jr. (to name a
few)—the festival has also mirrored—and, in no small way, influenced—
the struggle for, and growth of, jazz education in the schools.

Throughout the long, hard fight for academic acceptance of jazz,

173

the Collegiate Jazz Festival has been there, surviving its own battles with limited budgets, disapproving faculty, administrative red tape, cancellation threats, and, at times, perplexingly inattentive student bodies. The University of Notre Dame Collegiate Jazz Festival struggled and grew as did jazz in the schools. An educational and musical success, the festival became the model for many other collegiate and high-school festivals—none quite so soulful, well-produced, or laden with so much collegiate jazz talent.

All of which is valid historical fact. But what is the appeal, the real essence of the CJF?

The answer, I think, may lie in a dedication to an aesthetic integrity, an openness to diversity and change, and, simultaneously, a preservation of certain historically relevant jazz values and principles that, it is hoped, will never be lost.

Aesthetic integrity? Yes. Perhaps due to the unique union of what was once considered a "wanton" sound with a somewhat conservative Catholic university intent on preserving certain moral and ethical values for its student charges, the festival has remained free from often destructive commercial taint. Such freedom has, as a result, allowed the event to follow its own inner compass and path and present music in a rarefied environment that invites experimentation, excitement, and peak improvisational powers. From the very start, the festival has also been committed to providing a platform from which collegiate jazz talent could express itself as it saw fit. A mirror to changes, diversities, and developments in the professional jazz world (and, for a time in the experimental early sixties, perhaps even a forum for new ideas) the festival has continued to examine and alter its structure over the years (particularly with regard to competitive aspects) in order to keep pace with social, aesthetic, and musical evolutions and impacts. Much of the credit for this openness, of course, must rest with the Notre Dame students in charge of the event, who each year have brought—and continue to bring—new perspectives, energies, and a fresh approach to the CJF.

Finally, the festival preserves historically relevant jazz values and principles by honoring the contributions to jazz made by the judges—many of them legendary musicians, educators, and critics—in attendance each year and by presenting the traditional symposium and judges' jam.

As formalized jazz education has evolved, the number of clubs in which young musicians could sit in onstage and "jam" with professional musicians and later discuss backgrounds, interests, influences, and beliefs has dramatically decreased. Without a grip of some kind on the meaning of and benefits traditionally derived from this revered jazz institution, a whole generation of student musicians who are out-of-sync with jazz tradition and history might well evolve. The Collegiate Jazz Festival symposium and judges' jam, therefore, exist as both event highlights and educational necessities, offering CJF audiences and student musicians additional perspectives and insights into the culture of jazz.

Needless to say, the Collegiate Jazz Festival has made an impact. But, in the final analysis, perhaps it's best to return to the words of a student, *Scholastic* music-critic Pete Herbert, who in 1960 touched upon the real heart and purpose of this big "noise" from Notre Dame when he wrote: "If you've got something to say, come here and be heard—this is the lure of the CJF."

NOTES

Chapter 1. Beginnings

1. Although the history of Notre Dame's involvement with jazz actually dates back to 1917 and colorful student trumpeter/pianist/jazz combo and band leader Charlie Davis—friend of George Gipp and Knute Rockne and, after his graduation in 1921, the playing partner of Red Nichols, Hoagy Carmichael, and Bix Beiderbecke—an "official University Dance Band" didn't emerge on campus until the early fifties. Organized and run by Notre Dame student musicians, the dance band took the Lettermen name in 1955–56 while under the joint leadership of junior saxophonist Ed Pistey and sophomore guitarist Gene Bertoncini. Charlie Davis interviews, summer-fall, 1983; *Scholastic*, May 6, 1955, p. 11.

For in-depth looks at Charlie Davis and his famed Indiana band, see Duncan Schiedt's *The Jazz State of Indiana* (Pittsboro: Duncan P. Schiedt, 1977), pp. 124–47, or Charlie's own *That Band From Indiana* (Oswego, N.Y.: Mathom Publishing Co., 1982). A briefer profile of Charlie Davis (by the author) also appeared in the spring 1984 issue of *Notre Dame* magazine, pp. 45–46.

2. *Scholastic*, November 7, 1958, p. 22.

3. Ibid., p. 23.

4. Bill Graham notes that the overall festival concept—initially intended as a showcase for Notre Dame student jazz talent, but soon broadened beyond the campus to include a wider range of collegiate creativity in a "Newport-esque" setting—resulted from this "small bull session" (which may also have included other eventual festival staff members Jim Naughton, George Milton, Rudy Hornish, Gus Ludwig, and Jim Wysocki). Bill Graham interview, November 27, 1985.

5. In a *Scholastic* article published three weeks before the inaugural 1959 event, festival staff member Jim Naughton wrote: "When the committee first approached Mr. Suber with the idea for the festival, he became almost as excited as a ten-year-old in a penny arcade (which is not to suggest that the *down beat* office more than slightly resembles a penny arcade)." *Scholastic*, March 20, 1959, p. 15.

6. The term "stage band" developed in the late forties and early fifties as "a euphemism coined in the Baptist southwest to avoid the sinful aspects of dancing and jazzing." [Leonard Feather/Ira Gitler, *The Encyclopedia of Jazz in the Seventies* (New York: Horizon Press, 1976), p. 369.] Although stage-band origins stretch back to student marching bands in the early years of the century and later (in the twenties and thirties), university dance bands that adapted and presented popular music for a variety of student affairs, the real impetus for the stage-band movement was the end of World War II and the demise of many commercial bands (when swing discovered it was no longer king) in the late forties. With the job hunt on, many returning musicians took advantage of G.I. Bill opportunities and went back to school to obtain a music-education degree. By the early fifties, a large number of these music-degree recipients and ex-swing-era bandmen were scattered across the country teaching in high schools, instructing and organizing concert and marching bands—and, of course, "stage bands." For unknown reasons, the stage band movement found its earliest strengths in Texas, Missouri, and Oklahoma. In the Midwest, the movement took hold in the mid-fifties, due to the efforts of Fr. George Wiskirchen, Charles Suber, *down beat* magazine, and others. Once in college, these stage band-oriented high schoolers began to demand appropriate music opportunities thereby giving jazz education at the university level further impetus for growth. These demands eventually also resulted in events such as the University of Notre Dame Collegiate Jazz Festival, which offered the jazz-education movement even higher visibility, recognition, thrust, and unity. [Leonard Feather/Ira Gitler, *The Encyclopedia of Jazz in the Seventies* (New York: Horizon Press, 1976), pp. 366–374 (*Jazz Education* history and analysis chapter by Charles Suber); *Cavalier*, July 1967, pp. 73, 93–95 (article on collegiate jazz by James L. Collier); Allen Scott, *Jazz Educated, Man: A Solid Foundation* (Washington, D.C.: American International Publishers, 1973), pp. 17–26, 109–15.]

7. *Scholastic*, March 20, 1959, p. 15. Charles Suber interview, Chicago, January 7, 1983.

8. Bill Graham recalls that few results were expected when Tom Cahill and he first approached the elder Blue Note Club owner. "We thought we'd only get a few free drinks out of it, but Frank Holzfiend immediately took us under his wing. He was very encouraging from the start and probably did more for our morale than anyone in those early days." Bill Graham interview, November 27, 1985.

9. Tom Cahill interview, fall 1982.

10. *down beat* magazine, April 30, 1959, p. 13. Story retold in detail by Charles Suber during January 7, 1983, interview.

11. Thomas Schlereth, *The University of Notre Dame: A Portrait of Its History and Campus* (Notre Dame, Ind., and London: University of Notre Dame Press, 1976), pp. 184–87; Chet Grant, Bill LaFortune interviews, 1983.

12. *Scholastic*, March 20, 1959, p. 14.

13. Bill Graham interview, November 27, 1985; Tom Cahill interview, fall 1982.

14. *down beat*, April 30, 1959, p. 13. This number included: Dave's Band (Indiana University); the Octets (Marquette University); the UJW Quartet (University of Minnesota); the Trio (University of Cincinnati); the Chuck Lewis Sextet (Michigan State University); Keith Thomas Quintet (Indiana State Teachers College); Southern Illinois All-Stars (Southern Illinois); the Yeomen (Oberlin College); Duke's Men (Purdue University); Campus Owls' Quintet (Miami University); Ohio State University Jazz Forum (Ohio State University); University Jazz Workshop (University of Illinois); Johnny Jazz Quartet (St. John's University); DePaul Jazz Ensemble (DePaul University); the Lettermen (University of Notre Dame); and the Bob Pierson Quintette (University of Detroit). Midwest Collegiate Jazz Festival release, *Collegiate Jazz Festival* file, University of Notre Dame Achives.

15. *Scholastic*, March 20, 1959, p. 15. Bill Graham recalls that it was most likely Charles Suber's idea to invite Rev. Norman O'Connor. Bill Graham interview, November 27, 1985. Negotiations with Father O'Connor apparently continued up until a few weeks before the festival, as publicity articles in the *Scholastic* and *South Bend Tribune* including his name as a judging-panel possibility attest; *Scholastic*, March 20, 1959, p. 15; *South Bend Tribune*, March 26, 1959.

16. *down beat*, May 14, 1959, p. 4.

17. Bill Graham interview, November 27, 1985; Tom Cahill interview, fall 1982. Bill Graham recalls that the festival committee had little — if any — funding to draw on to assemble event paraphernalia, awards, etc.

> We didn't pay a penny for anything. The student government might have given us $200 or so, but, in reality, we had no investment money whatsoever. Charles Suber put me in touch with the music companies, [H & A] Selmer and [C. G.] Conn, and Tom and I had to go hat-in-hand to these guys. We gave them our story and they offered to sponsor some very nice prizes. I designed the first program and we got one of the sponsoring instrument companies — Conn, I think — to pay for the printing of the program, which was really just an 8-1/2 by 11-inch sheet of blue paper folded over once. We really put the strong-arm on one marketing vice president over there, just took advantage of him and put him in a position where — in light of the publicity we would receive in *down beat*, etc. — he just couldn't say no. We built a stage at one end of the basketball court and swiped a big blue-velvet curtain or drapery — it must have been twenty feet high — and draped it behind the stage. There was some tinfoil lettering that spelled out "The Midwest Collegiate Jazz Festival" pinned to the curtain. The Fieldhouse acoustics were awful, and everything we did was held together with baling wire. We were absolutely shocked with the results.

18. *down beat*, May 14, 1959, p. 12.
19. Ibid., p. 4.
20. *Scholastic*, April 17, 1959, p. 12.
21. *down beat*, May 14, 1959, p. 12.
22. Ibid.

23. *Scholastic*, April 17, 1959, p. 12.

24. A full list of individual 1959 winners includes: trombonist George West (Oberlin College); pianist Herb Pilhofer (University of Minnesota); drummer Ben Appling and string bassist Bill Woods (University of Detroit); tenor-saxophonist Sonny McBroom (Ohio State University); trumpeter Jim Benham (Michigan State University); guitarist Don Miller and vocalist Lois Nemser (University of Cincinnati); and Best Accordionist/Outstanding Instrumentalist Bob Sardo (Purdue University). *down beat*, May 14, 1959, p. 12; *Scholastic*, April 17, 1959, p. 12.

25. *down beat*, May 14, 1959, p. 12.

26. *Scholastic*, April 17, 1959, p. 12. Bill Graham recalls that Art Van Damme may have jammed on stage with one of the student groups during the festival. Bill Graham interview, November 27, 1985.

27. Ibid. After the festival, Blue Note club-owner Frank Holzfiend found himself "sorely tempted to book *all* seven finalists." *down beat*, May 14, 1959, p. 4.

28. *down beat*, May 14, 1959, p. 12. One of the budding talents Freddie Williamson "cornered" in 1959 was none other than Gene Bertoncini. After the festival, Williamson booked the Notre Dame student guitarist's Lettermen quartet into another well-known Chicago jazz club, the Cloister Inn, for a three-week July performance stint opposite singer Carmen McRae. Although Bertoncini would flirt with a career in architecture (initially as an apprentice to a disciple of Frank Lloyd Wright) for the next year, the booking was the first stepping-stone in what would become a successful jazz career. Gene Bertoncini interviews, 1983, 1985.

During a November 27, 1985, interview, Bill Graham stressed Gene Bertoncini's unsung importance to the first festival. "Gene was the first or second person we approached for advice. We talked to him about the festival idea, and he gave us a lot of input in terms of how to go about things. Although you won't find him listed as a member of the 1959 committee in the program or anywhere else in print, he made a big contribution to our efforts that year."

29. *Scholastic*, April 17, 1959, p. 12.

Chapter 2. The Sixties

1960

1. *down beat*, May 14, 1959, p. 4.

2. *Scholastic*, April 17, 1959, p. 5.

3. The National Stage Band Camp, Inc., a nonprofit corporation founded in 1958 by Ken Morris to "provide high school and college music students training in stage band jazz playing techniques," first took place during the summer of 1959 on the campus of Indiana University in Bloomington. Publicized as the "National Stage Band Camp, featuring the Stan Kenton Clinic" (approached by Morris before the gathering, Stan Kenton had readily agreed to

attend and lend his name to the proceedings), the one-week "camp" boasted an enrollment of 157. Featuring clinics, workshops, lectures, and rehearsals, the successful event was expanded to two weeks the following year and catered to 276 youths from 34 states and two provinces of Canada. Thereafter, camps were set up each summer both in Bloomington and at a number of universities across the country. Neither Kenton nor the other clinicians in attendance at the camps received any salary for their efforts. *down beat*, September 29, 1960, p. 23; October 24, 1963, p. 14.

4. *down beat*, November 12, 1959, p. 12.

5. Ibid.

6. Ibid., April 2, 1959, p. 11.

7. Ibid., April 28, 1960, p. 34.

8. *Scholastic*, March 18, 1960, p. 9.

9. Ibid., March 11, 1960, p. 15.

10. Allen Scott, *Jazz Educated, Man: A Solid Foundation* (Washington, D.C.: American International Publishers, 1973), p. 20.

11. There are a number of legends concerning Father Wiskirchen (also known from time to time in this period as "the Swinging Padre") that exist among ex-Melodons, educators, and musicians. One confirmed tale involves the time Father Wiskirchen—determined to obtain creative, exciting music charts for his high-school band—simply walked up to Count Basie between sets at a Chicago club, introduced himself (dressed, of course, in priestly garb and collar), and, after describing the sad plight of his young jazz charges, asked the legendary bandleader if he could just copy a few arrangements from Basie's music library. Perplexed, perhaps, by the incongruity of a man of the cloth teaching jazz, and touched by Wiskirchen's story, Basie agreed. Father Wiskirchen subsequently borrowed Basie's library, took it to his quarters, and copied a number of charts out for his band. *down beat*, October 30, 1969, p. 17; Charles Suber interview, Chicago, January 7, 1983. Another Melodon/Wiskirchen legend—unconfirmed—involves a meeting between the good Father and jazz legend Charlie Parker.

12. *South Bend Tribune*, March 20, 1960, p. 1.

13. Ibid., March 16, 1960; *down beat*, April 28, 1960, p. 29.

14. *down beat*, April 28, 1960, p. 4.

15. *Time* magazine, April 4, 1960, p. 74.

16. *Jazz Review*, June 1960, p. 36.

17. Ibid.

18. Ibid., p. 37. The University of Kansas Jays quartet performing at CJF 1960 also contained tenor-saxophonist Gary Foster.

19. *Time*, April 4, 1960, p. 73.

20. Ibid., p. 74. Regarding North Texas State's performance impact in 1960, 1961 festival chairman Dave Sommer wrote:

I had taken a break [from 1960 festival staff duties] to hear the North Texas State College Lab Band and, not finding a seat readily available, perched myself on the edge of the basketball court about 30 feet from the stage. The band worked its way through a difficult and powerful

Johnny Richards composition and then leader Leon Breeden announced that they would play "The Lamp is Low."

The band started out slow and sonorous, much as Ravel had intended his beautiful composition to be played. Then, with drummer Paul Guerrero leading the way, they moved into a Latin-tinged segment which almost lifted the Fieldhouse's rusty rafters. Almost, but . . . bang, the band leaped into an uptempo, all-stops-let-out-they-can't-keep-this-up-much-longer version of that old movie tune which just about blew me off the boards. I remember yelling "wow" or something, and sensing the complete spell this power had on the audience. Pure elation.

David Sommer, *CJF — First Four years: A Personal Recollection*, 1983 Collegiate Jazz Festival program, p. 23.

21. *down beat*, April 28, 1960, p. 4.
22. Ibid.
23. *Time*, April 4, 1960, p. 74.
24. *Fairmont* (West Virginia) *West Virginian*, March 25, 1960.
25. Ibid.
26. *Jazz Review*, June 1960, p. 37.
27. Other winners in 1960 included: guitarist Don Miller (University of Cincinnati); Most Promising Arranger Ralph Mutchler (Northwestern University); drummer John Tatgenhorse (Ohio State University); string bassist Dennis Behm (Iowa State University); and Most Promising Leader Lowell Latto (Ohio State University). Of the festival's student musician participants, Best Flautist Bob Pierson, found what was perhaps the most unique mode of paying one's way through college (in this case, the University of Detroit) — playing "bump and grind at a Detroit strip joint." David Sommer, *CJF — First Four Years: A Personal Recollection*, 1983 Collegiate Jazz Festival program, p. 23.

28. *down beat*, April 28, 1960, p. 34.
29. Ibid., p. 29.
30. *Time*, April 4, 1960, p. 73.; *down beat*, September 27, 1962, p. 20.
31. *Time*, April 4, 1960, p. 73. 1961 Chairman Dave Sommer (whose photo of 1959 Best Vocalist Lois Nemser accompanied the *Time* article) recalled that the *Time* piece was actually submitted by journalist Sidney Lazard, who was also covering the 1960 CJF for the *Chicago Sun-Times*. Dave Sommer interview, 1983.

32. *Jazz Review*, June 1960, p. 36.
33. *down beat*, April 28, 1960, p. 29.
34. Ibid., p. 34.
35. Jim Naughton interview, fall, 1982; Fr. George Wiskirchen, festival recollections, 1977 Collegiate Jazz Festival program, p. 6.
36. *down beat*, April 28, 1960, p. 34.

1961

1. *South Bend Tribune*, August 23, 1960.
2. Ibid.

3. *down beat*, September 29, 1960, p. 23.

4. 1961 CJF publicity brochure, University of Notre Dame Archives.

5. Ibid.

6. Ibid.

7. During the 1961 festival, Evans personalized his judging approach by offering each band and combo an extensive, often multiple-page critique. On occasion, he would even go so far as to write out long note-for-note transcriptions of student musician solos on paper during a performance and then notate exactly how the notes were ideally supposed to be played. Charles Suber interview, Chicago, January 7, 1983.

8. 1961 CJF information sheet, University of Notre Dame Archives.

9. 1961 CJF preliminary music session tapes, courtesy of Dick Klarich, Dave Sommer.

10. Ibid.

11. For their efforts, North Texas State band members reaped the Indiana Jazz Festival appearance prize offered by Hal Lobree, about whom CJF '61 chairman Dave Sommer had some things to say: ". . . a few words on Lobree. He was an Evansville businessman who thought it would be great to have a jazz festival, so he put on one. I think it lasted just that year. He came up to give the best group of CJF an appearance at the festival and proceeded to talk for at least twenty minutes in presenting the prize. Bored everyone stiff and gave me the willies for, as usual, we were running late and I never thought we would finish in time for the students to make it back to the halls in time for lockup." Dave Sommer correspondence, August 5, 1983.

12. In early 1983, Charles Suber bumped into Don Menza on a Chicago street only to be shocked during the course of the ensuing conversation as Menza said to him excitedly: "Well, this is the anniversary of that time at the CJF when you presented me with the saxophone that I had won as Outstanding Instrumentalist." Stunned at the vividness of Menza's memory of the CJF and that moment, Suber could only inquire as to how the well-known jazzman could recall the exact date. "Oh, that's easy," Menza replied, "because the day I received the award was also my birthday." Despite Menza's added memory-incentive, the exchange reveals much about the important meaning such prizes and recognition held for young, aspiring jazz musicians back in these early festival days. Charles Suber interview, Chicago, January 7, 1983.

13. *down beat*, June 8, 1961, pp. 16–17.

14. 1961 CJF brochure, University of Notre Dame Archives.

15. *down beat*, June 8, 1961, pp. 16–17.

16. Ibid.

1962

1. *down beat*, May 4, 1977, p. 18.

2. *down beat*, January 3, 1963, p. 17.

3. According to Ralph J. Gleason's liner notes for the Paul Winter Sextet album, "Jazz Premiere: Washington/The Paul Winter Sextet," issued in 1963,

Winter and Whitsell were enrolled at Northwestern University, Rout was about to begin work on a doctorate at the University of Minnesota, Evans had a degree in composition and would soon pursue a masters, Bernhardt was finishing a degree in organic chemistry at the University of Chicago, and Jones was a percussion major at Chicago's American Conservatory of Music. Ralph J. Gleason liner notes, "Jazz Premiere: Washington/The Paul Winter Sextet," Columbia Records album CL 1997, 1963.

4. *down beat*, January 3, 1963, p. 18.

5. Ralph J. Gleason liner notes, Columbia Records album CL 1997, 1963.

6. Little known amid the hoopla of the Sextet's Latin American tour was the disturbing fact that the trip had been poorly executed by the State Department, leading to numerous unfortunate complications. Provoked by a *down beat* article in late 1966 describing the poorly handled State Department tour of Russia made by legendary jazz-pianist Earl Hines earlier that year (*down beat*, November 3, 1966, pp. 18–19), Paul Winter Sextet/Latin American tour-manager Gene Lees wrote a blistering letter to *down beat* revealing that the Winter group was "treated as badly as the Hines group, perhaps worse. We were looked on by most U.S. government personnel only as live bodies, there to help gull the natives."

Citing a "cheapskate State Department policy of sending a group's equipment by air freight instead of as professional baggage," Lees went on to describe the difficulty he encountered in recovering misplaced baggage between Haiti and Mexico City. "Neither the airline, nor the U.S. government personnel seemed much interested in our predicament," continued Lees. "It took me thirteen days of searching and screaming over long-distance telephones to locate it." In the meantime, forced to dig up a replacement instrument, Winter-group trumpeter Dick Whitsell, "butchered his lip playing on a bad, borrowed instrument."

"Pianos," explained Lees, "were usually out of tune, some were unplayable; one was down so far that Warren Bernhardt played the entire concert transposing the music up a half step."

> In Costa Rica, two U.S. Information Agency types "forgot" about amplification for our concert. Trying to get adequate volume without it, bassist Richard Evans played until his fingers bled.
>
> We arrived in one town, having already been overworked by these two men to the point of collapse, to sit around a hotel lobby, waiting for people to check out; it seems these two men had "forgotten" to make hotel reservations. When we complained about this treatment, they sent back a "bad" report to Washington on us—and one of these men has now been promoted to a controlling position in setting up these tours.
>
> That was perhaps the most infuriating thing about it—the star-chamber system of reports to Washington on our "behavior." We were not, of course, able to send reports to Washington on their behavior. Yet I encountered misfits, incompetents, and fools in many critically important U.S. government posts in that troubled continent.

There were a few dedicated, capable and intelligent men, too, but the fools outnumbered them and it troubled me that this country's story is being told by such men. Many of them were condescending toward jazz and jazzmen but cynically indifferent to whether the music was good or bad so long as we softened up the people for them.

Although a curious five-years-after-the-fact artifact, Gene Lee's letter (excerpted above) remains a striking indictment of occasionally flawed State Department responsibility in regard to collegiate and professional jazz bands selected for foreign-tour duty in the early sixties. *down beat*, December 29, 1966, pp. 9–10.

7. *down beat*, January 3, 1963, p. 19. Once again, Paul Winter's pen proved as potent as his music, for, in reality, the Sextet's White House concert came about as a result of a letter Winter sent to President Kennedy's personal secretary. The letter, which inquired about the possibility of a performance for the Chief Executive, was subsequently shown to the President, who had previously taken note of the group's South American tour. An invitation to appear at the White House soon followed. *down beat*, December 6, 1962, p. 13.

8. *Scholastic*, March 30, 1962, p. 16.

9. Ibid., April 6, 1982, p. 10.

10. 1962 CJF press release, University of Notre Dame Archives.

11. *Scholastic*, April 13, 1962, p. 18.

12. Liner notes, Stan Kenton, North Texas State University Lab Band album, 90th Floor Records, SLL–904, 1961.

13. *Scholastic*, April 13, 1962, p. 19.

14. *down beat*, May 24, 1962, p. 15.

15. *Scholastic*, April 13, 1962, p. 19.

16. Ibid. Describing pianist Bob James's talents in the same *Scholastic* piece in 1962, Frank McConnell wrote: ". . . besides being a fine and firm leader of his group [Bob James] is one of the most technically proficient and swinging pianists I have heard. His style reminds one just a little of Thelonious Monk, perhaps because James, like Monk, has the sense to play with both hands, to play a piano and not an elaborate guitar, an attitude unhappily absent in most post-Bud Powell piano players. But James is primarily an individual; his treatment of the almost irrevocably cornball 'Ghost Riders In The Sky' was perhaps the best single performance of the whole series of concerts complete with a fine sense of humor (a terribly square tag ending played after each driving solo break), wonderful solo conception on the part of everyone in the group, and, of course, a firm swinging feel . . . a magnificent group."

17. Ibid.

18. Ibid.

19. Ibid.

20. *down beat*, May 24, 1962, p. 15.

21. Ibid.

22. *Scholastic*, April 13, 1962, p. 19.

1963

1. In 1963, for the first time in the history of the CJF, this number of 22 would include an opening festival performance by a 17-piece, student-run University of Notre Dame Lettermen big-band aggregate, led by alto-saxophonist/ student Bernie Zahren. In addition, a Notre Dame guest trio made up of guitarist Paul Leavis, drummer Robert "Gus" Duffy, and vocalist Buddy Hill (also a member of a local coffeehouse folk quartet known as The Four Winds) would appear while judges deliberated finalist choices on Saturday afternoon.

2. 1963 CJF program, p. 4. The 1963 *Dome* noted that Terry Gibbs and his quartet kicked off the jam session with a "frantic set," and that Bob Pozar, Ron Brooks, and Mike Lang "gave prodigiously of their talents" during the "all-night" proceedings which allowed "real aficionados the opportunity to greet the Saturday dawn." *Dome*, 1963, p. 53.

3. Ibid.

4. Ibid.

5. *Scholastic*, March 29, 1963, p. 26.

6. *Dome*, 1963, p. 52.

7. *down beat*, May 8, 1963, p. 10.

8. Ibid.

9. Leonard Feather liner notes, 1963 Collegiate Jazz Festival album, mastered and pressed by Crest Records, 1963. (Album courtesy of Paul Leavis, Bernie Zahren, Jack Carr, and Gus Duffy.) Recalling festival oddities in a March 7, 1969, *Scholastic* article, '69 CJF chairman Greg Mullen (who attended many early sixties CJF's as a Notre Dame High School Melodon band member) noted that at one point during the '63 event, Wright Jr. College's Frank Tesinsky "cast away the body of his horn" only to take ". . . . a solo on the slide . . . reminiscent of a constipated giraffe . . . heard in Lincoln Park Zoo." *Scholastic*, March 7, 1969, p. 21.

10. Ibid.

11. *down beat*, May 8, 1963, p. 10.

12. Ibid., p. 9.

13. Leonard Feather liner notes, 1963 Collegiate Jazz Festival album, Crest Records, 1963.

1964

1. *down beat*, September 26, 1963, p. 16.

2. In fact, an article on government-sponsored jazz tours (*down beat*, January 17, 1963) by Don DeMicheal reveals Paul Winter may have been one of the first to suggest that winners from the Notre Dame Collegiate Jazz Festival and the Villanova Intercollegiate Jazz Festival be chosen for foreign cultural-presentation tours representing the U.S. State Department.

3. Modeled on the well-known annual folk festival at the University of Chicago but geared to showcase collegiate folk groups, the first "CFF," which took "the Spirit of America" as its theme, featured sixteen participants from

a variety of midwestern colleges. Judges for the event were founder and president of Chicago-based Delmark Records Bob Koester, *down beat* associate editor Pete Welding, and University of Illinois folklorist/archivist Archibald Green. Among the groups taking part was a popular Notre Dame entry known as The Four Winds. *Dome*, University of Notre Dame, 1964.

4. *down beat*, April 23, 1964, p. 13.

5. *Voice of Notre Dame*, University of Notre Dame, April 15, 1964, p. 1.

6. Frustrated by a seeming standoff between four composer/arrangers and one "performing" musician (himself), Cannonball Adderley, concerned with the possible exclusion of the North Texas State University Billy Harper Sextet from the finals, raised his huge forearms at one point during the session, sent them crashing into the table, looked his peers in the eye, and exclaimed: "Did they swing? Did they? Did they have balls!?" Whether the direct result of this passionate outburst or not, the committee broke previous Collegiate Jazz Festival finals tradition and expanded the number of selected combos to four so as to include the Billy Harper group. Charles Suber interview, Chicago, January 7, 1983; Robert Share interview, Boston, 1983.

7. A founding member of the well-known pioneering jazz-rock group "Chicago," Jim Pankow's Melodon band days were recalled by Melodon band member/1969 Collegiate Jazz Festival chairman Greg Mullen. "Jim didn't write for the band back then," explained Mullen, "he played in a sub group of Melodons, a Melodons combo. He could improvise very well, but he never really promoted himself. We didn't know he'd go on like that." Conversation with Greg Mullen, summer 1983.

8. Due to a jaw injury incurred in an automobile accident in the early sixties, Baker, one of the outstanding trombonists in jazz (in 1962 he was named New Star trombonist in *down beat*'s International Jazz Critics Poll) had given up playing the instrument professionally and turned to cello instead.

9. *Scholastic*, March 7, 1969, p. 21.

10. *Indianapolis News*, August 13, 1962, no page.

11. *South Bend Tribune*, April 17, 1964.

12. *Chicago Daily News*, April 24, 1964, no page.

13. Many legends exist regarding Bunky Green and the 1964 Collegiate Jazz Festival. The most riveting of these tales concerns Cannonball Adderley's reaction while seated at the judging table as Green began to play in the preliminaries with Wright Junior College's big band. Listening for a moment to Green's solo prowess, Cannonball suddenly looked at the program listing and shouted loudly: "Vernice Green? Hell, that's no Vernice Green, that's Bunky Green!" Green, who was actually able to hear this remark all the way from the judges' table to the stage, was momentarily shaken, but continued to play. (Cannonball, of course, had good reason to recognize the saxophonist, for he had supervised the recording of Green's first album, "Blues Holiday"—cut when Green was barely twenty years old—for Riverside Records in 1960.) Conversations with Charles Suber and Bernie Zahren, 1983. Riverside information from *down beat*, December 15, 1966, pp. 20–21 and 42.

14. *down beat*, September 24, 1964, p. 24.

15. Gary McFarland liner notes, Collegiate Jazz Festival album, Crest Records, 1964.

16. Ibid.

1965

1. *Tulsa* (Oklahoma) *World*, January 20, 1965. The 1971 CJF program reveals an intriguing fact about the University of Michigan's 1965 Latin American Tour: "This tour was climaxed by a revolution in the Dominican Republic with the band being evacuated by U.S. Marine helicopters (sans luggage and instruments) amid a hail of rebel machine-gun fire."

Certainly a different kind of collegiate jazz experience! CJF '71 program, p. 7.

2. *Atlantic City* (New Jersey) *Press*, April 21, 1965, and Leonard Feather's liner notes to the Exodus Records album (EXS-6001) entitled "My Babe," released by Bunky Green in 1966 (in actuality, the album was recorded in 1960–61 for Vee Jay Records but was not released in record form until 1966). *down beat*, December 15, 1966, pp. 20–21, 42.

3. *down beat*, December 3, 1964, p. 9.

4. After the 1964 Collegiate Jazz Festival, the Northwestern band was offered the tour, and in late July, a deal and contract with the group were tentatively finalized by a representative of the State Department's Cultural Presentations committee and members of Northwestern's School of Music (including the dean, two assistant deans, and the comptroller), subject to the approval of school authorities.

Throughout the summer, the student-organized band, which had drafted Father Wiskirchen to be its unsalaried director, planned the tour, only to be jolted in early October when a university vice president announced that since the band was not an official university organization and Father Wiskirchen was not a member of the university faculty, the school was not "legally empowered to effect a contract with the government for the band's services, nor could the school assume any responsibility for the group while on tour." Strangely, though "unofficial," the Northwestern band had been in existence eight years, made use of university facilities, rehearsed weekly, presented concerts during the year and represented the school at outside festivals and functions such as the Notre Dame Collegiate Jazz Festival, at which numerous Northwestern band members had won soloist awards over the years. Even more curious is the fact that it was a Northwestern University student, Paul Winter, who had first broken ground in the State Department-sponsored collegiate-jazz foreign tour game. *down beat*, November 19, 1964, p. 13.

5. *down beat*, October 8, 1964, p. 13.

6. *Voice of Notre Dame*, April 7, 1965, p. 1.

7. Bernie Zahren correspondence, February 28, 1983. In something of a controversial move, the Notre Dame Lettermen group entry in CJF '65 presented a Larry Dwyer arrangement of Charlie Mingus's turbulent "Suite Freedom" during the festival-preliminaries sessions. Making use of Mingus's half-

sung/half-spoken song text (read on stage by Notre Dame student/poet Paul Reiter) the song—complete with handclaps and provocative tales of the black struggle for freedom—so moved the judging panel that they considered presenting the group with a special award. Although such an award was not forthcoming, the group nonetheless achieved for its efforts a courageous and meaningful niche in CJF history.

In 1983, Bernie Zahren, leader of the Notre Dame Lettermen, the group that performed the Mingus piece at CJF '65, recalled the presentation as the "most significant thing" he had done in music. Conversations with Bernie Zahren, 1983.

8. *down beat*, May 20, 1965, p. 12.

9. Ibid.

10. *Dome*, 1965, pp. 56–57.

11. Charles Suber interview, Chicago, January 7, 1983. (In a telephone interview in the summer of 1983, former Notre Dame trombonist and Collegiate Jazz Festival award-winner Larry Dwyer recalled that both Paul Horn and Clark Terry took part in the jam session at Robert's Supper Club.)

1966

1. *Scholastic*, March 18, 1966, p. 15.

2. *Indiana University Alumni Magazine*, April 1966.

3. Although unsure of whether it occurred in 1962 or 1966, Charles Suber recalled that judge Quincy Jones was so impressed with the overall Collegiate Jazz Festival experience that he turned over the check he received from CJF committee members at one festival for his transportation, hotel, and meal expenses and signed it back over to the event, refusing to take any money at all. In one of his judging years, Jones also volunteered to stay an extra day and come out to Notre Dame High School in Niles, Illinois, after the CJF in order to rehearse Father Wiskirchen's impressive Melodon jazz ensemble. Charles Suber interview, Chicago, January 7, 1983; Collegiate Jazz Festival program, 1977, p. 6.

4. *down beat*, May 5, 1966, p. 15.

5. *Scholastic*, March 7, 1969, p. 21.

6. *down beat*, May 5, 1966, p. 15. During its finals outing, the Indiana band performed a "wild and humorous version" of Charlie Mingus's "II B.S." replete with "plungers, hollers and sure-footed stomping." (*down beat*, May 5, 1966, p. 15.)

7. Ibid.

8. Ibid.

9. *Dome*, 1966, p. 218.

1967

1. *Cavalier*, July 1968, p. 94.

2. *Austin* (Texas) *American/New York Times* News Service (article by John S. Wilson), February 28, 1968.

3. *Billboard*, March 11, 1967.

4. CJF press release, November 1966. According to John Noel and Paul Schlaver, the negotiations with Bob Yde lasted roughly four to five months, beginning in the summer of '66 and continuing through October of that same year. Yde apparently pursued the Notre Dame Collegiate Jazz Festival aggressively during this period, eventually using such high-pressure tactics as "free-ride" offers to the Intercollegiate Music Festival finals in Miami. (Paul Schlaver even recalls making a bus trip to Miami at Yde's expense in late summer to discuss the IMF's direction and plans and that Fr. George Wiskirchen — whom Schlaver turned to in Miami for advice on numerous occasions — also took part in the meetings.) Essentially, Yde told Paul Schlaver and John Noel, "Here's the money to run your festival and here are the rules," fully expecting Notre Dame to join the Yde/Miami IMF team.

Though tempted at first by the offer, Schlaver and Noel eventually had reservations about Yde's plan, mainly because it allowed each regional feeder festival to recruit bands only from those respective regions, whereas the CJF had long been known for its national character. Confused, the two students turned to *down beat* editor Don DeMicheal and used him as a sounding board for their troubles. A longtime fan and backer of the CJF, DeMicheal expressed his belief that the Miami extravaganza might well be a highly commercial event and that by joining it, the CJF might lose much of its unique independent character. Bolstered by DeMicheal's comments and those of Fr. Wiskirchen, Schlaver and Noel gave the matter some additional thought and backed away from Yde's plan altogether (no easy decision in light of the CJF's pressing financial needs).

Greatly displeased with this rebuttal, Yde continued to badger the two students. Turned down for the last time, Yde (according to John Noel) remarked angrily, "Well, just remember you've had your chance," only to follow these words with a threat to "drive the CJF out of existence." Attempting to make good his curse, Yde tried to set up a Midwest regional event that year as part of the Miami feeder festival chain. Ironically, arrangements for such a Midwest festival at Northwestern University eventually fell through, and plans for the event were "quietly cancelled in early '67." Thus, concluded a *down beat* blurb of April 20, 1967 (p. 15), "the ballyhooed 'World Series of College Jazz' (at Miami) will not have a representative from the Midwest, where some of the country's best college jazz bands are located." As a result, despite Yde's vaunted event, the 1967 CJF would play host to a triumvirate of national powerhouse collegiate bands from the University of Illinois, Indiana University, and Ohio State.

(In all fairness to Yde and the IMF, it should be pointed out that each of the feeder festivals held a clinic with name jazz educators and musicians — all organized by music educator Clem DeRosa.)

Conversation with John Noel, July 15, 1983; conversation with Paul Schlaver, November 30, 1985.

5. Conversation with John Noel, July 15, 1983; conversation with Paul Schlaver, November 30, 1985.

6. CJF press release, November, 1966.

7. Ibid.

8. Ibid.

9. Ibid.

10. Notre Dame trombonist/two-time CJF soloist award-winner Larry Dwyer recalls an informal symposium in 1966 that took place in the LaFortune Student Center with the University of Illinois's John Garvey and various CJF judges in 1966. Conversation with Larry Dwyer, summer 1983.

11. CJF '67 program, p. 29.

12. At the jam, the piano was so out of tune that Herbie Hancock had to transpose and play each tune a half-step up. Notre Dame trombonist Larry Dwyer (who took the jam-session stage with Herbie Hancock and Donald Byrd) still recalls Hancock's feat with astonishment, for the pianist didn't miss a note on the thoroughly worn-out piano all night. John Noel also recalled the piano's unusual characteristics, noting that it sounded as if it had recently been reclaimed "from the bottom of St. Mary's Lake." Conversations with Larry Dwyer and John Noel, 1983. (John Noel also recalled that Hancock—upon realizing that the student musicians would actually be receiving and reading the judges' written critiques—skipped dinner one evening in order to rewrite all his judging sheets and offer each band and combo extensive, thorough critiques.)

13. *Miami* (Florida) *News*, February 10, 1967.

14. *down beat*, July 14, 1966, p. 15.

15. *South Bend Tribune*, March 4, 1967.

16. Ibid.

17. Long a leading figure in stage band activity throughout the country, Father Wiskirchen's impressive list of credentials had expanded by 1967 to encompass summer-faculty status at the prestigious Eastman School of Music, three books on music and stage bands (*Developmental Techniques for the School Dance Band Musician*, Berklee Press; *A Manual for the Stage or Dance Band Trumpet*, written with Frank "Porky" Panico; and *Building a Stage Band*, LeBlanc Publications), two regular *down beat* columns on school jazz developments and new arrangements, countless yearly Selmer music clinics, a position as director of instrumental music for the Archdiocese of Chicago, and selection as one of the ten outstanding band directors for 1966 by *School Musician* magazine.

18. Former Melodon/CJF '69 chairman Greg Mullen recalled Jim McNeely—currently a rising jazz-piano soloist/star and Stan Getz sideman for several years—in the summer of 1983 as "a great musician and a straight 'A' student."

19. *South Bend Tribune*, March 6, 1967.

20. Ibid., March 4, 1967.

21. *down beat*, April 20, 1967, p. 17.

22. Ibid.

23. Ibid.

24. *Scholastic*, March 7, 1969, p. 21.

25. As a result of this CJF/Best Combo selection, the Leon Schipper Quintet left in March of 1968 on an eight-week State Department sponsored African tour. *down beat*, February 22, 1968, p. 9.

26. Ibid., April 20, 1967, p. 17.

27. Summing up CJF past and present history, the festival program contained an article on the Stage Band movement (reprinted from *down beat*), a piece by Nat Hentoff on jazz developments and black nationalism (reprinted with permission from *down beat*'s '67 music yearbook), a well-researched bit on CJF history by John Noel examining CJF origins and evolutions of festival philosophy, and a recap of Melodon high-school band successes and history. In regard to renewed and strengthened relations with CJF sponsors, the program also contained full-page ads taken out by Selmer, *down beat*, Harmony, Zildjian, Verve Records, Getzen, BMI, and Wurlitzer.

1968

1. *down beat*, April 20, 1967, p. 18.
2. CJF '68 application form, University of Notre Dame Archives.
3. CJF '68 press release, February 5, 1968.
4. Ibid.
5. *Scholastic*, March 1, 1968, p. 17.
6. The story behind Wayne Shorter in this judging-panel instance also involves the CJF's first and only known contact with trumpeter/jazz innovator Miles Davis. After briefly getting to know pianist Herbie Hancock at CJF '67, Chicago schemers John Noel and Paul Schlaver discovered that legendary trumpeter/innovator Miles Dewey Davis would be playing at Chicago's Auditorium Theater in the summer of 1967. Naturally, the two young jazz fans decided that they'd say hello to Herbie Hancock, a member of the influential mid-sixties Davis quintet, before the show. On the appropriate date the two went to the auditorium with tickets in hand, but, once there, decided on impulse to make their way to the backstage door.

Figuring that Davis and crew would arrive sometime before the performance, Noel and Schlaver waited patiently for nearly forty-five minutes. Finally realizing that the show was due to start in a few minutes, they trudged down the alley alongside the auditorium, not a little disappointedly, back toward the entrance, barely noticing the cab that was headed their way. Suddenly, just as the vehicle pushed abreast of them, the cab window rolled down, and Herbie Hancock leaned out of the window to excitedly shout both their names. Shaking hands hurriedly with a surprised Noel and Schlaver, Hancock told the two to come backstage after the show.

Stunned that Hancock had recalled them at all, Noel and Schlaver sat through the show and after its completion promptly made their way back behind the curtains. True to his word, Herbie Hancock met and introduced them to Tony Williams, Ron Carter, Wayne Shorter, and Miles Davis, the latter of whom Noel noticed, was none too excited about the meeting (or, for that matter, about anything at all). Eventually, someone mentioned that trumpeter Dizzy Gillespie was playing at the London House (a well-known Wacker Drive Chicago jazz club at the time), and the whole group—Miles Davis included—piled into a cab. Once there, the group commandeered a table and ordered drinks. At one point, Miles even got up to play a few tunes with Dizzy, and as a result, the show and the table talk didn't end until about 4:30 in the morning. Somewhere in the conversation din, the CJF was described by Hancock, Noel, and Schlaver in detail and, of the quintet members, Wayne Shorter tentatively agreed to be a judge at CJF '68 (as did—in an unrelated matter—trombonist Bob Brookmeyer). For various reasons, neither jazzman could attend.

7. DeMicheal was no doubt aware of the fact that Schlitz had been moving toward backing jazz activities. In fact, the company had termed 1967 a "Schlitz Salute to Jazz" year. One of the first "donations" made by the company (through the Schlitz Foundation) was to the Longhorn Jazz Festival in Austin, Texas, for "education scholarships to young jazz musicians." *down beat*, May 4, 1967, p. 13; June 29, 1967, p. 15; August 10, 1967, p. 10.

8. This, no doubt, resulted from the interconnections between Schlitz CJF funding and other Schlitz monies directed toward George Wein-produced jazz events in 1967. *down beat*, May 4, 1967, p. 13; June 29, 1967, p. 15; August 10, 1967, p. 10. (Once the Newport arrangements had been finalized, Newport festival organizer George Wein also agreed to pay a visit to the 1968 CJF.)

9. In a July 15, 1983, conversation, John Noel noted that at times, it seemed as if the Schlitz funding plan had to be approved by "the holy Trinity itself." Noel also recalled that, as a gesture of goodwill toward the festival and the university, Schlitz eventually printed up huge, 40-inch-high posters for CJF/Schlitz publicity purposes. Lugging such posters around South Bend to hang in various watering holes, Noel also noted that he nearly lost his life to an obstreperous jazz-hating hillbilly who tossed him bodily out of one particularly rough South Bend bar.

10. *Observer*, February 21, 1968, p. 7.

11. *South Bend Tribune*, March 9, 1968, p. 11.

12. *down beat*, May 2, 1968, p. 36.

13. Ibid.; and Richard Bizot notes, CJF '72 program. During the performance, Cuomo and other Quartet members stopped playing at one point, sat down, lit-up pipes, and puffed away while the tape machine rambled on. *Scholastic*, March 7 1969, p. 21.

14. *down beat*, September 19, 1968, p. 19. (The word, "Grooveness"— meaning a "state of being groovy"—was coined by McIntosh himself.)

15. *South Bend Tribune*, March 9, 1968, p. 11.

16. Ibid., March 6, 1968, p. 11.

17. Ibid, March 10, 1968, p. 13, and *down beat*, May 2, 1968, p. 23.

18. *down beat*, May 2, 1968, p. 23.

19. *Scholastic*, March 7, 1969, p. 21. ('68 judge Ray Brown would later remark in a *down beat* magazine article—September 19, 1968, p. 9—that the Ohio State band walked onstage at the CJF "like they owned the place.")

20. *down beat*, May 2, 1968, p. 23.

21. *Chicago Daily News*, March 11, 1968.

22. Ibid.

23. Ibid.

24. *New York Times*, March 11, 1968.

25. *down beat*, May 2, 1968, p. 36.

26. Ibid. Despite this disclaimer by Morgenstern, the Sandke group must bear a certain, undeniable degree of responsibility for the incident, particularly in light of the fact that group-leader Sandke had performed with various groups—including finalists—for several years prior to 1968. There is, therefore, little doubt of Sandke's familiarity with CJF finals' rules.

More likely than not, the Sandke "Warm Valley" affair was the result of enormous naïveté, bravado, youth, impetuousness, and an acute sense of late-sixties theatrics.

27. *New York Times*, March 11, 1968.

1969

1. Conversation with John Noel, July 7, 1983. (Gates Chevrolet would continue to donate this service through 1979.)

2. CJF '68 program, p. 22.

3. Ibid., p. 5.

4. *Scholastic*, March 15, 1968, p. 24.

5. *down beat*, May 2, 1968, p. 2.

6. Ibid., p. 23.

7. Ibid., p. 22.

8. Ibid., p. 36.

9. *The Encyclopedia of Jazz in the 70's* (New York: Horizon Press, 1976), p. 370.

10. Although Dave Brubeck, George Wein, and Rev. Norman O'Connor had held an informal jazz discussion session during the 1958 St. Louis MENC biennial convention, the first formal jazz seminar as such sponsored by the conference occurred during the 1960 biennial in Atlantic City, New Jersey.

Attending the 1960 MENC affair were Billy Taylor (working the first of countless later clinician appearances to come), Hall Overton, Dr. Gene Hall (who had written and published the first school jazz article in the *Music Educator's Journal*), Dr. Ralph Pace of Columbia University's Teacher's College, and moderator Charles Suber. "The success of the seminar," wrote Suber in his chapter on jazz education contained in Leonard Feather's *The Encyclopedia of Jazz in the 70's*, "led to more jazz-related sessions at various state and national MENC events during the sixties." As a matter of course, such expansions undoubtedly led to the eventual formation in 1968 of the auxiliary National Association of Jazz Educators (NAJE).

11. *down beat*, May 16, 1968, p. 15.

12. Ibid., November 14, 1968, p. 27.

13. *The Encyclopedia of Jazz in the 70's*, p. 370.

14. *down beat*, November 14, 1968, p. 27.

15. Ibid., June 7, 1968, p. 34.

16. Ibid., August 8, 1968, p. 21.

17. Ibid., June 27, 1968, p. 14.

18. Ibid.

19. CJF '69 program, p. 32.

20. *Champaign* (Illinois) *News Gazette* (quotation taken from *New York Times* article), no date; University of Notre Dame Archives, "Collegiate Jazz Festival" file.

21. Ibid.

22. *down beat*, September 5, 1968, p. 34.

23. Ibid., p. 36.

24. CJF '69 program, p. 32.

25. *Time*, June 7, 1971, p. 67.

26. By 1969, Schlitz was fully involved in the jazz arena, supporting George Wein-produced jazz festivals across the U.S.

27. *Dome*, 1968, p. 262.

28. *Observer*, March 14, 1969, p. 3.

29. *South Bend Tribune*, March 15, 1969, p. 5.

30. Ibid.

31. *Commercial Appeal*, Mid-South, Memphis, Tennessee, May 4, 1969, p. 6.

32. Ibid., p. 5.

33. Ibid., p. 6.

34. In 1969, the CJF high-school festival broadened its previously localized scope to include bands from as far away as Akron, Ohio, and Memphis, Tennessee.

35. The idea of a jazz mass, of course, was by 1969 hardly new. In fact, the first attempts to incorporate popular-music elements into liturgical services had been made in the mid-fifties by Rev. Geoffrey Beaumont, vicar of St. George's Church in Camberwell, London, whose "Twentieth Century Folk Mass" soon received performance in the U.S. in Boston, Providence, and Norwalk, Connecticut [Frank Tirro, *Jazz: A History* (New York: W.W. Norton Co., 1977), p. 33; John S. Wilson, *Jazz: The Transitional Years, 1940-1960* (New York: Appleton-Century-Crofts, 1966), pp. 155–57]. A few years later, in 1959, a North Texas State University instructor, Ed Summerlin, set a traditional church service to jazz to assuage his grief over his nine-year-old daughter's battle with a congenital heart defect. In the early sixties, variations of Summerlin's jazz/mass conception were performed both on television and at the first International Jazz Festival in Washington, D.C. (Author Frank Tirro also notes that his own liturgical jazz composition, "American Jazz Mass," was written in 1959.)

Despite numerous jazz-mass efforts in the sixties (Lalo Schifrin's masterful "Jazz Suite on Mass Texts"; Duke Ellington's "Concerts of Sacred Music"; Joe Master's superb recording, "The Jazz Mass"; and jazz mass concerts performed by Mary Lou Williams, Don Ellis, and others), jazz did not appear as part of a Roman Catholic service in the United States until mid-1966. In addition, a joint statement issued by Pope Paul VI and two Vatican offices in January 1967 cast a baleful eye toward "distortions of the liturgy," particularly "music of a totally profane and worldly character not worthy of a sacred action." *down beat*, February 23, 1967, p. 11.

Fortunately, barely four months after this initial decree, Pope Paul VI reversed his decision on the use of jazz and other nonsacred music in Roman Catholic services. Authorizing a modernization of the rules governing Catholic Church music, the Pope issued a new, generally worded papal document entitled "Instruction on Music in the Liturgy," which, though not officially specifying which types of music could be used in services, offered a system of procedure to enable bishops to use their own judgment in regard to the acceptance or rejection of such music for worship purposes. *down beat*, May 4, 1967, p. 13.

Thus, barely three years after the first attempted jazz mass (in a Roman Catholic Service), and just two years after the papal reversal, the incorporation of a jazz mass into the framework of a jazz festival held on the campus of the best-known Catholic bastion of higher learning in the U.S., Notre Dame, was no small feat, particularly in light of the fact that attempts had been made to hold the jazz mass in conjunction with the CJF in 1968, less than a year after the new papal decree.

36. *Commercial Appeal*, May 4, 1969, p. 11.
37. Ibid.
38. CJF '69 program, pp. 10–11.
39. *Commercial Appeal*, May 4, 1969, p. 11.
40. *Observer*, March 17, 1969, p. 2.

Chapter 3. The Seventies

1970

1. *down beat*, May 15, 1969, p. 8.
2. CJF '70 program, p. 24.
3. Ibid.
4. Ibid.
5. Ibid.
6. Ibid.
7. *The Encyclopedia of Jazz in the 70's*, p. 370.
8. CJF '70 program, p. 33.
9. Ibid.
10. Ibid.
11. Ibid. Clark Terry was also involved in a somewhat spectacular postfestival airport run-in in 1969. As it turned out, on reaching Michiana Regional Airport on the outskirts of South Bend, Terry discovered that United Airlines had overbooked both his own and '69 judge Ernie Wilkens's return flights. As Richard Bizot would later recall in the '72 CJF program, "the normally mild mannered Terry," raised "spectacular hell" until United chartered a private

plane to make the Chicago connection. "Wilkens," continued a clearly bemused Bizot (who had driven the two judges to the airport), was "last seen looking somewhat forlorn and skeptical as a very fragile-looking Piper Cub (or something) taxied away from the terminal."

12. *Observer*, March 20, 1970, p. 5.

13. Ibid., p. 3.

14. *down beat*, May 14, 1970, p. 39.

15. Ibid.

16. Ibid., p. 37.

17. Ibid.

18. Ibid., p. 38.

19. Ibid.

20. Ibid., pp. 38–39.

21. Ibid., p. 38.

22. Ibid.

23. Ibid., p. 37.

24. Ibid., p. 39.

25. Convinced by '70 CJF chairperson Ann Heinrichs that the geodesic dome of Stepan Center presented an acoustical challenge fit for testing out new equipment, Buchanon, Michigan-based Electro-Voice, Inc. (a well-known manufacturer of microphones, speakers, and sound-amplification systems) offered in 1970 to donate microphone and amplification facilities to the CJF, along with the expert services of technicians Bill Raventos and Bill Southerland free of charge.

On the back cover of the 1972 CJF program, Electro-Voice elaborated a bit on the reasons for aiding the festival:

> Today's musical concepts demand sophisticated sound reinforcement. So we're happy to work with the Notre Dame students and musicians to create better sound for the CJF as we've been doing for years.
>
> The benefits are manifold. We satisfy our personal urge to participate in a great jazz festival. At the same time we learn more about our microphones and speakers under truly demanding conditions impossible to duplicate in the laboratory. But most important you hear the jazz you've come to enjoy under the best possible circumstances.

26. *down beat*, May 14, 1970, p. 40.

1971

1. Tom Schlereth, *The University of Notre Dame: A Portrait of Its History and Campus* (Notre Dame, Ind., and London: University of Notre Dame Press, 1976), p. 216.

2. Charles Suber interview, Chicago, January 7, 1983.

3. ACJF '71 poster, courtesy of Charles Suber.

4. Ibid.; Charles Suber interview, Chicago, January 7, 1983.

5. Allen Scott, *Jazz Educated Man: A Solid Foundation*, (Washington, D.C.: American International Publishers, 1973), pp. 25–26.

6. ACJF '71 poster, courtesy of Charles Suber.

7. *Observer*, March 2, 1971, p. 3.

8. '72 CJF program, p. 5.

9. *Observer*, March 8, 1971, p. 5.

10. '71 CJF program, p. 4.

11. *Observer*, March 8, 1971, p. 5.

12. Ibid.

13. Ibid.

1972

1. Another bluesman scheduled to perform on the same bill as Luther Allison, Robert Pete Williams, unfortunately received improper directions to South Bend and spent the night in an Indianapolis bus depot. Also mistakenly given directions to Indianapolis, Allison was able to backtrack and turn up two hours late—but ready to play—for the show. *Scholastic*, November 12, 1971, p. 8; reprint of article by Richard Bizot, *down beat*, November 12, 1970.

2. '71 judge/festival adviser Willis Conover had urged '71 CJF chairperson Ann Heinrichs to apply for the grant, and she had wisely followed the well-known Voice of America broadcaster's advice. '72 CJF program, p. 6.

3. Such clinics and lectures were possible in 1972 as the direct result of the National Endowment for the Arts grant, which, according to '72 chairman Bob Syburg's correspondence files, allowed the CJF to offer for the first time an honorarium of $225 for such additional services and efforts to each attending judge. As in previous years, the CJF picked up all transportation, room, meal, and phone costs incurred by judges.

(According to an early invitational letter sent by Bob Syburg to Dan Morgenstern, the first invitations for the '72 CJF were forwarded to Herbie Hancock, Gunther Schuller, Roberta Flack, Jim Pankow, Randy Brecker, and Frank Zappa. Aynsley Dunbar's appearance at CJF '72 may well be linked to the Zappa invitation. In addition, an invitation was also initially extended to AACM reedman/member Joseph Jarman—who accepted, no doubt, after a quick CJF recommendation from two-time CJF judge/AACM member Richard Abrams. Unfortunately, Jarman was later informed that another judging commitment had been made and did not attend; Gil Evans was also scheduled to attend in 1972, but backed out at the last minute and was replaced by veteran CJF judge George Russell.) Bob Syburg CJF correspondence files, 1971–1972.

4. For the record, between 1959 and 1972 the CJF hosted black-led bands in '59, '60, '62, '63, '64, '69 (three groups), and '71 (two groups). Black musicians, of course, appeared as members of other bands or combos each year from 1959 on. The first entirely black group to appear at the CJF is believed to be the five-man Crane Junior College Jazzmen/1963 finalist group, from which Earth, Wind & Fire-founder Maurice White and Earth, Wind & Fire-sidemen Don Myrick and Louis Satterfield emerged.

As for the judging panel, between 1959 and 1972, one-third of the judges invited to attend were black.

5. According to Bob Syburg's correspondence files, attempts were also made in 1972 to find local sponsors who could help to finance a trip by Leon Breeden's North Texas State Lab Band to the '72 CJF. These attempts, however, proved unsuccessful. Undated letters, Bob Syburg CJF correspondence file, 1971–72.

6. *Observer*, March 9, 1972, p. 2.

7. The "Blindfold Test" was inaugurated by critic Leonard Feather in 1946 in *Metronome* and, since 1951, has appeared regularly in *down beat* magazine. Basically, a well-known jazz musician is asked to listen to seven or eight musical recordings played by Feather—who gives no information about song titles, personnel, styles, instrumentations, etc., whatsoever before the selections are played. The musician's reactions are then recorded and released each month in the one-page feature in *down beat*. (Presently, several other critics often submit blindfold tests that supplement Feather's yearly output.)

8. *Observer*, March 10, 1972, p. 9.

9. *down beat*, May 25, 1972, p. 30.

10. Ibid.

11. Ibid.

12. Ibid.

13. *South Bend Tribune*, March 11, 1972.

14. '72 CJF program, pp. 5–6.

1973

1. CJF '73 program, p. 16.

Although student dance/jazz aggregates such as the Lettermen had existed in the fifties and sixties (four groups of which acted as CJF host bands from 1963–66), along with various CJF-participating Notre Dame combos ('59, '60, '62, '63, '66, '70, '71, '73), this reference is basically true. Until '72–'73, only the University Dance Band (most often the Lettermen) had been given official university sanction.

Though not yet fully recognized academically by the university (no credit was offered for student participation in the band), the formation of the Notre Dame Jazz Band in 1972–'73 was a step toward full, official university recognition and academic acceptance. In this uphill fight, Father Wiskirchen's esteemed presence at the university, no doubt, provided the jazz band with a major backing force.

2. *Dome*, 1973, p. 79.

3. *down beat*, January 18, 1973, p. 4.

4. Allen Scott, *Jazz Educated Man: A Solid Foundation* (Washington, D.C: American International Publishers, 1973), p. 67. (For in-depth coverage of the Utah debacle, see chapter 6, "Salt Lake Saga," in Scott's book, pp. 57–67.)

5. *South Bend Tribune*, April 13, 1973, p. 17.

6. CJF '73 program, p. 26.

7. *South Bend Tribune*, March 29, 1973, no page.

8. CJF '73 program, p. 26.

9. *South Bend Tribune*, April 14, 1973, p. 16.
10. Ibid., April 16, 1973, p. 36.
11. Ibid.

1974

1. *down beat*, August 16, 1973, p. 46.
2. *Observer*, March 28, 1974, p. 5.
3. Ibid. The word "ntu" (taken as the name of Gary Bartz's group) means "the spiritual and physical unity of all things" in Bantu philosophy. Joachim-Ernst Berendt, *Jazz: A Photo History* (New York: Schirmer Books, 1978), p. 309.
4. *Observer*, April 4, 1974, p. 9.
5. Ibid., March 27, 1974, pp. 3, 7.
6. Ibid., p. 7.
7. 1974 Student Government records show that, in actuality, some reimbursement was made to Electro-Voice by the CJF for truck shipment costs of equipment used at the festival—a total of $175.45.
8. *South Bend Tribune*, April 6, 1974, p. 8.
9. Ibid.
10. Ibid.
11. Ibid.
12. Though GSU's seven awards were entirely admirable, the unofficial CJF record of ten awards (garnered by the magnificent 1969 University of Illinois Band) still stood intact. In 1969, Illinois took awards for Best Big Band, Best Overall Group, Best Combo, Outstanding Instrumentalist, Outstanding Composer/Arranger, Best Trumpet, Best Piano, Best Big Band Bass, Best Big Band Drums, and for Special Recognition/Instrumentalist.

1975

1. Conceived by student-body president Pat McLaughlin in April 1974 and put into effect by senior Ralph Pennino (also a coproducer of the 1975 CJF), the Nazz Coffeehouse featured a variety of weekly campus folk and light-rock artists from 10 P.M. to 1 A.M., along with light snacks and nonalcoholic refreshments. Quickly established as a popular late-night haunt for music-hungry students, the Nazz soon reached out to Father Wiskirchen and his band and discussed the possibility of live performance.
2. *Scholastic*, March 7, 1975, p. 5.
3. *Observer*, April 11, 1975, p. 7.
4. *South Bend Tribune*, April 12, 1975, p. 6.
5. Ibid.
6. Ibid.
7. Ibid.
8. *Observer*, April 14, 1975, p. 5.
9. *South Bend Tribune*, April 14, 1975, no page.
10. Ibid.
11. Ibid.

1976

1. *The Encyclopedia of Jazz in the 70's*, p. 372.
2. Ibid.
3. Ibid., p. 373.
4. Ibid.
5. *Music Educator's Journal*, November 1975, p. 69.
6. *Scholastic*, November 7, 1975, p. 23.
7. In 1983, Damian Leader recalled that judge Bob James offered student musicians at the festival "extensive critiques," while Lester Bowie "once just just scrawled across the [adjudicating] sheet, 'Do it! Do it! Do it!' Another time he ran backstage to grab a young trombonist and shook him with both hands, according him the highest praise." About judge Malachi Favors, Leader also recalled:

> The whole [festival] experience was marvelous and ended only on Sunday when, sleepless, I drove Malachi Favors to the South Shore [train] station. We had the times wrong and he had to wait an hour for the train. I offered to take him somewhere for coffee, but he said, 'No, that's cool, I'll just practice a bit.' I left him in the deserted waiting room quietly playing [his bass]. It was great. — 1983 Collegiate Jazz Festival program, pp. 7-8.

8. *Scholastic*, November 7, 1985, p. 23.
9. *Scholastic*, March 28, 1977, p. 19.
10. Ibid.
11. *Observer*, April 5, 1976, p. 5.
12. Although this is fact, it is also undoubtedly true that (given the CJF awards structure after 1973) the 1966 Notre Dame finalist combo featuring saxophone sensation Bill Hurd and the 1960 Notre Dame combo containing saxophonist/flautist Bob Pierson would have also won Outstanding Performance awards.
13. *Observer*, April 5, 1976, p. 5.
14. Ibid.
15. Ibid.

1977

1. *Living Blues* magazine, November-December, 1976, p. 28.
2. *Observer*, March 31, 1977, p. 7.
3. *Living Blues* magazine, p. 28.
4. In 1977, an all-session CJF pass was priced at $8, while individual-session tickets ranged from $2.50 (Saturday afternoon) to $5.50 (Friday evening — including the judges' jam). In addition, Notre Dame/St. Mary's students could purchase CJF tickets at lower prices.
5. *Observer*, April 4, 1977, p. 6.
6. Wayne Darling of Ball State was the first in 1970, John Clayton, Jr., of Indiana University the second in 1973.

7. Rodby would go on to become the bassist in the widely popular, acclaimed Pat Metheny Group.

8. *Observer*, April 4, 1977, p. 6.

9. Ibid.

10. Ibid.

11. Ibid.

12. Ibid.

13. Ibid.

1978

1. *Observer*, November 22, 1977, pp. 5–7.

2. Author's personal recollections.

3. Ibid.

4. Ibid.

5. *Observer*, April 10, 1978, p. 5.

6. Ibid.

7. Ibid.

1979

1. Although the festival had operated primarily on verbal agreements over the years, I decided to ensure my commitments by sending out basic one-page, self-designed contracts to all the judges involved—Philly Joe Jones, Richard Davis, Buddy DeFranco, Joe Sample, etc. As it turned out, all but the Richard Carpenter/Stanley Turrentine team signed and returned the form.

2. The Tatum Group Masterpieces (Art Tatum & Buddy DeFranco), Pablo Records, 2310–736, 1975.

3. Father Wiskirchen's course (which made use of extensive reel-to-reel recordings featuring representative samples of jazz taken from various stages of its evolution and extensive text summaries) was one of the best-taught, most riveting classes in my four years at Notre Dame. As small but patent proof of his classroom talents, Father Wiskirchen was one of the few educators in any field I've ever come across to receive a spontaneous, sustained burst of applause from his students on the final day of class. During the year—at the request of the class—Father Wiskirchen devoted the majority of one class session to the music of Frank Zappa, complete with a riveting, often hilarious reel-to-reel compilation of excerpts from Zappa's varied work. (In the mid-to-late seventies, it was traditionally assumed the year's CJF chairman would take Wiskirchen's class, not only out of deference to Father George, but to keep in constant touch with the CJF's faculty adviser.)

4. Paul Peppin, a former Melodon and a sound technician with Master Recording Associates in Kettering, Ohio, for many years attended the CJF each spring to tap into the soundboard and system and make reel-to-reel recordings of festival bands and combos. Since 1968, Peppin had offered cassette or reel-to-reel tapes of festival groups to CJF attendees on a by-order basis. For the NPR "Jazz Alive!" series taping, Tim Owens merely contacted Peppin, specified

the tape quality required for broadcast, and asked permission to use the sound technician's finished product at a later date.

5. Nat Adderley, Philly Joe Jones, and Joe Sample had no previous festival judging experience. Fortunately, in 1979, Buddy DeFranco (an old adjudicating hand and frequent clinician), Bunky Green (a full-time educator), and Richard Davis (also an educator) did.

6. Personal recollections/Jethro Burns interview, Hanover, New Hampshire, July 23, 1983. (It should also be noted that had Jethro turned down the '79 CJF guest-band slot, he most likely would have attended as one of the judging-panel members, for serious consideration was being given to such a matter in the early months of 1979.)

7. As custodian of the Old Fieldhouse/student arts center in 1978–79, I had a chance to corral various talented art students to create silk-screened CJF posters, take program photographs, and, in the case of senior painting wizard Mike Cantwell (who, it seemed, stayed awake all night—every night—in the boxing room above my Fieldhouse abode painting wild, energetic pictures on canvases, boards, doors, and walls—and who often hung his just-finished works in my high-ceilinged room to dry), to paint the twenty-foot-wide (or more), seven-foot-high canvas work for the CJF. Painted with cans of spray paint, the work contained flowing abstract jazz musicians, a CJF logo, and wild splashes of energetic color, all emerging from an orange background. Mike Cantwell may well still retain the massive canvas. When last I heard of him, Mike was hobnobbing with painter Robert Rauschenberg somewhere in Florida. (In addition, Mike provided original artwork for the back of the '79 program and a festival publicity brochure.)

8. During breakfast that morning, Sample recalled some of his renowned studio-musician recording sessions, most notably, jazz singer/songwriter Michael Franks's early albums (which featured practically the entire Crusaders band and according to Sample, "just really clicked") and albums by singer Joni Mitchell. ("I just came in to do the session," he admitted, "I didn't know who she was.") In addition, the pianist made the somewhat startling admission that he was presently listening seriously to the music of Fats Waller.

9. During 1978–79, I negotiated with Master Recording Associates sound-technician Paul Peppin in order to have him go through his extensive CJF tape files, make copies of past outstanding bands and combos, and then send them along for deposit in Notre Dame's audio/visual library for student/faculty listening purposes and use. Unfortunately, the National Endowment for the Arts grant that I had hoped could free up some CJF budget money for Peppin's services in this regard fell through, and the plan never came to fruition.

Chapter 4. The Eighties

1980

1. *down beat*, January 1980, p. 71.
2. Ibid.

3. In recognition of the rise in the number of collegiate-jazz albums, *down beat* began to offer its annual deebee Awards for student recordings—classical as well as jazz—in 1978.

4. *Observer*, March 29, 1980, p. 7.

5. By 1980, the University of Notre Dame could boast of an impressive two-jazz-band program that also included three combos and an improvisational workshop.

6. *South Bend Tribune*, March 26, 1980, p. 30.

7. *Observer*, March 26, 1980, p. 5.

8. Ibid.

9. *South Bend Tribune*, March 26, 1980, p. 30.

10. Ibid.

11. *Observer*, March 26, 1980, p. 5.

12. Ibid.

13. *South Bend Tribune*, March 26, 1980, p. 30.

14. Ibid.

15. CJF '80 festival program, p. 5.

1981

1. *Observer*, April 11, 1980, p. 1.

2. Ibid. Although obviously the remarks of an impassioned blues-lover and critic, Aberli's comments contained a grain of truth. Like the CJF, the MBF had long been a maverick Cultural Arts Commission event, and its educational efforts were often overlooked amid poor profit and attendance figures.

Still, faced with dwindling student blues interest in 1980—due, perhaps, to poor scheduling, weather woes, and 1979 budget-cut weakened MBF publicity efforts as much as anything else—the Student Union, organized as it was to meet student needs, had little choice in the early eighties but to try a different musical tack. Taking up the musical slack somewhat, the Notre Dame Black Cultural Arts festival featured a month of activities in February 1981, including a performance by musician/poet Gil Scott-Heron.

3. *South Bend Tribune*, April 14, 1981, p. 28.

4. *Dome*, 1981, p. 150.

5. *South Bend Tribune*, April 14, 1981, p. 28.

6. Ibid.

7. *Observer*, April 8, 1981, p. 3.

8. CJF '81 festival program, p. 8.

1982

1. *Observer*, April 2, 1982, p. 9.

2. Interview with Nat Adderley, Boston, March 1982.

3. *University of Iowa Spectator*, (May 1982): 1, 7.

4. Ibid.

1983

1. Author's symposium notes, April 15, 1983.
2. CJF '83 program, p. 21.
3. Ibid., p. 29.
4. Ibid., p. 25.

1984

1. As had often been the case in CJF history, the usual spring down-pour served to delay incoming flights and upset judge/festival-staff dinner plans. So that the meal wouldn't be a total loss, staff members carried out a number of orders of filet mignon in protective Styrofoam plates to offer the judges when they finally arrived. As it turned out, however, three of the judges were practicing vegetarians, and the rest were simply too exhausted to eat at all. Rising to the task, judge Paquito D'Rivera "improvised" and set about consuming several steaks out of Styrofoam "dishes" late that night in the lounge of the Americana Hotel. 1985 Collegiate Jazz Festival program, p. 5; Bob O'Donnell interview, December 4, 1985.
2. In 1984, the University of Notre Dame Jazz Band once again embarked on a concert tour that took band members to Illinois, Indiana, and Michigan. In addition, the band was set to present two Dimensions in Jazz concerts on campus during the year and perform at other events such as Junior Parents Weekend and, in what was certainly a bow to the music's acceptance at the university, at the President's Black Tie Dinner (president here referring to Notre Dame's Fr. Theodore Hesburgh). 1984 Collegiate Jazz Festival program, p. 14.
3. Ibid., p. 27.
4. Ibid., p. 19.
5. John Cerabino interview, November 29, 1985.
6. Ibid.
7. Ibid. Bob O'Donnell interview, December 3, 1985.
8. 1984 Collegiate Jazz Festival program, p. 31. O'Donnell also became the first festival chairman to perform in the event itself—as a section trombonist in the University of Notre Dame Ensemble. Bob O'Donnell interview, December 3, 1985.

1985

1. *Brighton-Pittsford Post*, August 8, 1981. Little known is the fact that Bertoncini actually once turned down an offer to join what later became Weather Report, the widely acclaimed jazz-fusion group. "I did an album [*Odyssey of Iska*] with [tenor-saxophonist] Wayne Shorter," Bertoncini explains, "and Wayne called me up not long after that and asked me to join this group he was forming with [pianist/composer] Joe Zawinul, [drummer] Alphonse Mouzon, and [bassist] Miroslav Vitous, but I said 'No,' I wanted to do my own thing. If I had . . . " Gene Bertoncini interviews, 1983, 1985.

2. The albums (*Bridges*, Omnisound Records, GJB 3333, liner notes by Willis Conover; *Close Ties*, Omnisound Records, GJB 3334, liner notes by Gene Lees) feature Bertoncini adaptations and arrangements of selections by Rachmaninov, Bach, Ravel, Fauré, and Chopin, as well as John Lennon and Paul McCartney and more traditional jazz fare by Ellington, Gershwin, Rodgers & Hart, and Antonio Carlos Jobim. (Although a stellar jazz guitarist, Bertoncini did not neglect his University of Notre Dame-acquired architecture skills, for he has, over the years, designed one house for his parents and another for his brother. In a February 19, 1982, edition of the *New York Times*, critic John S. Wilson also discovered that Bertoncini's architecture background helps the guitarist to think "in terms of structure, of balance, of reaching climaxes" while performing.)

3. John Cerabino interview, November 29, 1985.

4. Ibid.

5. *South Bend Tribune*, April 14, 1985, no page.

6. Ibid.

7. Ibid.

8. John Cerabino interview, November 29, 1985.

9. 1985 Collegiate Jazz Festival program, p. 25.

10. *South Bend Tribune*, April 14, 1985, no page.

COLLEGIATE JAZZ DISCOGRAPHY

Today, few student musicians participating in collegiate jazz bands or combos complete their education without a recording of some kind. Although the majority of such recordings are ordinarily made in university studio facilities and distributed by the schools themselves, there are also several firms—such as Mark Records and Crest Records Inc., and West Coast outfits such as KM Records, AM-PM Records, and Sea Breeze Records that master and press collegiate (and often high school) jazz band and combo albums and (particularly Mark) simplify the album packaging/distribution process.

In late 1983, a questionnaire soliciting collegiate jazz album information was sent out to 285 colleges and universities in the United States offering jazz curricula and/or jazz degrees. A second questionnaire was sent out in August 1985 to an additional 160 schools (including those in Canada). From these mailings, 178 responses were received, 85 of which offered information regarding collegiate jazz band or combo albums and cassettes. In all, firm collegiate recording data was received from twenty-eight states (California to Maine, Texas to Minnesota) and Canada—a total of more than 200 recordings.

The following discography of nearly 250 collegiate jazz recordings (culled from questionnaire results, past Collegiate Jazz Festival programs, and a variety of other sources) is intended to offer student musicians and educators a framework for exchange and appreciation of jazz developments and talents on the collegiate level as well as to provide a basis for further such discographic research.

State	School	Album Title	Record Company	Leader	Year
Alabama	University of Alabama	"Hilaritas"	Nashville Record Productions Inc.	Steve Sample	1982-83
		"Jazz Ensemble"	Tom Britton & Assoc.		1972-73
		"The Stage Band"	Mark Custom Records		1970-71
Arizona	Arizona State University	"ASU Jazz-Basking"		Chuck Marohnic	1985
California	University of California/ Berkeley	"Orange Blossom Special" Vol. I"	Polydor 28MX2024	Dr. David Tucker	1981
				Dr. David Tucker	1979
	California State University at Fresno	"Live at the Satellite 1984"		Larry Sutherland	1984
		"Jazz 83"		Larry Sutherland	1983
		"Jazz 82"		Larry Sutherland	1982
	California State University at Pomona	1983-84 album (title unknown)		David Grasnick	1983-84
	Cerritos College	"College Neophonic Orchestra"			1970
		"Cerritos Jazz Rock Ensemble			1969
		"Wow" (Bud Brisbois with the Cerritos College Stage Band)		Jack Wheaton	1968
	Chaffey College	"Live and Kickin' "	Independently produced	Jack Mason	1984
		"Live At Gilberto's"	Independently produced	Brian Bettger	1983
		"Le Bebop Montreux"	Independently produced	Jack Mason	1982
		"Hollywood"	Independently produced	Jack Mason	1980
		"Pack Your Axe"	Independently produced	Jack Mason	1979
		"Imagination Flight"	Independently produced	Jack Mason	1978
		"Mandrake"	Independently produced	Jack Mason	1977
	Fullerton College (Jazz Band)	"Escape to Asylum"		Terry Blackley/ Jim Linahon	1984-85
		Fullerton College Jazz Band/ "Time Trippin"	JFLC 32883		1982

Institution	Title	Label/Catalog	Director	Year
Fullerton College (Lemon Street Stompers)	"Time For Dixie"	Mark/FC-1		1984-85
Los Angeles City College	"Zinger" (L.A. City College Big Band)		Dr. Woody James	1983
	"L.A., Si Si"		Dr. Woody James	1981
	"Alice In Welfareland"		Dr. Woody James	1980
	"L.A. Times"		Dr. Woody James	1979
Los Medanos College	"Mucho Gusto!"/The Los Medanos College Jazz Ensemble	Los Medanos College		1985
Mt. San Antonio College	"Lizard Power"	Lizard Power	Ashley Alexander	1980
	"We're on the Move"	Mt. San Antonio College	Ashley Alexander	1975
Orange Coast College	"Orange Coast College Big Band with Pepper Adams and Ted Curson"		Charles Rutherford	
San Diego State University	"Evolution"	Golden Track Studio	Bob Holtz	1982
College of the Siskiyous	"College of the Siskiyous Jazz Choir" (with Mark Murphy)	COS Records, Vol. 2	Dr. Kirby Shaw	1980
	"College of the Siskiyous Jazz Choir"	COS Records, Vol. 1	Dr. Kirby Shaw	1979
Southwestern College (2 yr.)	"Southwestern College Jazz Festival"		J. Merrill/R. Robinette	1968-81
Colorado				
University of Colorado at Denver	"Sampler"		Walter Barr	1983
University of Denver	"October Morning"	Mark Records/MCJS-20385	David Caffey	1983
University of Northern Colorado (UNC Jazz Band I)	"Alive IV"	Eaglear 122983	Gene Aitken	1983
	"Alive III"	Soundmark R982/BSCR	Gene Aitken	1982
	"Alive II"	Soundmark R839/KM5546	Gene Aitken	1980
	"Alive"	Soundmark R740/KM2079	Gene Aitken	1979

State	School	Album Title	Record Company	Leader	Year
	(UNC Vocal Jazz Ensemble I)	"Hot III"	Eaglear 112983	Gene Aitken	1983
		"Hot II"	Soundmark R981/BSCR	Gene Aitken	1981
		"Hot"	Soundmark R840/KM4987	Gene Aitken	1980
Connecticut	University of Bridgeport	"University of Bridgeport Jazz Ensemble"	Trutone Records	Mike Carubia	1981-82/83-84
		"New Kids On The Block"	Mark Records/MC20155	Neil Slater	1981
		"University of Bridgeport Jazz Ensemble Tour '80"	Mark Records/MC20068	Neil Slater	1980
		"University of Bridgeport Jazz Ensemble Live"	Mark Records/MC5937	Neil Slater	1979
District of Columbia	Howard University	"Howard University Jazz Ensemble-1984"	Mark/MCJS-20517		1984
		"Howard University Jazz Ensemble-1983"	Mark/MCJS-20375		1983
		"Howard University Jazz Ensemble-1982"	Mark/MC-20285		1982
		"Howard University Jazz Ensemble-1981"	Mark/MC-20166		1981
		"Howard University Jazz Ensemble-1980"	Mark/MC-20064		1980
		"Howard University Jazz Ensemble-1979"	Mark/MC-5684		1979
		"Howard University Jazz Ensemble-1978"	Mark/MC-5581		1978
		"Howard University Jazz Ensemble-1977"	Mark/MCJS-20002		1977

State	Institution	Title	Label	Director	Year
Florida	Florida State University	"Spontaneous Combustion"/Florida State Jazz Ensemble	Mark/MCJS-20547	Whit Sidener	1984
	University of Florida	"Just Friends"/University of Florida Jazz Band	Mark/MC-20246	Whit Sidener	1983
		"Strike Up the Band"/University of Florida Jazz Ensemble	Mark/MCJS-20503	Whit Sidener	1979
		"Versicolor"/University of Florida Vocal Jazz Troupe	Mark/MCJS-20388	Whit Sidener	1978
	University of Miami (Jazz Ensemble)	"Picadilly Lilly"	Independently produced	Whit Sidener	1976
		"Estamos Ahi"	Independently produced	Larry Lapin	1983
		"Jumbo Face"	Independently produced	C. Owen	1985
		"Halcyon Days"	Independently produced	C. Owen	1984
		"Seventh Sign"	Independently produced		
	(Vocal Jazz Ensemble)	"No More Blues"	Independently produced		
	University of Southern Florida	"Day of the Sun"	Mark Records		
		"Moleids"	Mark/MCJS-20463		
Georgia	University of Georgia	"UGA Jazz"	Mark Records	Roger Dancz	1967
	Georgia State University	"The Music Market"		Robert Morsch	1983
		"A Night In Tunisia"		Robert Morsch	1982
		"Just Messin' Around"		Robert Morsch	1981
	Georgia Southern College	Two albums put out in late seventies/early eighties		Duane Wickiser	
Illinois	DePaul University	"The Cutting Edge"/DePaul University Jazz Ensemble	DePaul University	Charles Anslinger	1984
	Elmhurst College	"Five 'N Live"		Doug Beach	1983
		"Nutville"		Doug Beach	1982
		"Just Friends"		Doug Beach	1981
		"A Song For You"		Doug Beach	1980
		"1979 Elmhurst College Jazz Band"		Doug Beach	1979

STATE	SCHOOL	ALBUM TITLE	RECORD COMPANY	LEADER	YEAR
	University of Illinois	"University of Illinois Jazz Band and Dixie Combo"		John Garvey	1969-70
		"University of Illinois Jazz Band"	Electrorecord Records (Romania)	John Garvey	1968
	Illinois Wesleyan University	"Stretchin' Out"	Mark Records/MC24589	Tom Streeter	1983
		"IWU Big Band Jazz"	unknown/NR11929	Tom Streeter	1980
		"Tour Concert 1979"	Mark Records/MC8158	Tom Streeter	1979
	Milliken University	"Milliken University Jazz Band Plays The Music of Carroll DeCamp"		Roger Schueler	1984
	(Only 1984, 1983, and 1982 albums presently available)	"M.U. Band Plays Bill Holman"	Sounds Fantastic	Roger Schueler	1983
		"M.U. Jazz Band"	Sounds Fantastic/NR2186	Roger Schueler	1982
		"M.U. Jazz Band"	Sounds Fantastic/(studio)	Roger Schueler	1979
		"Serate Musicali"	Mark/MC-8105	Roger Schueler	1976-77
		"M.U. Jazz Band"	Mark/8073	Roger Schueler	1976
		"Milliken Jazz Band"	Mark/MC8053	Roger Schueler	1975
		"Milliken Jazz Band"	Mark/MC8028	Roger Schueler	1974
		"M.U. Jazz Band"		Roger Schueler	1973
		"Milliken Jazz Band"	Mark/MC1813	Roger Schueler	1972
		"M.U. Jazz Band On Tour"	Mark/2845	Roger Schueler	1969
	Northern Illinois University	"Live At Montreux Jazz Festival"	NIU	Ron Modell	1984
	(Albums #3, 5, and 6 are available)	"Reflections of You"	NIU/NIU 6	Ron Modell	1982
		"Sea Urchins"	NIU/NIU 5	Ron Modell	1981
		"Magic Carpet Ride"	NIU/NIU 4	Ron Modell	1980
		"Space Train"	NIU/NIU 3	Ron Modell	1978
	Waubonsee Community College	four albums put out between 1972-1976		Duane Wickiser	1972-76
	Western Illinois University	albums from early to mid-1970's		David Fodor	

State	Institution	Album/Title	Record Label	Director	Year
Indiana	Indiana University	"Dave Baker's 21st Century Bebop Band"		Dave Baker	1981
	University of Notre Dame	"Collegiate Jazz Festival" (3 album finalists set)	Crest Records		1966
		"Collegiate Jazz Festival" (3 album finalists set)	Crest Records		1965
		"Collegiate Jazz Festival" (3 album finalists set)	Crest Records		1964
		"Collegiate Jazz Festival" (3 album finalists set)	Crest Records		1963
		"Collegiate Jazz Festival" (3 album finalists set)	Silver Crest Records		1962

Collegiate Jazz Festival tapes (reel-to-reel & cassette) of festival finalists/bands 1967-1981 reside at Master Recording Associates, Kettering Ohio. In addition, tapes of 1982-86 festivals were made by local South Bend, Indiana, audio recording firms. Reel-to-reel tapes of CJF finalists 1959-1961 also exist; these tapes were, however, never distributed in any form.

State	Institution	Album/Title	Record Label	Director	Year
Iowa	Coe College	"Mississippi River Rat"	Sound Aspects/SAS-1004	Paul Smoker	1985
		"QB"/(with Anthony Braxton)	ALVAS/AR-101	Paul Smoker	1984
		"Coe Jazz Band"	Audio House/177F76	Jerry Owen	1976
	Cornell College	"On The Road, Cornell Jazz '78"	Recorded Publications Co. (RPC)/#z 496321	Jesse Evans	1978
	University of Iowa	"Johnson County Landmark"		Dan Yoder	1979
	University of Northern Iowa	"Creative Cooking"	Rec. at U. of Northern Iowa/pressed by RMR, Cheyenne, Wyo.	Bob Washut	1983
		"UNI Jazz Band I In Concert"		Ashley Alexander	1973
Kansas	University of Kansas	"Jazz Ensemble I 'Live At KMEA'"	Crest Records	Dr. Ronald C. McCurdy	1982
	Kansas State University	various albums up to 1979			

STATE	SCHOOL	ALBUM TITLE	RECORD COMPANY	LEADER	YEAR
Louisiana	Loyola University (New Orleans)	"Loyola Jazz Band I"	H&G Recorded Productions/HG61183	Joseph Hebert	1983
		"Loyola Jazz Band I"	H&G/MC 15502A	Joseph Hebert	1981
		"Loyola Jazz Band I"	H&G/HG 52079	Joseph Hebert	1979
		"Loyola Jazz Band I"	H&G/#01074	Joseph Hebert	1974
	Southern University (Baton Rouge)	"Southern University Live At The American College Jazz Festival"		Alvin Batiste	1971-72
Maine	Bowdoin College	"The Emanons"	private issue	unknown	1960
Massachusetts	Berklee College of Music	"Jazz In The Classroom Series, Vol. I-XV"	Berklee Recordings	Herb Pomeroy	1957-85
Michigan	Aquinas College	AFTGRN. Jazz Ensemble	River City	B. Early	1984
	Michigan State University	"Back On Track"	A&S Records (Dallas)	Ron Newman	1981
	Western Michigan University	"The Jazz Orchestra 1984"	(unknown)	Trent Kynaston	1984
Minnesota	Gustavus Adolphus College (St. Peter, Mn.)	"Gustavus Stage Band"	SMR E-871	Mark Lammers	1982
		"Gustavus Stage Band"	Mark/25020	Mark Lammers	1980
		"Gustavus Stage Band"	Mark/4711	Mark Lammers	1978
		"Gustavus Stage Band"	Mark/4241	Mark Lammers	1974
		"Gustavus Stage Band"	Mark/4030	Mark Lammers	1972
	Hamline University	tapes of jazz band albums exist, but no clearance for commercial sale		Paul A. Pizner	
	University of Minnesota/Duluth				
	University of Minnesota	"University of Minnesota plays the music of Nestico, Brookmeyer, and Jones"	Mark/MJS-57598		

State	Institution	Recording	Director	Label/Number	Year
Missouri	Central Missouri State University	"Remembrance"	Bill Crain	Mark/MCJS 20609	1985
	Meramec Community College (St. Louis Community College at Meramec)	8 "Jazz Lab Band" albums (1972-83)	various directors (Dr. Ron Stillwell, Steve Terry, Bob Waggoner)		1972-83
Nevada	University of Nevada	"Musical Montage"	Mack McGrannahan	Crest Records/UNR 1983 A-B-C-D	1983
	University of Nevada/Las Vegas	"University of Nevada/Las Vegas Live in South America"	Frank Gagliardi	UNLV Records	1981
		"After Midnight"	Frank Gagliardi	UNLV Records	1980
		"University of Nevada/Las Vegas Behind the Iron Curtain"	Frank Gagliardi	UNLV Records	1979
		"Split Session"	Frank Gagliardi	UNLV Records	1978
		"University of Nevada/Las Vegas in Europe"	Frank Gagliardi	UNLV Records	1976
New Jersey	Princeton University	"Princeton University Jazz Ensemble Live at Alexander Hall"	Justin DiCioccio	AMP Recording/AMP 8426	1983
		"Princeton University Jazz Ensemble"	Jim Capolupo	Vogt Quality Records/CSRV 2623	1979
New York	Eastman School of Music	"Hot House"		Mark Records	1985
		"Eastman Jazz Ensemble/Montreux"	Rayburn Wright	Mark/MJS 57605	1982
		"Eastman Jazz Ensemble/Holiday"	Rayburn Wright	Mark Records/MES-57582	1979
		"Eastman Jazz Ensemble/Live"	Rayburn Wright	Mark Records/MES-54600	1976
	(combo)	"Saxology"	Rayburn Wright	Mark Records/MJS-57612	1984

State	School	Album Title	Record Company	Leader	Year
	Ithaca College	"Song for the Asking"/Ithaca Vocal Jazz Ensemble	Mark Records		1975
		"A Tribute to the 'Duke' "/Ithaca Vocal Jazz Ensemble	Mark Records		1969
	State University of New York at Binghampton	"Concert/Studio Session" (Harper Jazz Ensemble)	Mark/MC5685	Al Hamme	1975
		"Stage Band Showcase, Rec. 6, Vol. I"	Crest Records	Al Hamme	1969
	State University of New York at Buffalo	"Clark Terry At Buffalo State"	Mark/MC5685	James Mabry	1979
	State University of New York at Fredonia	"Wah, Wah, Wah"/Fredonia Jazz Ensemble	Mark/MCJS-20486		1984
		"Royal Flush"			1983
	State University of New York at Oswego	5 albums through 1981 various albums, but not for commercial sale			
	State University of New York/College at Potsdam	"Potsdam College Jazz Ensemble"	Crest Records/POT 42882	Anthony Maiello	1982
		"Potsdam College Jazz Ensemble"	Crest Records/PB 4308	Anthony Maiello	1981
Ohio	University of Akron (Jazz Ensemble)	"Now!"	Mark/MCJS-20382	Roland Paolucci	1983
		"Live—Montreux Jazz Festival"	Queen City/no number	Roland Paolucci	1980
		"Jazz At The University of Akron"	Advent/AUJ-1-789	Roland Paolucci	1979
	University of Akron (Steel Band)	"Puttin' The Shoes On"	Mark/MCJS-20419		
	Ashland College	several albums through 1974			
	Bowling Green State University	"Just Friends"	cassette recording (available)	David Melle	1983

Institution	Album	Label / Notes	Director / Arranger	Year
	"BGSU Lab Band"	cassette recording (not available)	David Melle	1982
	"Celebration"	album (available)	David Melle	1981
	"Thumbs"	album (available)	David Melle	1980
	"BGSU Lab Band"	album (available)	David Melle	1979
	"BGSU Lab Band" 1969-72, 1974-78	locally produced albums; stock sold out	David Melle	1969-72 1974-78
Capital University (Columbus, Ohio)	"Ray's Recipe"	Capital University	Vaughn Weister	1982
Central State University	"Bout Time" (combo)	Central State University	Don Miller	1983
University of Cincinnati	"The Four Axemen"	King Records		1959-60
Kent State University	"Famous Arrangers"/Kent State University Lab Band	Mark/MES-39091		
Ohio State University	"Ozone Park"	OSUJE Records/700	Tom Battenberg	1983
	"Music To Clean The Garage By"	OSUJE Records/1000	Tom Battenberg	1981
	"Acorn's Tavern"	Mark Records/MES-57581	Tom Battenberg	1979
	"Live At The Montreux Jazz Festival"	OSUJE Records/1000	Tom Battenberg	1978
	"Fourtunes" (direct to disc)	Clear Blue Records/300	Tom Battenberg	1978
	"The Adventures of Cap'N Wake-Up"	OSUJE Records/1500	Tom Battenberg	1977
	"OSU Jazz Ensemble with Clark Terry"	OSUJE Records/500	Tom Battenberg	1973
	"OSU Jazz Ensemble"	OSUJE Records/500	Tom Battenberg	1972
	"OSU Jazz Ensemble"	J.T. Records/1000	Tom Battenberg	1971
	"OSU Jazz Forum Big Band"	Constellation	Lowell Latto	1960
Oklahoma — Central State University	"Central State University Jazz Ensemble" (4 albums 1978-81)		Dr. Kent Kidwell	1978-81

State	School	Album Title	Record Company	Leader	Year
	Phillips University	"Phillips University Jazz Orchestra"	Fantastic/NRI U607 (manufactured by Nashville Record Productions)	Robert Hearson	1978
Pennsylvania	Villanova University	"Jazz At Villanova: The Fourth Intercollegiate Jazz Festival"	Villanova University		1964
Tennessee	Austin Peay State University	"APSU Jazz Collegians"	Crest/81-Ten-3A, 81-Ten-3B	Aaron Schmidt	1982
	Memphis State University	"Southern Comfort"		Gene Rush	
		"Memphis State Statesmen with Doc Severinsen"		Tom Ferguson	1968
Texas	Lamar University	"Lamar Jazz Bands In Concert"	RPC/Z502661	J. Simmons & Wayne Dyess	1978
		"Lamar Jazz Live"	(out of print)	Jimmy Simmons	1974
	North Texas State University	"NTS One O'Clock Lab Band/ Lab '83"	NS83	Neil Slater	1983
		"Lab '82"	NS82	Neil Slater	1982
		"European Tour '82 (Live At Montreux)"	NS82B	Neil Slater	1982
		"Lab '81"	NS81	Leon Breeden	1981
		"Lab '80"	NS80	Leon Breeden	1980
		"Lab '79"	NS79	Leon Breeden	1979
		"Lab '78"	NS78	Leon Breeden	1978
		"Lab '77"	NS77	Leon Breeden	1977
		"Lab '76"	NS76	Leon Breeden	1976
		"Lab '75"	NS75	Leon Breeden	1975
		"Lab '74"	NS74	Leon Breeden	1974

Institution	Album	Label/Catalog	Director	Year
	"Lab '73"	NS73	Leon Breeden	1973
	"Live! '72-73"	NS72-73	Leon Breeden	1972-73
	"Lab '72" (double album)	NS72	Leon Breeden	1972
	"Lab '71"	NS71	Leon Breeden	1971
	"Lab '68"	Century 30178	Leon Breeden	1968
	"North Texas Lab Band"	90th Floor Records/SLL-904 (mono & stereo)	Leon Breeden	1960-61
Other *North Texas State* albums:	"The Spirit Soars"/North Texas State University Zebras	Mark/MJS-57600		
	"So . . . Easy to Love"/North Texas State University Jazz Guitars	Mark/MJS-57604		
	North Texas State University Jazz Singers/"Fantabulous"	Mark/MJS-57592		
	North Texas State University Jazz Singers/"More Than Just Friends"	Mark/MJS-57607		
	North Texas State University Jazz Singers/"Icarus"	Mark/MJS-57608		
Odessa College	"Putting It Together"/ The Odessa College Jazz Band	No Mountain Recording	Dr. Bernard Rose	1985
Sam Houston State University	"Catabiandol!"	Silver Crest Records/ SHS–11678–B	David Caffey	1978
University of Texas at Austin	"Sublime In Time" (with Toshiko Akiyoshi)	Mark/MCJS 20400	Richard Lawn	1983
Texas Christian University	"Southern Exposure"	Texas Christian University	Curt Wilson	1985
	"The Wide-Mouthed Frog"	Texas Christian University	Curt Wilson	1983
	"From Russia and Poland with Love"	Rainbow	Curt Wilson	1980
	"What Have They Done to My Song, Ma?"	Vestige	Curt Wilson	1978

STATE	SCHOOL	ALBUM TITLE	RECORD COMPANY	LEADER	YEAR
	Texas Southern University	"3rd Ward Vibration Society"	SUM Concerts, Inc./NR 612X04-A 761208 A+1	Lanny Steele	1976
Utah	Brigham Young University (all available)	"Synthesis: In Orbit"	KM Records	K. Newell Dayley	1982
		"Synthesis II"	Century Records	K. Newell Dayley	1981
		"Synthesis"	Allied Records	K. Newell Dayley	1976
	University of Utah	"Jazz '82" (The University of Utah Mon-Wed-Fri. Big Band)	/USR 7871	Henry Wolking	1982
	(all albums available)	"Jazz '78"	/SCS 223	Henry Wolking	1978
		"Jazz '76"	/SCP-76-LP	Henry Wolking	1976
		"The University of Utah Jazz Ensembles '75"		Henry Wolking	1975
	Weber State College	Weber State College Jazz Band (cassette)	Watson Recording	Dr. Ron Elliston	1985
West Virginia	Marshall University	Jazz Ensemble (tapes available)		J.D. Folsom	
Wisconsin	Lawrence University	"Lawrence University Jazz Ensemble Plays the Music of Student Writers"	Lawrence University	Fred Sturm	1983
		"Lawrence University Studio Orchestra"	Lawrence University	Fred Sturm	1978
	University of Wisconsin/EauClaire	"Doodle Oodle"	private pressing	Henry Mautner	1983
	University of Wisconsin/Whitewater	"Wisconsin State University Whitewater Jazz Ensemble"	/SS #16204	Frank Ferriano	1969
Canada	York University (Ontario)	York University Jazz Sextet	York University Records/YUR01		1982

Other Collegiate Jazz albums of note:

"Intercollegiate Jazz Festival" (festival finalists)

Impulse A 9145

produced by Bob Thiele

1968